PLAY UP SKY BLUES

PLAY UP SKY BLUES CHAMPIONS 1967

COVENTRY CITY'S RISE TO THE TOP

JIM BROWN

pitch

First published by Pitch Publishing, 2017

Pitch Publishing
A2 Yeoman Gate
Yeoman Way
Worthing
Sussex
BN13 3QZ

www.pitchpublishing.co.uk
info@pitchpublishing.co.uk

A CIP catalogue record is available for this book
from the British Library.

ISBN 978-1-78531-332-5

Typesetting and origination by Pitch Publishing

Printed in the UK by TJ International, Cornwall

Contents

Foreword

IN 1966, I was 14-years-old and a football nut. Growing up in Leamington Spa, just ten miles from Highfield Road, I was in the right place at the right time to be on Jimmy Hill's Sky Blue bandwagon. Since my first visit to see Coventry City in 1962, I hadn't been a regular at home games because of Saturday school but got to Highfield Road whenever I could, otherwise it was Lockheed Leamington's Windmill Ground to watch the free-scoring Brakes. Halfway through the 1965/66 season, as City's promotion challenge became serious, I started to design strategies to skip school and see Saturday home games.

As the 1966/67 campaign began I had honed these strategies and was able to see every home game, bar the solitary loss to Crystal Palace. When I look back at my records I can see that although I saw the Manchester United cup defeat in 1963, I didn't see the team lose a home league game until they reached the First Division!

And 1967 was a fantastic year.

In the so-called 'Summer of Love', my football team reached the First Division for the first time in thrilling circumstances, my favourite music acts – The Beatles, The Rolling Stones, Bob Dylan, The Who – were at the peak of their powers and I discovered the opposite sex. The euphoria of promotion was followed by parties galore and a host of new experiences for a spotty 15-year-old.

In most of my books I acknowledge the influence on me of the late Derek Henderson, the *Coventry Telegraph* football writer throughout the JH era. It was Derek who inspired me as a teenager to begin to study the club's history and his match reports from the 1960s were an invaluable resource in writing this book. As far back as 1969 Derek allowed me access to his scrapbooks and the *Coventry Telegraph* archives and started my love affair with the club's history. Once again, I hope my recounting this momentous season meets his approval.

Another author to thank is Marshall Stewart who wrote the book *Miracle in Sky Blue* in a matter of weeks in 1967. Marshall has generously given me lots of cuttings and memorabilia from his time covering City from the press box in the 1950s and 1960s.

Many thanks to others who have given me assistance with the book, including former players and staff: Ron Farmer, Dietmar Bruck, Mick Kearns, Bobby Gould, Dudley Roberts, Mick Coop, Andy Harvey and Norman Pilgrim. Their memories are invaluable. I am grateful to the numerous City fans and friends who have given me their memories of the season including Dean Nelson, Rod Dean, Jonathan Strange, David Brassington, Mike Young, Alan Ludford, Nick Cook, Brian Chaston, Kevin Shannon, Mick Williams, Ian Davidson, David Smith, Keith White and Geoff Moore.

To fellow writer Steve Phelps, thanks for the encouragement to write this story. To my friends from the *Coventry Telegraph*, Alan Poole (now retired) and Andy Turner for their constant support of what I do for the club's history. I am also grateful to Paul and Jane Camillin of Pitch Publishing for their faith in me, to Duncan Olner, who designed the impressive cover of the book, to Tony Brown and the ENFA website that has been so helpful in checking facts, and to the late Edna Davis, who is the source of many of the pictures in this book.

Finally, thanks to my football club, Coventry City, who have been and continue to be such a big part of my life. I am sure there were others and if I have not mentioned you I apologise.

The majority of pictures used in the book were obtained from some of the above named and the origin of them is unknown. A number were identified as being from publications no longer in print. The holders of copyright on the photographs are difficult to identify but the publishers will be pleased to correct any omissions brought to their notice at the earliest opportunity.

Last but not least thanks to my wonderfully supportive wife Doreen who has been loyal and patient with my obsession with Coventry City for too many years to mention.

Introduction

PRIOR to the 1960s Coventry City's most successful period was in the 1930s. Under the hard-nosed management of Harry Storer, the Bantams, as the club was nicknamed, won the Third Division South championship in 1936 with a tough centre-half and captain in George Mason and a prolific scoring centre-forward called Clarrie Bourton. The three pre-war seasons in Division Two saw the club come close to reaching the First Division. They twice finished fourth but many fans accused the directors of not wanting promotion after the sales of key players.

After the war, the club's momentum faded and they were relegated in 1952. The next decade saw the club stagger from one crisis to another and they even became founder members of Division Four in 1958. Promotion from the basement division in 1959 was almost repeated a year later but again the momentum faded.

In 1960 local businessman Derrick Robins, who had been on the board of directors since the mid-50s, became chairman, and just over a year later with the club languishing in the lower reaches of Division Three and playing in front of crowds under 10,000, he persuaded former Fulham player and recently retired chairman of the Professional Footballer's Association, Jimmy Hill, to become the club's manager. After a low-key start, Hill began to transform the club in the summer of 1962, signing a completely new five-man forward line and introducing a revolutionary all-sky blue kit.

An exciting FA Cup run in 1963 got the club's supporters behind him and a year later the club were champions of Division Three with an average attendance of 26,000. 1964/65 was a season of consolidation and the club finished tenth but, in the following campaign, the Sky Blues were in the promotion hunt from the start. From mid-September onwards they were never out of the top four and although Joe Mercer's and Malcolm Allison's Manchester City were always favourites for the title, the Sky Blues were neck and neck with Huddersfield, Southampton and Wolves for the second promotion place.

Ultimately, they were pipped by one point by Southampton and finished third after two disastrous away defeats at Easter. Some unhappy fans pointed fingers at Hill for selling their favourite player, George Hudson, in March when promotion was in their sights, a decision that was only vindicated much later. The disgruntled fans repeated the accusation of supporters in the late 1930s: 'City don't really want promotion'. Hill responded: 'If we go up I shall get an increase in salary as well as the players. If anyone thinks I am going to pass up a chance like that they must think I am a very funny person.'

After narrowly missing out on promotion City's fans needed to know that the club's momentum under Hill was not going to falter. In addition, they needed a new hero to worship following the loss of Hudson. These were the issues that chairman Robins, manager Hill and his management team grappled with in the summer of 1966.

The Sky Blues Cast

The Players

Bill Glazier (Goalkeeper)

Many shrewd observers of the game believe that, but for a broken leg in April 1965, Bill Glazier would have been a member of Alf Ramsey's 1966 World Cup squad. At the time of the incident Bill was on a fast track to success. Six months previously, Coventry manager Jimmy Hill had splashed out £35,000, a British record fee for a goalkeeper, to bring Glazier to Highfield Road. Sceptics had questioned Hill's sanity in paying big money for a goalkeeper untried at the highest level, but his gamble had been rewarded as City's defence had looked more comfortable than for a long time and Glazier won England Under-23 honours.

The Nottingham-born keeper had started his career on the books of Torquay United and joined Crystal Palace in October 1961. Within months he had displaced Welsh international Vic Rouse and in three-and-a-half years in South London he played over 100 games for the club who in those days were nicknamed the Glaziers!

In the 1963/64 season, he helped Palace win promotion to Division Two in second place behind the Sky Blues, but had a horrendous game at Highfield Road which Bill remembers: 'It was the first game of the season and City were strong favourites for promotion. We really struggled to contain them and ended up giving away two penalties and losing 5-1. Ron Farmer scored both penalties and a 35-yard free kick which I didn't see until the last minute.'

A week after signing for City, Glazier was selected as a reserve for the England Under-23 team and a month after his move he played in a 5-0 victory over Romania at Highfield Road.

The following February his career received another boost when he was one of 23 players involved with the full squad preparing for the upcoming Scotland game. Two more Under-23 caps, when he again kept clean sheets, increased hopes that he could emulate another City goalkeeper, Reg Matthews, and win a full England cap.

Tragedy struck at Maine Road on 17 April 1965. Bill came out bravely to save from Manchester City's Glyn Pardoe and the two players collided. Glazier's left leg was broken in two places and he spent five weeks in Manchester Infirmary and was in plaster for three months. It took Bill a year to return to first team action and his World Cup chance had gone.

Mick Kearns (Right-back)

Mick Kearns was a product of Coventry City's youth policy before there was even a policy. He was a great servant for the club and is the only man to have made over 350 appearances for Coventry City as his sole club. Along with George Curtis and Brian Hill, he holds the extraordinary record of having played in five different divisions of the league with one club. Between 1957 and 1968 he made 385 appearances and was a virtual ever-present for most of that period.

Nuneaton-born Mick came from a footballing family. His great uncle Jack played in Aston Villa's 1910 Championship side. He was spotted playing for Stockingford Villa and joined City as an amateur in 1955. He combined his football with work as an apprentice motor mechanic at Massey Ferguson and used to train two evenings a week at Highfield Road under the watchful eye of part-time youth coach Billy Frith. Mick acknowledges the help he got from Frith: 'I owe him a lot, he was not only a great coach but a nice man too.'

One evening in September 1957 Mick caught the bus into town and was walking to the ground from Pool Meadow when he spotted on the newspaper billboards 'Kearns makes debut'. Manager Harry Warren had selected him for that night's Division Three South game with Bournemouth.

Mick has vivid memories of that time: 'Everything was so disorganised at the club then, nobody had bothered to tell me I was playing and I was hardly prepared. I'd spent a hard day on the production line and the last thing I felt like was playing a game. We were a bit of a shambles and lost 3-0 and it was probably the worst prepared City team I ever played in.'

Knee problems, which would dog Mick during his career, slowed his progress and it was 12 months before he won a regular place in the team, now in Division Four under his old mentor Frith. Playing at wing-half he was a key player in City's promotion team and continued to perform consistently throughout his career.

Mick was one of a few players that Jimmy Hill did not jettison soon after his arrival in 1961 and it was the Farmer-Curtis-Kearns half-back line which would be the constant as City climbed out of the lower reaches of Division Three and won two promotions in four years. Hill later converted him to full-back and Mick, although preferring the wing-half role, happily obliged.

In 1966 he was granted a well-deserved testimonial, with George Curtis, and Jimmy Hill wrote: 'He reads the game like a bibliophile, and just when the defence looks like collapsing his brain will have taken him into just the right spot to heal the breach. There has not been a more pleasant player on the books of Coventry City in its existence.'

Dietmar Bruck (Left-back)

Born in Gdansk during World War Two but brought up in Coventry, Dietmar was outstanding for Coventry Schools and it was no surprise when he joined the club's groundstaff after he left school. He was given his debut as a raw 17-year-old by Jimmy Hill's predecessor Billy Frith at the end of 1960/61 season and was City's third youngest player at the time.

Dietmar made his big breakthrough in 1962/63 under Hill. His performances in the cup run that season were extraordinary, from man-marking Portsmouth's danger man McCann in the second replay to his stunning goal that brought the house down against Sunderland. However, he had stiff competition for a place with Farmer, Kearns and Hill also contesting the wing-half positions.

Originally an attacking wing-half, Bruck was successfully converted to a left back in 1966 after the departure of Allan Harris and easily took to the new role. 'Brucky' played in that position for the rest of his career and his strong tackling and no-nonsense defending made him perfect for the role.

Ronnie Farmer (Attacking wing-half)

Born in Guernsey in 1936, Ron's family were evacuated from the Channel Islands days before the Nazis invaded. After returning to the island after the war he made his name at the North Athletic club and attracted the interest of Nottingham Forest. Along with his elder brother Bill (a goalkeeper) he moved, aged 16, to the mainland to try and carve out a professional football career.

Ron, a tough-tackling half-back, had stiff competition for a first-team place but finally got his chance in 1958 when he made nine appearances in Forest's First Division side. City manager Billy Frith signed him in a £6,000 double deal with goalkeeper Arthur Lightening in November 1958 and he went straight into the team for a 5-1 home win over Chester. The double signings were a major boost to the club's Division Four promotion hopes and Ronnie played in 26 successive games as City finished runners-up and won promotion.

Ronnie blossomed in the higher league and over the next few seasons was a virtual ever-present in the side. The half-back line of Farmer-Curtis-Kearns became the lynchpin of the team in the early 1960s. Ronnie was a good footballer, but his main strength was winning the ball and feeding his forwards with penetrating passes. His penchant was for scoring long-range goals and taking penalties. He was entrusted with spot kicks soon after Jimmy Hill's arrival in 1961 and over the next five seasons he missed only one out of 23 attempts – at Millwall in 1964 when his shot hit the post and bounced to safety. His nonchalant penalty-taking style fooled many goalkeepers. The kicks may not have been powerful but they were always deadly accurate in their execution.

In August 1963, he became the only City defender to score a hat-trick when, against Crystal Palace at Highfield Road, he scored two penalties and a stunning 35-yard free kick past future City goalkeeper Bill Glazier in a 5-1 victory. That season he ended with 11 goals – eight from penalty kicks – as City won the Third Division title.

George Curtis (Centre-half and captain)

Affectionately known as 'The Iron Man', George Curtis ranks alongside George Mason as the greatest centre-half and captain in the club's history. He was the son of a miner who had left the coalfields of south Wales to move to Kent around the time Curtis Junior was born in 1939. George was a prodigious talent, playing for Snowdown Colliery, a Kent junior side managed by former City star Harry Barratt. Barratt recommended him to Coventry in 1955 and within months George was given his league debut at left-back as a 16-year-old.

It was not until the start of the 1958-59 season that manager Billy Frith switched him to centre-half and he took to the role like a duck to water. He would miss only six games in the next nine seasons. During this period he became one of the most feared defenders in the Football League. Considered by many opposition fans to be over-physical, he always maintained he played the game in a fair but hard manner. He turned out for Coventry on many occasions when lesser mortals would have gone sick and his style epitomised the spirit of the club during this period. Jimmy Hill's faith in him was rewarded as George captained the side to the Third and Second Division titles.

By 1967 Curtis was approaching 500 City appearances but his contribution to the club's rise cannot be measured in statistics alone. That year Hughie Spencer, the club's long-serving team-coach driver who had probably seen most of Curtis's games over the years, described George's part in the club's progress: 'I often think that, but for George, the club would never have been where it is today.' Curtis led with his courage and strength, and his example earned the respect of colleagues and opponents alike. Opposing fans booed and baited him, but he was one of those players you wished you had on your team.

When Jimmy Hill arrived at Highfield Road in 1961 Curtis was already the captain of the side and Hill quickly recognised that he had a jewel on his hands. Not only was he a fearsome and courageous centre-half but he was also a wonderful ambassador for the football club. According to some of his team-mates Curtis went out of his way to cultivate the captain's role under Hill, acting as the manager's chief lieutenant in the dressing room and as the players' go-between with the manager.

Dave Clements (Defensive wing-half/Outside-left)

The Larne-born player joined Wolves as a 17-year-old in 1962 and played for his country's youth side at Wembley in the 1963

European Championships. When he was made available by Wolves a year later Jimmy Hill pounced and paid £1,500 to bring him to Coventry. He would prove to be one of Hill's most astute purchases. After some promising reserve displays he made his first-team debut at Northampton in early 1965, scoring City's goal in a 1-1 draw.

Playing as an inside forward in place of the injured Ernie Machin, he had a massive impact, scoring eight goals in his first ten games and after only seven appearances he made his Northern Ireland debut in a 2-1 win over Holland. His left-wing partner against the Dutch was 19-year-old George Best and Dave didn't let the side down.

John Key (Outside-right)

After taking over as Coventry City manager in 1961 Jimmy Hill only signed one player who he had played with, his former Fulham colleague Roy Dwight, a stop-gap acquisition who appeared sporadically in the 1962/63 season. That was until May 1966 when JH swooped to sign another Fulham man, John Key, who had been released on a free transfer by the First Division club.

Key, by then 29 , had been at Craven Cottage since leaving school in 1956. The Chelsea-born player was a direct winger who loved to beat his full-back for speed and cross accurately for his forwards as well as getting a good share of goals. He was an outstanding athlete as a schoolboy and won the Southern AAA long jump championship. He came to Highfield Road after 181 games and 37 goals for Fulham, and although he and Hill played together at Craven Cottage his career only really blossomed after Hill retired from playing.

Ernie Machin (Inside-forward)

Jimmy Hill's scout Alf Walton spotted Ernie playing for Lancashire League side Nelson in early 1962 and he was forever described as Hill's 'blue eyed boy,' probably because JH persisted with him in his early career when the fans gave him some stick after a dip in form. Machin denied this later: 'That was a load of rubbish about being his favourite – we used to argue like cat and dog. He almost kicked me out once when he discovered I was going back to Bolton every midweek on the milk train after a Tuesday night game.'

Hill gave him his debut in April 1963 as an inside-forward and at the start of the 1963/64 season he was the first choice in the number 10 shirt, having displaced Jimmy Whitehouse. Playing as a scheming inside-forward Ernie was soon on the verge of England Under-23 honours but then suffered a serious knee injury against Watford. He ended up having several operations and it was 18 months before he was fully recovered. In 1965/66 he was a virtual ever-present.

Bobby Gould (Centre-forward)

As a 15-year-old, the former Caludon Castle schoolboy had been released by Billy Frith in 1961 but fortunately Jimmy Hill called him back for a trial that led to him becoming an apprentice. A favourite of Hill's from the start, JH gave him his debut in place of the injured Hudson in October 1963, in a 0-0 draw at Shrewsbury. Over the next two and a half years the young centre-forward played only 15 games but his bustling style left its mark on opposing defenders and he also chipped in with a few goals.

In March 1966, when crowd favourite George Hudson was surprisingly sold to Northampton, Bobby stepped up and made the centre-forward position his. Many supporters made the mistake of comparing him to their hero and he took a lot of unwarranted barracking from City fans. By the summer of 1966 he had played only 31 games and scored just nine goals.

Ian Gibson (Inside-forward)
Born in Newton Stewart in southern Scotland in 1943, Ian Stewart Gibson was a schoolboy prodigy and played at Wembley for Scotland Schoolboys against England in 1958 whilst on the books of his local club Stranraer. In July 1958, he moved south to join Third Division Accrington Stanley – a 15-year-old boy thrown into a high testosterone dressing room – and he quickly grew up in a world of snooker halls, betting shops and pubs. Within months he was given his league debut a week before his 16th birthday, one of the youngest ever league debutants, and three days later netted his first league goal.

Bradford Park Avenue had spotted him and cash-strapped Accrington had to sell him to the Yorkshire club. In his second season Park Avenue won promotion from Division Four under their tough Scottish manager Jimmy Scoular when Gibbo was almost ever-present and netted seven goals. In March 1962 Second Division Middlesbrough, then managed by Bob Dennison who later became chief scout at Highfield Road, paid a club record £20,000 for the diminutive Scot. He was an instant hit at Ayresome Park, netting twice on his home debut against Bristol Rovers.

A virtual ever-present for the next four years, Gibbo made 184 appearances and scored 47 goals. He won two Scottish under-23 caps alongside starlets such as Charlie Cooke, Neil Martin and Billy Bremner. Boro went close to promotion in 1963 when they rejected a £40,000 offer from Hibernian, but finished in mid-table in the two subsequent seasons and were relegated in 1966. That year, in their penultimate game Boro, desperate for points, lost 2-1 to the Sky Blues at Highfield Road. Gibbo scored and caught the eye of Nemo in the *Coventry Telegraph*: 'Without the wiles of chunky Ian Gibson, their skipper – one of the best inside-forwards we have seen on the ground this term – they would have been sadly adrift. Time and time again, he was in the centre of the picture trying to rally his men.' No doubt Hill was impressed that day.

Hill had been under pressure after selling George Hudson to Northampton in March 1966 with some fans blaming him for costing the club promotion. JH needed a marquee signing and despite interest from First Division clubs Gibbo chose City. By City's standards the fee of £57,500 was enormous.

Ronnie Rees (Outside-right/left)

When Jimmy Hill was given £30,000 by Derrick Robins in the summer of 1962 he bought a completely new forward line – for younger readers that means five players. Four of them – Willie Humphries, Hugh Barr, Terry Bly and Jimmy Whitehouse – were successes and played a key part in the Sky Blue revolution. The other, left-winger Bobby Laverick, was a mistake that Hill realised very quickly. Fortunately for him he had an outstanding but unknown 18-year-old winger in the reserves called Ronnie Rees.

Hill's gamble in promoting the Welsh youngster to the first team in September 1962 came off and for the next six years he was a virtual ever-present, making 262 appearances and scoring 52 goals. International honours soon arrived. He first won under-23 honours and in 1964, after being an ever present in the Division Three championship side, he won the first of his 39 full caps. The lad from Ystradgynlais was in illustrious company, playing with greats such as John Charles, Ivor Allchurch and Cliff Jones, but was not overawed.

In that memorable 1963/64 promotion season he scored 15 goals, including a hat-trick in the 8-1 thrashing of Shrewsbury. He took the Second Division by storm, setting up many goals with his speedy wing play which demolished many full-backs over the years. The left wing was his preference but if injuries or tactics demanded he was just as effective on the right.

Brian Hill (Defensive wing-half)

Born in Bedworth in 1941, Brian was still three months short of his 17th birthday when he made his debut in what was City's last ever game in the old Division Three South in April 1958. It had been a miserable season – a 13-game run without a win from Boxing Day to mid-March had consigned them to the new Fourth Division – and manager Billy Frith was already planning for the new league by blooding youngsters.

Looking back, Brian had only dim and distant memories of that time. 'I think I only got a game because the season was as good as over and it was a chance for the manager to look at some of the kids. I had barely played for the reserves before and it was a big surprise to play for the first team.'

After leaving school in 1956 Brian went to work at the Jaguar factory but soon he was invited to trials with City and was offered an apprentice contract. In April 1958, with both main strikers Ray Straw and Jimmy Rogers injured, Frith decided to play Brian at inside-right and his namesake Ray at centre-forward in the final game on a warm early summer's evening at Gillingham. With Peter Hill at inside-left City played three Hills in the side for the first time.

Brian had a dream start to his career when, with only seven minutes on the clock, he scored. Nemo in the *Coventry Telegraph* described it in glowing terms: 'He took just seven minutes to score, and what a peach of a goal it was. The ball came down the middle. Brian took it in his stride and drove it grass-high into the corner with the aplomb of a veteran.'

For the next four seasons Brian struggled to get a first team game and it wasn't until Jimmy Hill took over in 1961 that he came to the fore. Hill, recognising his speed as his major asset, converted him to a defensive half-back and in 1962/63 season he became a regular. He earned a reputation as a tough tackling man-marker and was even tipped for England Under-23 honours.

Brian was first choice at either wing-half or full-back until 1967, except when his niggling hamstring injuries kept him on the sidelines, but it seemed whenever he returned to the side their fortunes picked up.

John Tudor (Centre-forward)

Jimmy Hill's knack for spotting young talent is largely overlooked when considering the great man's career but Coventry City benefited from that ability enormously in the 1960s. He encouraged the development of youth players such as Mick Coop, Willie Carr and Ronnie Rees and had an eye for late developers such as Ernie Machin, Dave Clements and John Tudor.

The 19-year-old John had almost given up hope of playing professional football after being turned down by numerous clubs including Derby, Nottingham Forest and Middlesbrough. He was playing for his local team Ilkeston Town in the Midland League and his manager Jim Rayner recommended him to City in late 1965. City took him on a month's loan.

He made a big impression scoring 12 goals in five 'A' team games, including six in one match and soon got a call-up for the reserves. A professional contract was forthcoming at the end of the season but Bobby Gould and Ray Pointer were ahead of him in the pecking order as the season started. Little did he know what was in store for him in the ensuing months.

Brian Lewis (Wing-half)

Woking-born Brian started his career as a 16-year-old at Crystal Palace in 1959 and was given his league debut two years later. In 1963, after 33 games for Palace, he got his dream move to Portsmouth, the club he had supported as a boy. A grafter rather than a skilful player, he won a regular place in Pompey's Second Division side and played almost 150 games for the south coast club, scoring 24 goals. Brian was an effervescent player who could play in a variety of positions, something that appealed to Jimmy Hill, but he had a reputation for being over enthusiastic in the tackle, a euphemism for a dirty player.

In Brian's obituary in 1998 Ivan Ponting in the *Independent* aptly wrote: 'Lewis occupied every outfield position, but was at his best as an attacking right-half who packed a savage shot, whose sweeping crossfield passes were a trademark, and who was wirily resilient in the tackle. A lovable scamp both on and off the pitch, he was feted by his supporters, especially at Portsmouth, for cheeky dribbles which lured opponents into rash tackles, thus securing free kicks in menacing situations.'

Ray Pointer (Centre-forward)

Cramlington-born Ray signed for Burnley in 1957 and over six seasons he made 270 appearances in claret and scored 133 goals, the second highest number in the club's history. Burnley were one of the top sides in the country at that time and in 1959/60 they lifted the League Championship and ever-present Ray notched 23 goals. Another 26 goals followed the next season and in October 1961 his displays finally earned him three full England caps.

Despite scoring two goals he was surprisingly not included in the 1962 World Cup party. That season Burnley were probably at their peak and for a long time they were in contention for the league and cup double. They eventually lost in the FA Cup Final to Tottenham and were pipped for the league title by Alf Ramsey's Ipswich Town. Ray scored a spectacular goal for Burnley in a post-season friendly at Highfield Road.

His form had fallen away by 1965 and he was allowed to leave Turf Moor for Bury for £8,000 but soon rediscovered his form with 17 goals in 19 games. That persuaded Jimmy Hill to splash £20,000 on him that December when City's promotion push was stuttering through lack of goals. Pointer's arrival had the desired effect and he scored on his debut, a 1-1 draw at Norwich and a hat-trick in a 5-1 New Years' Day win over Preston.

Eleven goals in 19 games convinced Hill that the fan's idol George Hudson was dispensable and 'The Hud' was controversially sold to Northampton.

Peter Thomas (Goalkeeper)

Peter grew up in Coventry and was an 18-year-old apprentice electrician playing in goal for GEC in 1965 when he was invited for a trial at Ryton. First-choice Bill Glazier was recovering from a broken leg and with his understudy Bob Wesson promoted Jimmy Hill wanted a back-up keeper. Peter and youth team goalkeeper Martin Clamp shared the reserve-team duties during 1965/66.

John Burckitt (Left-back)

John had joined City as an apprentice at Highfield Road in 1962 and played his early football alongside youngsters such as Bobby Gould, Peter Denton and Dudley Roberts. The 1964/65 campaign was John's golden season. He captained the City youth team and in October 1964, at the age of 17, he made his first-team debut as a left-back in a 2-2 home draw with Manchester City. In only his fifth game he played in a disastrous 8-1 League Cup defeat at the hands of Leicester City. He became a regular in the England Youth training squad and in April 1965 he was rewarded with five international caps as England reached the final of the European Championships. Also in the England squad were Chelsea's Peter Osgood and Wilf Smith who later became City's first £100,000 signing.

John was a regular for the reserves but amazingly did not get another chance in the first team for almost two years, mainly due to the outstanding form of left-back Allan Harris and later Dietmar Bruck.

John Mitten (Outside-left)

The outstanding form in the mid-1960s of Ronnie Rees and Dave Clements meant that John Mitten, a good winger in his own right, had few chances to shine for the Sky Blues. In three and a half seasons he played 42 first-team games, scoring seven goals. A prolific dribbler with a vicious shot and an excellent corner-taker, with a bit more luck he could have been a big success at Highfield Road.

Born in Manchester in March 1941 he was the son of Manchester United winger Charlie Mitten, who controversially left the English game in 1950 to play in the unrecognised Colombian League. Later, Charlie became manager of Newcastle United and caused a stir in 1958 by picking John, who had won schoolboy and youth honours for England, for the first team. He hardly endeared himself to a Geordie crowd already whispering nepotism when he missed a penalty on his debut.

In 1961 John moved to First Division Leicester and played briefly alongside Gordon Banks and Frank McLintock. In 1963, after a brief spell at Old Trafford where he could get no further than the reserve team, he was signed by Jimmy Hill on a free transfer as cover for Rees. He made four appearances in the Third Division promotion season and was never on the losing side. By the summer of 1966 he had made 30 starts in three seasons but was getting frustrated. John was also an accomplished cricketer for Leicestershire.

Mick Coop (Right-back)

Although born in Grimsby he grew up in Leamington and attended Cashmore and Oken schools where he was an outstanding footballer and cricketer. He was spotted playing for Milverton Villa and joined City as an apprentice on leaving school in 1963, before signing professional forms in early 1966. By the summer of 1966 the 18-year-old had been a regular in the reserves for 12 months and was on the verge of a first-team call-up.

Barry Lowes (Outside-right)

Barrow-born Barry, a qualified electrician, had started his career with his home-town club before a £6,000 move to First Division Blackpool in 1961. With stiff competition from Mandy Hill, he failed to break into the first team and in the summer of 1962 moved to Workington. Here he played under legendary manager Ken Furphy and alongside players such as Kit Napier and future Spurs boss Keith Burkenshaw. A tally of 34 goals in 121 games convinced Bury to sign him in 1966 and he scored six goals in 33 games at Gigg Lane.

Pat Morrissey (Attacking wing-half)

Although born in Enniscorthy in County Wexford he grew up in Coventry and was playing for Priory School when he was spotted by the Sky Blues in 1964. He turned professional in July 1965 and played in a strong City youth team which included Mick Coop, Trevor Gould and a 15-year-old Willie Carr. Pat, or Paddy as some called him, was a skilful wing-half with a strong tackle and his reserve appearances impressed not only City's management team but also the Irish selectors who gave him an under-23 cap in early 1966.

Dudley Roberts (Centre-forward/Centre-half)

In 1965/66 season Dudley Roberts burst on to the scene when he scored five goals in his first five league games, including two on his home debut. The son of post-War City hero Ted Roberts, Dudley never fulfilled his early promise but was a regular reserve team player for the remaining two years of his career at Highfield Road.

Dudley inherited his father's heading skills and displayed them by scoring prolifically at Cheylesmore School. After joining the

Sky Blues as an apprentice in 1961 he was converted to a defensive wing-half and played in City's youth team with Bobby Gould and Pat Morrissey. In the autumn of 1965 he was called up to play at centre-forward for the reserve team after injuries to the regular strikers. Impressive performances earned him a first team call-up at Preston and he did not let the side down in a 0-0 draw. His home debut against Charlton a week later coincided with his 20th birthday and he celebrated with two goals in a 3-1 win, one a close range shot from a Ken Hale cross, the second a trademark header.

Dudley later recalled: 'I still can't remember the first goal as I was concussed when I scored it. George Curtis and I clashed heads going for a cross and the first half of the game was a blur to me. The second goal though is vivid in my memory, I headed in a Ronnie Rees cross.'

Goals against Plymouth, Portsmouth and Ipswich took his total to five in five. He missed several games through injury and when he was fit Jimmy Hill had signed Bury's Ray Pointer to boost the attack.

Benny Glover (Attacking wing-half)

Born in Birmingham he was the eighth of 14 children and was pinched by the Sky Blues from under the noses of Aston Villa and Birmingham City. He came for a trial at Ryton in 1964 and agreed to play as an amateur. He played as a wing half in the club's youth team that season, appearing in the same side as Mick Coop, John Burckitt, John Matthews and Pat Morrissey. By the summer of 1966 he had made sufficient progress to be offered a professional contract. He made rapid strides and after less than a dozen reserve appearances he was considered for the first team.

On a Friday afternoon in early November 1966 club captain George Curtis walked up to him in the corridor outside the dressing rooms at Highfield Road and asked: 'Chicken or steak for lunch tomorrow, Benny?'

The staff

Jimmy Hill (Manager)

Born in Balham, South London in 1928 he was first spotted by Reading manager Ted Drake playing for his regiment whilst doing National Service in 1948. He never made the first team and in 1949 joined Brentford after being released where he soon got a first team chance as a centre-forward. Converted to a wing-half, he spent three years at Griffin Park making 87 appearances before making the short journey to Fulham, then a First Division club.

He spent nine happy years at Craven Cottage before a knee injury ended his career and was a wholehearted and enthusiastic member of the team that almost reached Wembley in 1958 and won promotion to the First Division in 1959. During his time there he became the chairman of the Professional Footballers Association and was instrumental in the abolition of the maximum wage for players in 1961.

When chairman Derrick Robins offered him the City manager's job he only agreed to join if he had complete control – the first City boss to have such power. A 2-1 home FA Cup defeat by Kings Lynn was the catalyst for change, although he had been offered the post a week earlier.

Hill made enormous changes. In came a new continental-style sky blue strip, out went the complete back-room staff including loyal servants such as Alf Wood and Ted Roberts. The club was never out of the limelight and his innovations were admired nationwide. He introduced the Sky Blue train, pre-match entertainment, the Ryton training ground and the Sky Blue song as well as developing the ground into a modern, well-equipped stadium.

His greatest attributes were his ability to deal in the transfer market and the strength of his convictions. He was never afraid to make what were, at the time, unpopular decisions and see them through. The sale of top scorer Terry Bly in 1963 was a case in point. The fans were in uproar when he was sold but within weeks it proved to be an inspired decision as Bly's career tailed off and his replacement, George Hudson, became the most idolised player in the club's history. Three years later there was further hullabaloo when Hudson was sold but a year after, when promotion was secured to Division One, Hill's judgement was proved correct. In his first full season in charge the FA Cup run to the quarter-finals put them back into national view and although they missed out on promotion from Division Three they made it the following year as champions. A season of consolidation in Division Two was followed with a narrow miss in 1966.

Bobby Gould names Jimmy Hill as the best manager he played under 'by a mile'. 'He was a genius and knew how to get the best out of every player. He was supremely professional, he believed the team had to work and play together, and kept strictly to routines. For example, at home games we always had to be at the ground for 11am (no one was ever late!) and we were taken by coach to the Leofric for lunch – he instilled a togetherness which you don't always see these days.'

Alan Dicks (Assistant manager)

Born in Kennington, South London in 1934, Alan was signed by Chelsea in 1951. A centre-half or wing-half, he failed to gain a regular place at Stamford Bridge and played 35 games in six years, including a solitary match in the Blues' First Division championship season of 1954-55. A move to Southend in 1958 gave him regular first team football and he made 88 appearances over the next four years. In early 1962 Jimmy Hill lured him to Coventry as his assistant.

Dicks was still playing for Southend and transferred as a player with City agreeing to pay Southend £100 per match up to a maximum of £1,000 if Dicks played for the first team. Alan was a regular at centre-half for the reserves for the next five years but never pulled on a first team shirt and Southend went empty handed. Hill gave Alan a pretty free hand with the reserves and his man-management skills were honed as the club's Football Combination side won promotion to Division One in 1965.

Pat Saward (Head coach)

Born in Cork, southern Ireland in 1928, Pat Saward lived in Singapore and Malaysia before his family came to London at the end of the war. Remarkably he didn't play organised football until the age of 18. He played as an amateur for Crystal Palace before moving to Millwall as a professional in 1951. Over the next four years he was a regular at wing-half or inside-forward for the Lions, making 126 appearances and winning the first of 18 Republic of Ireland caps. In 1955, he joined Aston Villa for £7,000 and made a scoring debut in a 4-4 draw with Manchester United. The tall, broad-shouldered, darkly handsome Saward won an FA Cup winners medal in 1957 as Villa upset the odds to beat the Busby Babes, and three years later captained Villa to the Second Division title. In 1961 he joined Huddersfield where he played until Jimmy Hill approached him in 1963.

Huddersfield were ordered to reduce his fee to a free transfer by a Football League tribunal and Jimmy Hill explained that whilst his main job at Coventry would be coaching the youngsters 'he could come into the first team if the occasion arose'. A week later he was in City's reserve team.

Pat became a popular character around the club over the next few years and had a reputation for his dapper fashion sense. He was always immaculately attired, an attribute he also instilled into his young players. He was a hugely influential figure in the rise of the club during the 1960s and was credited with playing a significant role in the development of key players such as Willie Carr, Mick Coop, Jeff Blockley and Dennis Mortimer.

Peter Hill (Trainer)

Although Peter Hill was born and brought up in the Derbyshire village of Heanor he made his home in Coventry and gave his heart to Coventry City. Arriving in the city in 1947 as a 16-year-old, he had a 16-year playing career with the club followed by five years as trainer under Jimmy Hill.

Peter was one of many Derbyshire youngsters brought to Highfield Road in the years following the war. His performances for Ilkeston team Rutland United caught the attention of several league clubs and Peter's father urged him to reject Derby County and sign for Coventry. He cut his teeth with City's nursery club Modern Machine Tools FC alongside many other talented teenagers and played in the Coventry Works League. Lol Harvey, another son of Heanor and four years younger than Peter, spoke highly of him: 'Growing up he was a natural sportsman and could have had a career in cricket he was that good. He was a very skilful footballer. In those days, inside-forwards were expected to get up and down the pitch and needed lots of stamina, Peter had both and scored more than his fair share of goals.'

Legendary manager Harry Storer handed Peter his debut as a 17-year-old at Sheffield Wednesday in a Second Division game in February 1949 and he was the club's youngest debutant at the time, aged 17 years and 181 days. It would be 1952 before Peter became a first-team regular and in September of that year he scored his first hat-trick in a 3-0 home win over Leyton Orient, including two rare headed goals. Around this time it was common knowledge that Arsenal were interested in signing him.

The years from 1952 to 1958 were dark days for the club with managers coming and going, boardroom disagreements and financial crises and Peter was the one constant through the period. Playing at either inside-right or left, he was never a prolific scorer but got his fair share of goals and reached double figures on three occasions.

In 1958, after City were relegated to Division Four, manager Billy Frith switched Peter to the right wing where his speed was put to best advantage – he was a natural on the wing and gave many full-backs a nightmare time. Injuries kept his first team appearances down in 1961/62 but in November 1961 he was a member of the City team humbled by Southern League Kings Lynn in the FA Cup, an event that sparked the arrival of Jimmy Hill as manager. His widow Barbara told me that he knew after the Kings Lynn game that it was time to pack in and he made one final appearance in March 1962, before hanging up his boots at the premature age of 30. Jimmy Hill asked him to stay on and be the first-team trainer. He became the man with the 'magic sponge' and was first to tend the serious injuries of Ernie Machin, Bill Glazier and George Curtis.

Peter played 309 senior games for the club and scored 78 goals. He is second only to Ray Straw in the post-war period and the fifth highest in the club's history.

Norman Pilgrim (Physiotherapist)

In July 1964, there was little fanfare when 28-year-old physiotherapist Norman Pilgrim arrived at the club. Norman was born and grew up in West Ham, watching his local team for the first time in 1945. He was working in St Giles hospital in South London when he spotted an advert in the *Physiotherapy Journal*: 'Progressive football league club seeking ... etc.' Interviews with club doctor Peter Coghill and Jimmy Hill followed and he was offered the job. He told me: 'At the time qualified physios were rare in football – at most clubs injured players were treated by former players who largely had very little knowledge and their role was often a sinecure for many years' loyal service.'

His major early success involved Ernie Machin, as he recalled: 'When I arrived in 1964 Ernie had been out for almost a year with a knee injury which had been operated on by a London surgeon who had doubts whether he would play again. However, after further surgery in 1965 by Tom Sargeant, who later became a director of the club, and six months of intense rehabilitation, he continued to play for many years.' Norman was also influential in Bill Glazier's recovery from a broken leg in 1965 and Mick Kearns's from knee problems in 1966.

Chapter 1

Preparations for new season

AS Coventry City reported back for pre-season training in late July 1966 the World Cup was capturing the imagination of the public. Hosts England were through to the semi-final where they would face Portugal and little attention was paid to the City players arriving at Ryton in glorious weather where Jimmy Hill and his back-room team would put them through their paces. After the near miss at promotion the previous season the Sky Blues were one of the favourites for success in Division Two.

Before the summer break the club had undertaken a tour of Europe to promote Rover Cars with the blessing of Prime Minister Harold Wilson. Rover provided eight sky blue Rover 2000 cars which were driven on a 2,500-mile tour of Frankfurt, Vienna, Zurich and Brussels, stopping off at 'promotional conferences' in each city and at the same time City would play one of the local teams. The tour matches were generally friendly affairs except for the game in Frankfurt against Offenbach Kickers who lived up to their name. Ronnie Rees, tired from a tour of South America with the Wales team, got himself sent off for a clumsy tackle.

At the start of the summer Hill and Robins knew that they needed to strengthen the team to win promotion to Division One. Despite the excellent gates and a raft of other money-making enterprises, another major source of funding was needed if City were to gain promotion and compete with the big boys.

That summer a new Sky Blue Pool was launched with the aim of generating £100,000 a year. Launched as 'Rocket the Sky Blues into Europe', chairman Robins donated £10,000 to kick-off the competition which boasted it would have a £1,000 weekly first prize by Christmas. The aim was recruit 250,000 members from the city and surrounding areas.

The £100,000 generated would largely go towards signing players. Hill explained: 'Last season we wanted Charlie Cooke, the Dundee inside-forward who this week signed for Chelsea for £70,000. And I had another player in mind, who would have cost only a little less, who would almost certainly put us into Division One. But sadly, the money was not available. My board of directors decided there and then that I must have the cash in future. I know the players to buy and I haven't made a bad transfer yet.'

Numerous other players were linked with the Sky Blues including Preston's young star Howard Kendall, Tottenham's Alan Mullery and Grimsby centre-forward Matt Tees. Hill, however, refused to comment on any rumours including a strong one that Arsenal wanted him as their manager to replace Billy Wright, who had been sacked in June.

Hill had made just two new signings in the close season. His former Fulham team-mate, 28-year-old John Key, a right-winger with bags of First Division experience, was signed on a free transfer just days after the season ended. The Londoner had played almost 200 games for the Cottagers and was fast and able to get in a good cross.

Hill's other signing, in the first week in July, had the City fans purring. Scot Ian Gibson, 23, had left a strong impression playing for Middlesbrough in City's final home game the previous campaign. An old-fashioned dribbling inside-forward who could create and score goals, Gibson's fee of £57,500 had smashed the club's transfer record and big things were expected from him.

The first Scot signed by Jimmy Hill, had been linked to First Division clubs Southampton and Leeds, as well as Birmingham and Blackburn from the Second Division. National newspapers tipped him to sign for Don Revie at Leeds if the Yorkshire club failed to win the signature of Alan Ball. But on 4 July Nemo reported in the *Coventry Evening Telegraph* that Hill had got his man. Gibson had travelled south the previous day and needed just 15 minutes with Jimmy to be persuaded to sign. At the same time Middlesbrough boss Stan Anderson was in Gorleston, Norfolk, trying to persuade City's reserve winger Peter Denton, on holiday at his parents' home, to join 'Boro as part of the deal. Denton thought long and hard before rejecting the offer, one which would have reduced City's cash expenditure by around £10,000. Ultimately Denton decided to stay and fight for a place, a decision he may have later regretted.

Two first team players had departed – full-backs John Sillett and Allan Harris. Left-back Harris and his wife had found it difficult to settle in the midlands after his move from Chelsea in December 1964 and after 69 games for the club he moved back to Stamford Bridge for a £45,000 fee, which represented a profit of £10,000 for City.

A year later Allan would be a member of Chelsea's FA Cup Final side against Tottenham, alongside his brother Ron. Hill's plan to cover for Harris's departure was to switch half-back Dietmar Bruck to left-back. Dietmar recalls the conversation with JH: 'He said he thought I had the attributes for a good full-back – I had a lot of stamina and pace, I was hard in the tackle and liked to get forward. He was looking for a left-back who could bomb up the wing. It seemed to work right from the start of the season, I enjoyed the new role and I played in 39 league games and only missed three through injury.'

John Sillett, 30, had been one of Hill's first signings for the club in 1962 but four years later JH wanted to play Mick Kearns at right-back and in young Mick Coop had an adequate back-up. Plymouth wanted a replacement for Tony Book, who had joined Manchester City and 'Sill' fitted the bill. John had made 128 appearances for the club, winning a Third Division championship medal in 1964 and had been a key man in the Sky Blue Revolution. Hill banked a further £5,000 from this sale.

Hill was one of the BBC 'experts' during the World Cup and appeared several times on television during the competition, making comments and giving interviews. Many in the broadcasting world were impressed with his performances in front of the camera but few City fans could have imagined that Hill's future career would be in that world. He recalled in his autobiography that on the day of the final he stood next to Joe Mercer at Wembley and both of them were in tears at the final whistle as England beat West Germany 4-2. Meanwhile City director John Camkin was used as a pundit on ITV's coverage during the tournament.

City's excellent scouting network had discovered another batch of outstanding prospects and the club had signed a good number including two Leicester schoolboys, centre-half Jeff Blockley and goalkeeper John Spiers. The club's Lancashire scout, Alf Walton, who had discovered Ernie Machin and Graham Paddon, had recommended Manchester-born winger Tom Sinclair whilst Nuneaton schoolboy sensation Bobby Allen, fresh from scoring goals for England Schoolboys had walked into Highfield Road and asked to sign for the Sky Blues in preference to Manchester United to whom he had been 'tied' on schoolboy forms. The club's youth scheme was churning out talented players by the bucket-load and that summer Benny Glover, Malcolm Keley, John Tudor and Howard Moore became full-time professionals.

The *Coventry Telegraph Pink* of 30 July published a picture of the playing staff and directors. The following were included in the photograph: Full-time professionals (29): Bill Glazier*, Bob Wesson*, Peter Thomas, Martin Clamp, Mick Kearns*, Dietmar Bruck*, John Burckitt*, Brian Hill*, George Curtis*, Ronnie Farmer*, Ernie Machin*, Ray Pointer*, Ian Gibson, Ronnie Rees*, Dave Clements*, John Key, John Mitten*, Bobby Gould*, Mick Coop, Peter Denton*, John Tudor, Dennis Oakes, Howard Moore, Ben Glover, Dudley Roberts*, John Docker, Malcolm Keley, Pat Morrissey, Mick Cartwright.

*indicates a player who has previously appeared in the first team.

Apprentice professionals (13): John Spiers, Malcolm Knox, Tom Sinclair, Paul Bloodworth, Graham Paddon, Bob Allen, Brian Cocking, Geoff Brassington, Don Peachey, Trevor Gould, Willie Carr, Bob Dobbing, Jeff Blockley.

Manager and coaching staff: Jimmy Hill, Alan Dicks (assistant manager), Pat Saward (coach), Peter Hill (trainer), Norman Pilgrim (physiotherapist), Tom Sergeant (resident orthopaedic surgeon).

Directors: Derrick Robins (chairman), J.W.(Phil) Mead, John Camkin, Jim Stevenson, Dr. Peter Coghill, Paul Oliver (secretary).

The reserve team under assistant manager Alan Dicks would be playing in the Football Combination Division One alongside all the top London clubs. The third team, the 'A' team who had won the Midland Intermediate League the previous season, had been switched to the West Midlands League where instead of meeting the third-string teams of the other Midland clubs they would be pitched against tougher and more experienced non-league sides.

The club's fourth team, the 'B' team, mainly consisting of first-year apprentices, took the 'A' team's place in the Midland Intermediate League, moving up from Coventry local leagues. Coach Pat Saward had responsibility for both the 'A' and 'B' teams but if the team's fixtures clashed then former City, Tottenham and Birmingham forward Peter Murphy, would take over the 'B' team duties. There was also a 'C' team playing in the Coventry and North Warwickshire League.

Chapter 2

August – a stuttering start for Sky Blues

EXACTLY one week after England's dramatic 4-2 World Cup Final victory over West Germany at Wembley the Sky Blues kicked off a short pre-season campaign with a trip to the Black Country where they drew 1-1 with Dudley Town of the West Midlands League. Jimmy Hill was able to name a full-strength team and new signing Ian Gibson lined up alongside Bobby Gould and Ray Pointer with Ronnie Farmer rested in favour of Ernie Machin in midfield. Pointer netted City's goal in the 14th minute and Watson equalised in the 26th minute in what was described as 'a comfortable workout'. That evening a reserve team played at Dunstable Town.

Other than a brief report from Dudley, there was little news of the Sky Blues in the *Coventry Telegraph Pink* that Saturday. They had a couple of pictures from the Midland qualifying section of the Professional Footballers' Golf Championship that had taken place at Kenilworth the previous week. Bill Glazier was pictured alongside Wolves' Ernie Hunt – little did they realise that they would be playing in the same team in less than two years.

George Curtis, John Mitten, Mick Kearns and Mick Coop were pictured hauling their trollies and it reported that Coop would be the only Sky Blue out of eight entrants to qualify for the final to be held at Kenilworth in October. Wolves' Ron Flowers, an unused member of the England World Cup squad, was the leading qualifier.

Four days later on 10 August Highfield Road hosted a pre-season friendly against a Varna Select XI from Bulgaria. The World Cup had sparked keen interest in foreign opposition and over 9,500 watched an entertaining game. Machin grabbed a seventh-minute headed goal from Key's cross which did look suspiciously offside but Yanev headed an equaliser early in the second half. An impressive Varna looked more likely winners as the second half went on and eight minutes from time George Curtis brought down centre-forward Bilyalov.

Referee Jack Taylor awarded a penalty but Gogomilov blasted the spot-kick over the cross-bar. Seconds later Pointer inexplicably missed from six yards with only the goalkeeper to beat. Then, in the last minute, Ronnie Rees almost won the game for City after a series of hair's breath escapes in both goalmouths. The entertaining game finished 1-1.

The reserves warmed up with two games that week. Two Dave Clements' goals and one from Dudley Roberts gave them a 3-0 win at Wellington Town in Shropshire and Lower Gornal Athletic were seen off 3-1 with Dennis Oakes, John Docker and Clements on the score-sheet.

On Friday evening (12 August) City travelled to Hereford for the final warm-up game and trounced one of the Southern League's better teams 5-1. Hill rested Mick Kearns and Bobby Gould and gave starts to full-back John Burckitt and Ronnie Farmer and it was the latter who had an excellent game in central midfield to give the manager a problem of who to leave out for the opening league game with Hull City, only eight days away.

It was a slick team effort from the Sky Blues who peppered the home goal from the start. Ray Pointer hit an upright with a fierce drive and Hereford's Albert Derrick clipped a header against City's bar before Farmer put the Sky Blues in front on 26 minutes following good work by Rees and Key. Six minutes later Gibson sent Key away down the right and a pinpoint cross was met by a thumping header from Pointer. Three minutes before the break Pointer made it 3-0 from Machin's cross before making way for Gould at half-time. Dave Clements also came on for Key as City continued to dominate the home side. Derrick did pull a goal back on 58 minutes but Machin scored twice in six minutes to complete the scoring.

City skipper George Curtis came up against an old foe in John Charles, the famous Welsh centre-half/centre-forward. The 35-year-old 'Gentle Giant', ten years earlier Britain's most expensive footballer when he joined Juventus from Leeds for £57,000, had signed for Hereford in the close season and succeeded in beating Curtis enough times in the air to suggest he was still a considerable force in the game. Charles's presence helped boost the Edgar Street crowd to over 4,500.

The following night, seven days before the season started, Jimmy Hill was interviewed by the *Coventry Telegraph's* Nemo in the *Pink*. He described the new campaign as 'Our big pressure season', recognising that everyone in Coventry, and many outside, expected the club to clinch promotion to Division One.

Many supporters feared that there might be a reaction after the narrow failure to win promotion in the previous campaign and City could be also-rans. Hill's response was, as ever, positive: 'I firmly believe we have as good a chance of going up as any side in the division – including Birmingham, Wolves and Blackburn, who are being widely tipped.'

He outlined two major aims that the team had to achieve in order to attain the promotion that so many supporters craved:

'First, to make Highfield Road an unpleasant place for visiting sides to visit in terms of getting results and, second, to try to be more fluid in our attacking away from home and increase our goal power on opponents' grounds.'

On the first point, he told Nemo: 'In the old days this was a bleak ground, with a sloping pitch, and points were really hard for visiting teams to win. Now there is a tendency for visiting teams to look upon the place, with its terrific atmosphere, good playing conditions and suchlike as a challenge, and we have been a bit generous to them. We must be more ruthless and not leave as many holes in defence.'

On the second aim he admitted that although the team had conceded only 22 goals in 21 away games the previous season, their goals for of 19 was 'not good enough.' Hill concluded the interview with a confident forecast: 'This season, before the ball starts rolling, I'll say in all confidence that I believe about half a dozen sides will make the running and we'll be with them.'

In the *Pink,* Nemo made his annual predictions about the Sky Blues. In the previous two seasons his forecasts had been spot-on – a mid-table finish in 1964/65 and just missing out on promotion in 1965/66. Now Nemo believed that with the addition of Ian Gibson they would not fail to go up under the 'infectious and persuasive enthusiasm of Jimmy Hill, England's most modern-thinking manager'.

Bobby Gould, looking back, recalls that expectations were high amongst supporters: 'We thought we had won promotion the previous season when we won at Huddersfield and it was a blow to us when Southampton clinched promotion ahead of us.

'JH had signed Gibbo but in truth we didn't know much about him or realise what a talented player he was. When we couldn't beat Dudley and the Bulgarians in the pre-season games there was some nervousness that we wouldn't live up to the fans' expectations.'

Many pundits were tipping Birmingham City, rejuvenated the previous season after the appointment of the experienced Stan Cullis as manager in mid-season and bolstered by the signing from Chelsea of Barry Bridges and Bert Murray, as strong candidates for promotion. Nemo felt that there were question marks over Blues' prospects and preferred Wolves, especially if 'Ernie Hunt is buzzing'. Huddersfield, fourth the previous season, weren't amongst Nemo's strong contenders and he concluded by tipping relegated Blackburn Rovers as City's strongest challengers. The Ewood Park outfit had lost their best player Bryan Douglas to injury for much of the previous season but he was fit again and with a number of new signings they would be challengers.

A week before the season started in earnest it was announced that reserve goalkeeper Peter Thomas had joined League of Ireland champions Waterford, with whom he had just been on a tour of Europe. City had released Peter without a fee but there was an agreement that should the Sky Blues need him back at any future time he would be made available. The move was a great opportunity for Thomas, who had yet to make a first-team appearance for City, as Waterford as champions would be appearing in the European Cup and Peter was expected to play in their first-round tie against East German champions ASK Vorwaerts. After joining the club a year earlier from the GEC works team he had made rapid progress and kept goal confidently in a number of reserve games.

The club had a knock-back from the league days before the start of the season when they tried to re-arrange the home game with Birmingham, scheduled for the first Saturday in September. On the same day Warwickshire would be playing in the final of cricket's Gillette Cup at Lord's and Wembley was hosting the European Speedway finals. Many City and Blues fans would be expected to attend these two events and the club felt the attendance for the Highfield Road game would be 3-4,000 lower as a result. An attempt to switch the game to the Friday evening was rebuffed as there was 'not a legitimate excuse'.

The draw for the first round of the League Cup was made that week and City were given a home tie with fellow Second Division outfit Derby County with the tie scheduled for mid-September. It would mean another return to Highfield Road for City's former international goalkeeper Reg Matthews. Reg who had won all his five England caps whilst at Coventry in 1956, was now approaching his 34th birthday and it might be his last visit to his old stomping ground. The Football League also announced that substitutes would be allowed in League Cup games for the first time.

City's preparations for the opening league game, at home to Hull City, continued the following week. It would be the 11th time in 13 seasons that the Football League's fixture compilers had given City a home game on the opening day and the team had won ten and drawn the other in that time. There was a blow for manager Hill when Ernie Machin strained knee ligaments in training and was ruled out for two weeks.

With a good weather forecast, a crowd of 25,000 plus was predicted for the game against their newly-promoted opponents who boasted a strong defence and a high-scoring attack. The Tigers, under the chairmanship of local builder Harold Needler, were a go-ahead club. As champions of Division Three they had scored 109 goals with three forwards netting 20 or more goals – Ken Wagstaff (27), Chris Chilton (26) and Ken Houghton (22) and Wagstaff and Chilton were recognised as two of the best strikers outside the First Division.

The service was provided by the speedy winger Ian Butler. A pre-season injury to goalkeeper Maurice Swan had resulted in manager Cliff Britton having to sign Southend's Ian McKechnie on the eve of the game, and the former Arsenal keeper made his debut for the visitors.

The club's official programme boasted a clever new sky blue cover with the heads of the 22 Second Division captains around the edge. Inside there was no change to the design (that would come midway through the season) with many of the long-standing adverts unchanged, the teams displayed on the centre-pages in a 2-3-5 formation and no pictures. It was surprising that in almost five years at the club Jimmy Hill had done little or nothing to the contents of the programme.

JH's page gave the manager the chance to have his say on football matters, not just in the city but on the wider stage. After crowing about the 'outstanding excitement' of England's World Cup victory, he boasted that, having looked at the country's World Cup grounds, Highfield Road was 'second to none'. Finally, he had a pop at *Sunday Express* columnist Danny Blanchflower, the former Tottenham and Northern Ireland captain. Danny, who Hill described as his 'old pal' had, according to Jimmy, been writing for some time about the sky blue bubble bursting. Hill suggested Blanchflower take a trip to the club's £20,000 training ground at Ryton, gaze at last season's performances by the youngsters in the Midland Intermediate League, where the young Sky Blues had 'led the Midlands', and 'have a word with our bank manager, who will tell you that miracles have been done financially'. He concluded: 'No, Mr Blanchflower, the bubble cannot burst ... this is the original family club where everyone is welcomed and has a part to play. A club built on such foundations is not going to collapse overnight. No, Danny Boy, the sky is very blue in more ways than one.'

Jimmy Hill selected Ronnie Farmer in Machin's place, and gave debuts to summer signings Key and Gibson. On a sweltering hot day with temperatures in the high 70s the teams came out to a great ovation from the perspiring shirt-sleeved crowd of 27,740.

It was a gruelling encounter in the heat and a number of players on both teams were under par. City had the best chances with Ray Pointer failing to net from a good position in the first half and

Bobby Gould heading inches wide. Gibson had the crowd on its toes with a 60-yard surging run which resulted in a fine stinging drive. Three minutes into the second half, Dietmar Bruck, playing his first game in the unaccustomed left-back position, hit a shot from 35 yards. The low shot seemed to be going harmlessly wide and McKechnie was convinced it was passing outside the far post. Instead, to his horror, the ball crept inside the post.

It proved to be the only goal and although Wagstaff and Chilton both brought good saves out of Bill Glazier, the City defence, with Brian Hill shackling Wagstaff and Curtis mastering Chilton, held out under a little pressure in the final ten minutes. Two minutes from time a dust-up between Hull skipper Andy Davidson and Bobby Gould saw Davidson strike Gould in the back. Most of the crowd and the referee missed the incident but an eagle-eyed linesman spotted it and brought it to referee Cowen's attention and Davidson was sent off.

Talking about the incident 50 years later Gould remembers being a feisty young man back then: 'I had an aggressive streak and upset a lot of defenders that season and I remember Davidson getting angry with me that day. I think I fouled him and he retaliated but he raised his hands and even in those days you couldn't get away with it. My job was not only to score goals but to get under the skin of the opposition.' The Sky Blues had won on the opening day for the fifth consecutive season.

The reserves kicked off their season on the following Tuesday evening when a crowd of 5,640 watched a 1-1 home draw with Northampton. Transfer-listed Bob Wesson played in goal and there were a number of scouts including Newcastle and Bury there to see him put in a good display. Wesson, aged 25, had been at the club since 1958 but had lost his first-team place the previous Easter when Glazier had returned from a year out with a broken leg. As long as Glazier was fit he would be JH's first choice between the posts.

Bob wanted a move and told Nemo: 'I'm not fussy which club I go to, as long as I can establish a first-team place. I didn't expect much interest until I had played a few competitive games.' Rumours were rife in the midlands that First Division West Brom were interested but there had been no official approach.

On Wednesday the team travelled to Plymouth for their first away game. John Key was injured and Dave Clements came in on the left wing with Ronnie Rees switching to the right in an otherwise unchanged team. Plymouth's new signing from Coventry, John Sillett, had hoped to make his home debut against his former club but injury ruled him out. The trip to Home Park was a disaster with goalkeeper Bill Glazier having a nightmare. The home side were 2-0 ahead after nine minutes. First a Norman Piper drive from 30 yards was pushed to one side by Glazier but the ball crept over the line, then four minutes later Bryn Jones's left-foot shot from a similar distance seemed to catch Glazier unsighted and the ball crept in by a post as Glazier dived too late.

City pulled themselves back into the game and were level by half-time with Gould scoring off an upright on 36 minutes before Pointer volleyed in from Gibson's teasing free kick. At 2-2 Clements, City's best forward, had a great chance to score but missed and soon afterwards Pointer was brought down heavily and had to be substituted.

Almost immediately Plymouth re-took the lead when Farmer tackled Piper and the ball spun into the City six-yard box. Glazier and two defenders failed to stop Mike Bickle from forcing the ball home. The fourth goal, two minutes from time, was a howler on Glazier's part. He started to come out for Jones's cross but suddenly stopped dead in his tracks and, with Curtis thinking it was a keeper's ball, Bickle was left with an easy chance to head home from ten yards to make the final score 4-2. Glazier had earlier distinguished himself with two saves it would be impossible to better – twisting in mid-air to flick over a Bickle header and clutching a ferocious drive by Jennings.

The final scoreline must have been a severe shock to City's non-travelling fans who had come to expect better from away performances. Nemo's view in the following Saturday's *Pink* was that Ernie Machin's midfield constructive ability had been severely missed in both games and Ian Gibson was still 'finding his way in the City set-up'. 'Gibbo' would challenge that view three days later at Portsmouth.

The injuries to Machin and Pointer and the poor defensive performance had JH scratching his head ahead of the trip to Fratton Park. After a lacklustre start to the season the Sky Blues needed a result to get back on track. Pompey, too, had started poorly and suffered a 5-4 home defeat to Birmingham three days earlier. Pointer had recovered from his knock and took his place in an unchanged City line-up. Pompey included former City winger Albert McCann, a player released by Jimmy Hill in 1962 but who had been a key man for the south coast side ever since.

Only four months previously City's promotion hopes had collapsed at Fratton Park but there was to be no slip-up this time. In a defence-dominated first half City, playing in their change strip of red shirts and shorts, grabbed the only goal after 25 minutes. Ian Gibson, demonstrating why the club had paid a record fee for his signature, made it. In the *Coventry Telegraph* Nemo described it thus: 'Nineteen inside-forwards out of 20 would have immediately clipped the ball back from the by-line ... but Gibson, acclerating past Tindall from a Rees pass, waited, and then beautifully teed up the ball for Dave Clements to head home.'

Gibson was the main reason that City were well on top and 30 seconds into the second half he created the second goal. The diminutive Scot raced 40 yards with the ball before sliding it through for Bobby Gould to power his shot into the roof of the net. City's reliable defence did the rest, keeping a stranglehold on the experienced home attack to guarantee an away victory.

In the *Pink* the headline was: 'Gibbo The Great Sinks Portsmouth' and Nemo wrote: 'Inspired by a super-show from Ian Gibson, Coventry City came back fighting after that midweek defeat by Plymouth to outplay and outclass a limp Portsmouth side who were never able to worry a much tightened up Sky Blues' defence.'

Bobby Gould remembers the win at Portsmouth: 'Fratton Park was a great ground for me. I scored my first goal for City reserves there, then my first league goal in the 2-0 win in 1964, then again for City in 1966 and later playing for Bristol Rovers in 1978 we played Millwall, who had to switch the game to Portsmouth as a punishment for crowd trouble, and I scored a penalty in a 3-1 win.'

For 13-year-old David Smith it was a first City away game: 'Our summer holiday in 1966 was with my aunt, Mum and sister camping in France. My aunt lived in Portsmouth and we came back just in time to see Portsmouth v City and my Grandad felt duty bound to take me and we stood on the large terrace alongside the side of the pitch towards the Milton Road end.

'The Portsmouth popular end had two tiers and I recall seeing a lot of Sky Blue colour in one of the upper tiers. Two Sky Blues goals were enough to win it, I think both at the end we were closest to. I was at a boarding school in Sussex at the time and only saw City games during the school holidays. I saw the Plymouth game and then nothing until half-term. Whilst at school, Saturday afternoons were spent listening to the radio, hoping there would be some reference to the Coventry score, then it was off to the TV room to see the Teleprinter for away games but home games scores would be given later as the kick off was always 3.15. The results of evening games were harder to find so it was down to the library first thing in the morning to get results from the newspapers.'

Back in Coventry the potential of the apprentice professionals on the club's books was demonstrated at Ryton where the 'B' side met Aston Villa in a Midland Intermediate League game. The young Sky Blues were 7-0 ahead at half-time and the final score was 12-0. On the score-sheet were Graham Paddon (4), Don Peachey (3), Willie Carr (2), Tom Sinclair, Paul Bloodworth and Trevor Gould. After defeating Shrewsbury 6-0 in their first game, that made it 18 goals in their first two games!

The following Tuesday was wet and the rain kept the Highfield Road crowd down to 20,327 for the return game with Plymouth. City got their revenge for the 4-2 drubbing at Home Park six days earlier but it was a fortuitous 1-0 victory over a side who deserved at least a point. Argyle had done their homework and Norman Piper man-marked Gibson and as a result City looked like an engine running at half-power. City had a real let-off in the 22nd minute when Nicky Jennings met a Reynolds cross. Glazier somehow got down to block the effort but it bounced off his chest and in a furious scramble George Curtis cleared it off the line for a corner.

City got their goal after 37 minutes when Pointer met Mick Kearns's finely-hit cross and clipped in a right-foot drive from practically a horizontal position after falling. The pace picked up until half-time but after the break it was Plymouth who looked the more likely promotion candidates. Their best chance came in the last few seconds as Kearns hit a chancy back-pass towards Glazier. The City keeper had time only to block it, and as it bounced clear to Argyle left-back Doug Baird, he cleverly lobbed it back towards the City goal. Glazier scrambled back and two City defenders desperately scrambled back on the goal-line as Baird's lob flew inches over the bar.

It was later revealed that Gibson had been nursing a heel injury which may have ruled out some players but it was clear that the message was going around the division: stop Gibson and you'll stop Coventry. Portsmouth had not done their homework and paid the penalty but Plymouth could have easily done the double over the Sky Blues.

Ronnie Farmer remembers having a stinker in the game: 'I misplaced so many passes that I fully expected to be substituted. Nothing I did came off and I was crap but I kept running and tackling. Before the next game we had a team-talk and JH went around the room asking us how we thought we had played. I told him 'I was surprised you didn't take me off, I was hopeless' but he replied 'you kept running, you kept tackling and you blocked some passes, all that was wrong was your passing and the rest of your game was fine, so I wasn't going to take you off'

The one bright spot in the Plymouth game was the performance of centre-forward Bobby Gould who chased everything and never gave up the fight. He put in a number of powerful shots after bulldozing through but his efforts failed to inspire his team-mates and Rees and Pointer had again been well below their best.

In the programme Jimmy Hill was in confrontational mood once again. After aiming his sights at Danny Blanchflower in the Hull issue he now turned on two of the elder statesmen of English football in Bob Lord, the outspoken chairman of Burnley, and Sir Joseph Richards, chairman of the Football League. Jimmy reported that Lord had 'pontificated last week that toilet facilities and amenities will not attract fans to soccer, but the great magnet was a winning team playing attractive football'. Hill went on: 'Heaven help us if any of them fail to understand that point.'

Richards was called to account by Hill for stating that 'the English way of playing was the best, much better in fact than the Continental techniques and gimmickry'. Jimmy took offence to the use of the word gimmickry. 'How people love to use that word in derogatory fashion since the success of the Sky Blues. One is surely entitled to ask Mr Richards on what basis he feels qualified to advise anyone as to which methods bring success in 1966. His own Fourth Division team, Barnsley, played a League Cup match last Wednesday in front of a crowd of 2,495.'

Jimmy argued that Coventry had tried to 'fight the disease of disinterest in every way we know how. We have improved the playing staff, built toilets, offered amenities and I see no reason to apologise for one brick'. He went on to imply that nothing had been learned from England's 6-3 defeat by Hungary in 1953 by the men running the English game.

City's visitors four days hence were local rivals Birmingham City who had won their first four games and were the leaders of the first league table. The Sky Blues would have to up their game if they were going to avoid defeat against the Blues.

Top of Division Two (31 August 1966)

		Pl	*W*	*D*	*L*	*F*	*A*	*Pts*
1	Birmingham	4	4	0	0	12	6	8
2	Bolton	4	3	1	0	7	3	7
3	Blackburn	4	3	1	0	7	4	7
4	Ipswich	4	3	0	1	8	2	6
5	Crystal Palace	4	3	0	1	8	5	6
6	SKY BLUES	4	3	0	1	6	4	6

Chapter 3

September – Lack of goals a worry as Sky Blues fail to impress

ON the first Saturday of September there was a large away following from Birmingham City to boost the Highfield Road crowd to 36,400 – the fourth highest in the Football League that day – and the cricket and speedway attractions in London seemed to have had no effect on the attendance. Blues looked strong with their experienced new signings from Chelsea, Barry Bridges and Bert Murray. The legendary former Wolves manager Stan Cullis had taken over as manager at St Andrew's halfway through the previous campaign and had pulled the Blues away from the foot of the table to a respectable mid-table finish.

The signings, especially that of Bridges who had played for England just over a year earlier, were a statement of intent. Bridges had been on City's transfer radar before Ian Gibson had been signed but it was believed that Blues' better financial deal had won the race in their favour. The bookmakers had made Blues one of the favourites for promotion and their opening day win at Molineux had confirmed their threat. Bridges and Murray were there to provide some flair to what had been a tough, workmanlike team that included the dour wing-half Ron Wylie, who would later be head coach at Coventry under Gordon Milne, and the long-haired Trevor Hockey, a skilful but feisty midfield player.

For City, Ray Pointer was injured so Ernie Machin returned with young full-back John Burckitt on the bench. This was a much-improved performance from the Sky Blues and Nemo felt that: 'The team recaptured the admiration of their followers with a fiery performance that was more in keeping with the known ability of the side.'

City had a firm grip on the game for well over an hour against a defensive-minded Blues and George Curtis should have scored from Clements's corner in the first half but got his forehead under the ball. City finally got their breakthrough ten minutes into the second half with a goal virtually out of nothing. Ron Farmer's down-field pass was blocked, but Gould moved on to the loose ball with tremendous acceleration, cut past defenders Thomson and Martin and had it past keeper Jim Herriot with 'the skill of a seasoned player'.

Blues had to come out of their defensive shell and on 73 minutes Geoff Vowden eluded the attentions of Brian Hill for the one and only time to slide the ball past Glazier in what was their first effort on goal. Near the end Hockey was sent off after a bad foul on Farmer by the tunnel. He had already been booked and became the second visiting player to receive his marching orders. The result ended Blues' 100% record but they were still top of the pile with the Sky Blues moving up to fifth place.

The reserve side played out a 0-0 draw with Leicester City at Filbert Street in the Football Combination Cup. They came up against several promising youngsters including Peter Shilton, David Nish and Alan Woollett. The 'A' team lost 1-0 to Kidderminster Harriers and the 'B' team found Walsall a much tougher opposition than their two previous opponents and were held 2-2.

The Sky Blues then faced two successive away games, at Millwall and Norwich. The match at the Den took place on the Monday evening following the Blues game. Millwall were on the crest of a wave having won successive promotions from Division Four and they had not lost in the league at home for 49 games. Sadly, City's form, so promising against Birmingham, sagged in south London and resulted in a single-goal defeat with the Sky Blues rarely looking capable of ending the Lions' incredible run.

Millwall manager Benny Fenton, having notched the team's first win of the season against Northampton two days earlier, decided to keep an unchanged side which meant no place for the new centre-forward Bobby Hunt who had signed the previous week from Northampton.

City, with Ray Pointer in for Dave Clements, started well and Lawrie Leslie in the home goal had to tip over a Bobby Gould header after eight minutes. Soon after Leslie smothered another header before Pointer forced the keeper to save with his legs. Millwall soon took control, chasing everything and never gave the Coventry midfield time on the ball.

With over 15,000 inside, the Den was a cacophony of noise and any home attack was roared by the partisan crowd who also booed George Curtis every time he touched the ball. City's disjointed attack looked unlikely to score and with 65 minutes on the clock Millwall struck from a free kick. Tom Wilson touched the ball to tiny winger Joe Broadfoot who unleashed a shot that scraped just inside the post past a groping Glazier.

In the final ten minutes City at last showed some urgency and looked more menacing and a minute from time they beat Leslie.

From outside the penalty area Ronnie Farmer hit a fierce drive which beat the keeper but at the last moment swerved inches past the post.

The following Saturday's *Pink* reported that three young Coventry City fans had been the beneficiaries of kindness from manager Hill at Millwall. One had ridden down from Coventry on his motor-bike, only to find after the game that it had been stolen. Two others had their wallets stolen during the game and had no means of getting home. As soon as Hill heard of their predicament he said: 'Come on lads – ride home with us.' So the three unfortunates jumped on to the team coach and were brought back to Coventry.

The Second Division programme that week saw Ipswich displace Birmingham at the top by virtue of a 4-3 home win over Derby County whilst Blues were held 1-1 at Plymouth. There were signs that Ipswich, relegated from the First Division in 1964 and now managed by Bill McGarry, were getting their act together at the lower level and they had now won five out of six games.

Five days later at Carrow Road City faced the Canaries who had started the season poorly but had notched their first win in midweek, away at Northampton. Norwich had a new manager in the shape of Lol Morgan who had taken Darlington to their first promotion in 40 years the previous campaign. Morgan had the problem of re-moulding the attack following the summer sale of top scorer Ron Davies to Southampton. Gordon Bolland was wearing the No.9 shirt and Hugh Curran, a January signing from Millwall, was alongside him. There were no great expectations at Carrow Road that season for a club that had never played in the top flight.

On a sun-drenched afternoon, Jimmy Hill recalled Dave Clements in place of Ray Pointer in his only team change. Hill's set-up was a defensive one with Gibson playing extremely deep and as a result City didn't get enough attackers forward. Both sides had good chances in an even first half with Gould heading wide from a good position and Bolland shooting over following a free kick. Four minutes into the second half City were caught napping from a free kick and Curran had space to head powerfully past Glazier.

The goal brought City to life and on 68 minutes they drew level. Some nice passing between Farmer, Gibson and Rees saw the winger take the ball to the by-line and deliver the perfect cross for Bobby Gould to head home. City looked the more likely winners after that but a draw was a fair result. Nemo however was far from convinced in his match report: 'They [City] cannot go on in this fashion with goals at such a premium, and hope to keep raking in points.' Once again City's attack had failed to produce the goods and Nemo pointed the finger at Rees and Gibson who he argued 'are just not playing well enough'.

There were new league leaders on Saturday evening – the third different team inside a week – as leaders Ipswich drew 1-1 at Ashton Gate and were leap-frogged by Bolton Wanderers, 1-0 home winners over Huddersfield. City were seventh, three points behind Bolton.

City's reserves lost 4-3 at Nottingham Forest that day after leading 3-2 with 25 minutes left. Pat Morrissey pushed his claims for a first-team call-up by scoring twice and John Key netted the third goal but it now looked as though the team would not qualify for the next stage of the Combination Cup. The 'A' team lost 2-1 at Atherstone after leading through a John Docker goal. The 'B' team's incredible scoring exploits came to an end when a team with six triallists and three amateurs came up against West Brom's 'A' team at Ryton. Albion won 3-0 with 15-year-old Asa Hartford scoring one of the goals.

There was good news that weekend. The club announced that a former Forest youngster Trevor Shepherd, had signed for City on a free-transfer after impressing in City's West Midlands

League side as a triallist. At the same time, it was revealed that, in the face of opposition from 19 other clubs, they had signed 15-year-old Cheshire schoolboy Brian Wilks. Top flight clubs Leeds, Liverpool and Burnley had all sought Brian's signature but he and his family chose the Sky Blues.

In the *Pink* under the heading 'Sky Blues' magic never fails to lure best of boys', Jimmy Hill explained that money played an insignificant part in these transactions: 'We will not pay boys before they've done anything – it ruins them for life. We rely on our image. When they walk in the front door, they sense something different. The manager can put on a smile but he can't force everyone on the staff to do the same thing for the boy's benefit. It's the quality of the staff and the atmosphere that often sway things for us.'

Nemo explained how Brian, a strongly-built striker from Ellesmere Port, came to City: 'It came as the result of a routine tip-off from a scout in the Cheshire area. City receive hundreds of reports on boys during the course of a month and they all have to sifted carefully with the best of them invited for Sunday morning trials at Ryton where most of the coaching staff including JH, would be in attendance.'

The following Tuesday, 13 September City faced Derby County at home in a League Cup second round tie. Pointer was recalled in place of the injured Ernie Machin and John Burckitt made a rare appearance at full-back, allowing Dietmar Bruck to play alongside Curtis at the heart of the defence. Derby, managed by Tim Ward, were bottom of the league table with just three points from seven games but started the game strongly. Glazier had to tip Eddie Thomas's strong header over the bar and then the keeper failed to catch a corner but Gordon Hughes missed an open goal. City however struck in the 33rd minute – Gibson's cross was only partially headed away and Farmer hit a crisp shot into the net.

City were on top and former City custodian Reg Matthews, captain against his old club on the night, had to pull off some good saves to keep County in the tie. On 58 minutes City extended their lead. Mick Kearns's long ball down the middle found Clements running strongly. The Irishman brushed aside a challenge from Bobby Saxton, Matthews only partially stopped his first shot but 'Clem' followed up to score. There was a rare sound of Matthews being booed by a Coventry crowd when he fouled Pointer in a dash out of goal after 68 minutes and the home fans did not let him forget it.

Five minutes from time City, coasting to the third round, were stunned by Derek Draper's shot which Glazier failed to hold and Gordon Hodgson nipped in to score. Suddenly City looked vulnerable and the home crowd were biting their nails especially when a shot on the turn from Draper sizzled past an upright with Glazier groping. The final whistle came as a relief for the 14,800 crowd and the City players. The following day's draw for the third round gave City a long trip to Third Division Brighton in what would be the two club's first meeting in the competition.

On the same night, the 'A' team won 2-0 at Redditch in a West Midlands League Cup tie with goals from John Tudor and Pat Morrissey.

The Sky Blues had got back to winning ways although not convincingly. Now they could look forward to home games on successive Saturdays to attempt to catch up with the league leaders Bolton. For the eighth league game on Saturday, 17 September, Bristol City were the visitors to Highfield Road. The Robins's great servant John Atyeo had retired and the team were struggling for goals without him. With only one victory they were 20th in the table. In one change from the Derby game Jimmy Hill recalled Brian Hill for his 200th first team appearance in place of John Burckitt.

The visitors had a panic on the morning of the match when inside-forward Terry Bush woke to discover that his ankle was badly swollen and was ruled out. At 7.30 in the morning manager Fred Ford called 18-year-old youth player Dickie Down at his home in Bristol and told him to get to Highfield Road as he was making his debut that afternoon – against George Curtis!

Bristol were full of tall players, Bobby Gould recalls: 'They had the tallest defence in the country in those days, none of them were under 6ft and they kicked lumps out of me. The wing-halves were Gordon Low and Gordon Parr and Parr became my best mate when I was at Bristol City and we still see each other these days and talk about their giant back four. They had also had Jack Connor, an old-fashioned centre-half who if you went past him just brought you down.'

Bristol came to defend with nine and, sometimes, ten men behind the ball and for long periods City didn't have the guile to break down the packed visitors' defence. At the interval, there were murmurs of discontent amongst the 21,082 crowd after 45 minutes of infuriatingly inept finishing and an almost total lack of enterprise from Bristol. The visitors had almost scored just before the break when Dietmar Bruck had to leap to head Sharpe's goal-bound effort off the line with Bill Glazier beaten.

Ronnie Farmer didn't appear for the second half after being concussed in a clash of heads with Brian Clark and John Mitten came on as substitute for only his second appearance of the season, with Dave Clements dropping into midfield. The breakthrough came on 65 minutes. Ronnie Rees's shot hit Gordon Low's hand and although it looked unintentional the referee pointed to the spot. With regular penalty-taker Farmer off the field, Mick Kearns stepped up to take the spot-kick. He placed it too close to Mike Gibson in the Bristol goal and was relieved when the ball flew sharply up into the roof of the net off the keeper's body as he dived for the ball.

Only Ian Gibson showed any real guile but his shrewd crosses found no takers. Bobby Gould fought hard but Pointer and Rees continued to struggle to find their form. At the end it was two points but after the third 1-0 home win in a row the fans wondered how long the team could go on relying on a solitary goal for a result.

Dickie Down never became a regular at Ashton Gate but did score for City 48 hours later in a League Cup loss at Swansea and managed four more goals in seven games for the Robins that season, but after two games the following season he joined Bradford Park Avenue.

Elsewhere Bolton consolidated their top place with a 5-2 victory at Cardiff with Wyn Davies and Francis Lee both scoring braces. Ipswich slipped up 2-1 at home to Carlisle and Crystal Palace were up to second after a 2-1 home win over Derby.

City's 'A' team pulled off a creditable 5-1 win away to Port Vale Reserves in the West Midlands League with John Tudor and Trevor Shepherd both scoring braces in only the team's second win in the higher division.

In the *Pink* it was reported that coach Pat Saward was appealing for players for the 'C' team. He was finding it difficult finding young local amateurs to play regularly for the team as many thought that it wasn't worth it if there was no future for them. Saward appealed for young student teachers to turn out and invited them to training sessions on Monday and Thursday evenings. Saward also revealed that at the age of 38 he had applied for a permit to play in the West Midlands League in order to give the young team of 15-16-year-olds some experience. Saward hadn't played competitive football since leaving Huddersfield to become City's coach four years earlier.

The team's inconsistent form prompted criticism in a letter published from Mr Duncan of Long Buckby. Mr Duncan took Jimmy Hill to task for playing 'Ernie Machin at every opportunity, for not playing Gibson as a more positive attacker and for not picking Pointer as an attacker rather than at number 11'. Overall, he considered Hill's tactics to be 'too negative'.

Hill wasn't happy with the Bristol performance and acted decisively by selecting the out-of-form Rees and Pointer in the reserves against Forest three days later. JH told the press: 'They have both been going through a bad patch, and the sooner it ends the better. If not, other players have got to be tried.' Rees was on target in the 4-0 victory over a strong Forest team that included England international winger Alan Hinton. John Mitten and John Tudor, with two, were the other scorers and the latter's performance earned him his first-team debut on the following Saturday against Bury in place of Pointer.

The following evening Jimmy Hill travelled to Wolverhampton to see one of City's promotion rivals hammer Cardiff 7-1. JH referred to the game in his programme notes on the Saturday: 'Wolverhampton have suddenly forced themselves back into the picture with two overwhelming wins. I saw them on Wednesday destroy Cardiff ... and their forward line certainly knows how to rub it in when it's on top.'

In all Hill made five changes for the visit of Bury, three of them positional. Farmer wasn't fit to return so Clements continued at wing-half, Rees switched to the left wing with John Key recalled on the right and 20-year-old Tudor, who a year earlier had been playing for non-league Ilkeston, at inside-right. Hill explained: 'He [Tudor] has given a series of consistently good performances for the reserves.'

The changes worked as City romped to a 3-0 victory but it was a game with controversy. Bobby Gould gave the Sky Blues a fifth-minute lead with a flashing header from a Clements' corner but City failed to grab the goals their first-half performance deserved. On the hour came the first controversial moment. Bobby Owen, the division's leading scorer with eight goals in nine games, netted for Bury only for the referee to rule the goal out for hand ball. Furious Bury players surrounded the ref but he was adamant. Within seconds City were 2-0 ahead when Gibson's cross was headed out to Clements who hit a thunderous shot into the net.

Then with 15 minutes left Gibson's scorching shot came off the underside of the bar and spun back into keeper Neil Ramsbottom's arms. The referee and his linesman signalled a goal but again the Bury players were angry at the decision. It was Gibbo's first goal for the club and he was robbed of a second near the final whistle when two of his colleagues were standing offside as he netted.

John Tudor had a satisfying debut and impressed with his heading and the 22,000 crowd went home relieved that City had re-discovered their shooting boots. In the *Pink* Tudor explained how, after a frustrating three years trying to break into senior football, he had arrived at Highfield Road: 'I'd stopped thinking about going anywhere by Christmas last year, but then Jimmy Hill and Pat Saward saw me playing for Ilkeston in a match at Lockheed Leamington and Jim Rayner, the manager of the Derbyshire club, recommended me. Jim's lost his job since then but I owe him a lot. It was as a result of this that I came to Coventry. As soon as I walked into Highfield Road I knew my luck had changed. I said to myself "this is it – this is what you've been waiting for".'

Elsewhere, Second Division leaders Bolton were held 0-0 at home by Wolves and second-placed Crystal Palace lost 1-0 at Plymouth allowing Ipswich, back to winning ways (2-1 at Blackburn) and the Sky Blues to move ahead of them. City were up to fourth in the table, two points behind Bolton. The 'A' team lost 2-0 at Lower Gornal but the 'B' team won 5-2 at Shrewsbury after trailing 2-1 at half-time, with goals from Bloodworth, Trevor Gould (2), new boy Wilkes and an own goal.

The following Thursday it was reported that Walsall had made an inquiry about Bob Wesson, City's transfer-listed goalkeeper.

No fee was being disclosed but Jimmy Hill commented: 'Bob is a good goalkeeper and I would class him in the £20,000 bracket. But we will not ask that sort of sum for him, in fairness to the player.' The Saddlers were in the bottom half of the Third Division and had been beaten 4-0 at Workington the night before. Their manager Ray Shaw was not available for comment. There had been no firm inquiries about John Mitten, City's other transfer-listed player, but it was understood he had been watched by Plymouth Argyle.

A day later Wesson was on his way to Walsall with a £10,000 fee paid by the Saddlers and was lined up for his debut the following day at Darlington, curiously enough at a spot only ten miles from his native Thornaby-on-Tees. Bob had been the goalkeeper in the Third Division championship season 1963/64 but lost his place when Glazier had been signed only to regain the keeper's jersey when Glazier broke his leg in April 1965. Jimmy Hill paid tribute to him: 'I am most grateful to Bob for the way in which he has done his job here, and for suffering the ups and downs with good grace.'

Wesson's departure gave Hill a slight headache in the goalkeeping department and he quickly moved to recall Peter Thomas from Waterford. Thomas had been transferred to the Irish club in the summer but they had released him back to the Sky Blues on the understanding that he could return to Ireland, if required, at any time. There was no transfer fee involved.

Top of Division Two (30 September)

		PL	*W*	*D*	*L*	*F*	*A*	*Pts*
1	Bolton	9	6	2	1	18	8	14
2	Ipswich	9	6	1	2	18	10	13
3	Hull City	9	6	0	3	20	8	12
4	SKY BLUES	9	5	2	2	12	7	12
5	Crystal Palace	9	5	2	2	15	11	12

Chapter 4

October – Dark clouds over Highfield Road

COVENTRY City travelled to Preston on Saturday, 1 October and suffered an unlucky 3-2 defeat. Jimmy Hill kept an unchanged side but Preston were without Welsh inside-forward Brian Godfrey, who was injured, but were able to call on Nobby Lawton, a former Busby Babe, who was coming back from injury.

City went behind within two minutes after conceding their first penalty of the season. Mick Kearns was adjudged to have fouled winger Frank Lee and Alex Dawson, another former Busby Babe, hammered home a fierce right-foot shot that gave Glazier no chance. City came back strongly and had two good chances to score. First, Rees crashed a great shot against the bar and then the Welsh wizard put over a defence-splitting pass that Bobby Gould should have put away. The game was no picnic and the fouls came thick and fast. Preston goalkeeper Alan Kelly needed treatment after a collision with Gould and Preston gave Ian Gibson some rough treatment. Then Dawson grabbed Curtis around the waist and in another clash minutes later the City captain fell to the ground clutching his stomach and the referee spoke to both players.

On 27 minutes, against the run of play, it was 2-0 as Scot Ernie Hannigan was first to react to a loose ball after Glazier had stopped Lee's free kick. Gibson however was the best player on the pitch, pulling all the strings and he was mainly responsible for the Sky Blues reducing the lead five minutes before half-time. 'Gibbo' tricked Preston's Alan Spavin with a nutmeg before slipping the ball on to Gould who in turn found John Tudor unmarked and the young Derbyshire striker had the ball in the net for his first senior goal.

The fouls and rough play continued into the second half and after Dietmar Bruck tripped David Wilson the referee called the captains together, telling them to cut out the rough play. Within minutes City were level as George Curtis's thumping header from a Clements corner went through a forest of legs and into the net. City's joy was short-lived as on the hour Glazier misjudged Dawson's header, the ball hit a post and Wilson forced home the loose ball with City's defence, the best in the division before the game, at sixes and sevens. Despite strong City pressure in the last half-hour, the home side held on to gain the two points and leave Coventry still without a league win at Deepdale.

Hull City had crept into top place by virtue of a 2-0 midweek victory over Portsmouth but after losing at Plymouth they were usurped at the top by Bolton who fought out a 2-2 draw at Portman Road. Bolton's Wyn Davies netted his eighth goal of the season and the First Division scouts were keeping close tabs on him. City were eighth but only three points behind Bolton and second-placed Ipswich.

A midweek reserve-team friendly against Stoke City at Highfield Road enabled Jimmy Hill to run the rule over several key players. Ernie Machin and Ronnie Farmer were returning from injury and Ray Pointer was trying to recapture some form but these three senior players were overshadowed by two promising youngsters in the 2-1 victory. Trevor Shepherd, making his reserve debut, looked very sharp and was gaining in confidence when he had to go off as a result of a hard challenge from Jackie Marsh. Birmingham-born Benny Glover also impressed at wing-half with some tenacious tackling and scored the winning goal with a hard drive that took a deflection. Goalkeeper Peter Thomas, on his return from Waterford, also had a fine game.

The following night a trip to Brighton for League Cup action gave Jimmy Hill's team the chance to bounce back from the Preston defeat. Third Division Brighton had started the season poorly and had only just secured their first league win of the season – a win seemed a formality for the unchanged Sky Blues. The Seagulls were lucky to survive an early onslaught from Hill's men. Ronnie Rees and John Tudor had shots blocked on the line and Bobby Gould hit the post with the goal gaping. It was no surprise when Rees scored after 15 minutes, his first goal of the campaign. He received the ball from Gibson, cut inside his full-back and struck a strong ground shot past Brian Powney in the home goal. Ten minutes later Tudor, according to Nemo in the *Coventry Telegraph*, 'improving with every game', looked to have scored a second goal but Powney somehow tipped the fierce shot over the bar.

City failed to build on the early lead and for the second game running conceded a penalty on 35 minutes when Brighton's Turner seemed to fall over Brian Hill's legs. Jimmy Collins took the spot-kick but Glazier, playing in his home town, smothered the ball for a great save.

Brighton's frantic second half rally seemed to have petered out when, with ten minutes remaining, they scored a freak equaliser. Glazier had Collins's shot well covered but the ball spun off Mick Kearns's boot in flight and deceived the keeper. Suddenly Brighton smelt blood and threw everything at the Sky

Blues. Wally Gould headed just wide and, with the 13,097 crowd going wild, Glazier somehow got his hand to a goal-bound effort from the same player. At the final whistle the Sky Blues looked the more relieved team but would surely put the Seagulls to the sword at Highfield Road in the replay a week later.

City's players stayed at Worthing after the Brighton game and on Thursday they relaxed with a game of golf before the long trip to Carlisle for the game at Brunton Park on Saturday. They heard that the winners of the replay with Brighton would have a home tie with Northampton Town which opened up the possibility of the legendary George Hudson returning to Highfield Road.

Carlisle themselves had had a long journey in midweek having travelled to First Division Southampton in the League Cup and come away with an excellent 3-3 draw. Four successive league wins had lifted the Cumbrians into sixth place (ahead of the Sky Blues) and they were a formidable home side having lost only three games the previous season and one in the current campaign. Jimmy Hill recalled Ernie Machin and Ray Pointer in place of Key and Tudor. Carlisle meanwhile were without Gordon Marsland who had suffered a broken leg at Southampton. Peter Garbutt deputised.

City, playing in their all-red change kit, were badly out of touch for most of the game and Gibson and Pointer struggled against more physical opponents. They fell behind on the half-hour following a rare mistake by George Curtis who missed a long ball through the middle and left Dave Wilson free to score.

On 64 minutes it was 2-0 after Garbutt got his leg to a cleverly worked corner and gave Glazier no chance. There was a late rally from the Sky Blues with Dave Clements pushed into the lacklustre attack. He hit four of his searing shots and one of them went into the net via a post in the 77th minute but Carlisle saw out the final minutes despite considerable City pressure. The Sky Blues however did not deserve a point.

The defeat left City back in tenth place, five points behind the leaders Bolton who whipped Preston 4-2 with Wyn Davies hitting a first-half hat-trick. Second-placed Ipswich beat Birmingham 3-2 and these two teams were one point clear of Crystal Palace (5-1 winners over Northampton) and Hull City (4-2 winners away to Cardiff with Ken Wagstaff netting all four goals).

City's 'A' team drew 1-1 at Dudley Town with Dudley Roberts heading City's goal whilst the 'B' team won 5-2 at Aston Villa with goals from Don Peachey (3), Graham Paddon and Trevor Gould.

After the game at Carlisle there was trouble in the away dressing room. In his autobiography Jimmy Hill described his version of events: 'When the game was over in Carlisle I was as fierce as the Coventry players had ever seen me, I chastised Ian (Gibson), pointing out that his performance left a lot to be desired, or ungentlemanly words to that effect. "It seems to me you are more interested in the result of the three o'clock race at Kempton Park than you are in ours at the same time on Saturday." They were my final words.'

Eye witnesses describe a physical confrontation in the dressing room and confirm the fall-out was as much about Gibson's betting habits and money as his role in the team although Hill did think Gibson's play lacked discipline. He had had a poor game at Carlisle but also had been singled out for praise by Nemo seven days earlier at Preston. There were without question other players in the team who were underperforming to a greater extent. Although he didn't play, Ronnie Farmer was in the dressing room and recalls the incident: 'Gibbo had his head in the Sporting Life or some such paper and JH came in and let rip at him. I remember him saying "That's all you think about – horses. If you took your mind off that and did as I asked you to do." Gibbo had a poor game, he wasn't obeying instructions – he was coming too deep and then losing the ball in his own half and putting the team under pressure but he wasn't the only one who had a bad game.'

Bobby Gould also remembers the day well: 'I'd never seen JH blow a gasket the way he did that day. He blasted Gibbo with both barrels and I didn't want to be anywhere near Gibbo in case JH started on me so I tried to move away from him. Gibbo was one of the racing school in the club and could always give you a sure-fire winner that usually didn't win. I think JH, who to a large extent didn't like betting, thought his performance was affected by him concentrating on some horse or another and felt he deserved better from a player who had cost the club a lot of money. Up till then I'd never seen JH lose his rag but he certainly left the rest of us quaking in our boots and very clear who was the gaffer.'

Many of the pressmen covering the game had overheard the row and inevitably it made headlines in the Sunday papers. On the long train journey home there was, according to Nemo in his book *The Sky Blues*, 'an electric atmosphere'. Gibbo had decided there was only one course open to him. He slapped in a transfer request on the Monday morning. He told Nemo: 'I'm determined to get away. The sooner the better. Things don't seem to have worked out. I'm sorry.'

Hill, for his part, uttered a vague: 'We just don't see eye to eye on the way he should play in the team.' The club would not let the Scot go, he added, without a suitable replacement. In the meantime, Gibson was omitted from the team to face Brighton in the League Cup replay 'while we sort things out'.

The announcement the following day that secretary Paul Oliver was leaving the club only served to add to the feeling of unrest. 'What's going on at Highfield Road?, people asked. Oliver, 31, who had been at the club since April 1963, was leaving to join the new North American National Professional Soccer League in an administrative role. His replacement was 36-year-old Alan

Leather who had been assistant secretary at Tottenham Hotspur for nine years but had recently resigned and was about to join the Football Association when he was approached by Coventry and decided to come to Highfield Road instead. During the 1966 World Cup he was a team liaison officer and at one stage was attached to the England squad.

That Tuesday night was one of the worst of the Jimmy Hill era. On top of missing Gibson, the manager was forced to make changes owing to injuries to Bruck and Brian Hill. Mick Coop, 18, came in a full-back for his senior debut, Dudley Roberts made his first appearance of the season and Farmer returned from injury allowing Clements to play on the left wing with Rees switched to the right.

City took an early lead through a Bobby Gould diving header but former Chelsea and Watford forward Charlie Livesey soon equalised and a minute before the break the Seagulls went ahead through Billy Cassidy. As the teams re-took the field after the break City were booed by their own fans – something unheard of in the five years since Hill had arrived at the club.

With Gould suffering from a nasty eye injury incurred in heading the goal and Rees carried off just after half-time, the City second-half revival never arrived and 13 minutes into the second period Brighton struck again – Howard Wilkinson cracking home what looked suspiciously like an offside goal to make it 3-1. The visitors controlled the last half hour comfortably in front of a stunned and angry home crowd. Glazier, whose judgement was often at fault on a night of endless errors knew nothing about power shots from Livesey and Cassidy which struck the posts. He almost conceded a fourth goal three minutes from the end after a badly-timed run out of his goal, only to see a shot from Wilkinson – who had dribbled around him – pass across the goal and be cleared.

Brighton therefore became the first visiting side to win at Highfield Road since Huddersfield the previous November, ending a 17-game unbeaten home run. The crowd of 13,437 was the lowest at the stadium for two years. Nemo described it as 'an inexcusable performance' and 'no fluke defeat'. On top of the Gibson episode and two successive away defeats, the club seemed to be in crisis.

For debutant Coop it was a nightmare experience but Nemo felt that on a night when established players looked like fish out of water, he performed creditably. After the game Mick told the journalist: 'I think the behaviour of some of the spectators towards their own team was shocking. I've never heard anything like it playing for the reserves, and it was a bit shattering.'

The following day Nemo revealed that City were negotiating with a First Division club on a player-exchange deal involving Ian Gibson. Jimmy Hill would not name the club in case the deal did not go through but it was understood that it wasn't Leeds United, a club interested in Gibson before he signed for City. The following day it was reported that a Second Division club were supposedly keen on the Scot but Hill wouldn't speculate on whether a deal was likely before the weekend. On Friday a rumour went around that Fulham were prepared to do an exchange deal involving Gibson and former England international captain Johnny Haynes. Hill quickly quashed the story.

More problems faced the manager as the week from hell went on. Promising full-back John Burckitt asked for a transfer because of a lack of first-team opportunities. Mick Coop's promotion on the Tuesday night had clearly upset the former England youth international but John's progress had stalled in the last 12 months and Coop now looked the better prospect. If things could get any worse, Ronnie Rees had a foot in plaster following the Brighton game and would miss Saturday's visit of Blackburn Rovers.

There was no mention of the Gibson issue in Jimmy Hill's programme notes for the Brighton game as it had probably gone to the printers before the story blew up. However, for the

Blackburn issue Hill employed a novel and fascinating way of getting his point across to the fans. He used an imaginary conversation between himself and Joanna, his young daughter. Joanna begins by asking her dad 'Why are they booing the team as they come out', to which JH replies, 'Because they want them to do well'. 'Is that the way to help them do better?', queries Joanna. The conversation goes on with more probing questions: 'Why are they singing dirty songs about you, Daddy?' to which JH replies 'They like singing and dirt and they don't like me' and goes on to explain that what they really don't like is that the team aren't scoring goals and beating everybody. When asked 'What's that Gibson business?' JH replies: 'They want him in the team.' 'Do you want him in the team?' asks Joanna, to which JH replies, 'I want everyone whom I think will help get the Sky Blues into Division One'. After having a chuckle at the humour of the piece, one can see that Hill is using the dialogue to get over what he might not have been able to say overtly, that he's not impressed with the criticism and fans who think they know better than him, and that only a winning team would satisfy the supporters.

Newly out of Division One, Blackburn boasted six internationals including Keith Newton, Bryan Douglas, John Connelly and Ronnie Clayton. They had started the campaign strongly before three successive defeats had pegged them back but they were ahead of City and after all the extraordinary happenings at Highfield Road were favourites to win.

Hill had to rebuild confidence and Brian Hill, John Key and John Tudor came in for Coop, Roberts and Pointer, as well as John Mitten for the injured Rees. City started strongly and took a seventh-minute lead. Key raced past his full-back and sent over a low teasing cross. Gould almost turned it in at close range but the ball ran to Tudor who scored with ease. The pressure on the visitors' goal continued and after 19 minutes it became 2-0. In a slick and fast movement Mick Kearns fed Machin whose ball down field caught the Rovers defence in two minds and Gould raced through to crack the ball past Barton for his seventh goal of the campaign.

The difference from the Brighton game was tangible with players fighting for every ball and never giving Rovers' star-studded team a moment's peace. The crowd of 21,016, many of whom thought City would be sunk by the Lancashire club, got behind City from the start and came alive in reaction to the early goals.

City eased back at 2-0, allowing Blackburn a lot of possession but their play was over elaborate and with Clements marking danger-man Douglas like a limpet and Hill doing a similar job on winger Connelly, City rarely looked in trouble. On one occasion Clements slipped and Douglas looked certain to score but hit his shot against a post and Andy McEvoy could have scored in the second half but hesitated when clean through. At the final whistle there was relief that City, without Gibson, had come through with two points.

League leaders Bolton had lost 2-1 at Bury on the Friday night and second-placed Ipswich slipped up 4-2 at Portsmouth to allow Hull City, 3-1 victors at home to Wolves, to go top of the pile. Plymouth Argyle beat bottom team Cardiff 7-1 with Mike Bickle scoring four to go sixth – their sixth home win out of seven. The Sky Blues were eighth, four points behind Hull.

Gibson meanwhile was playing for the reserves at Ipswich and had a 'quiet game although he showed one or two flashes of brilliance'. He scored with a header but was unable to stop the side losing 2-1. The 'A' team lost 4-0 at Ryton to Bromsgrove whilst the 'B' side, with four 15-year-olds, beat Birmingham 4-0 with Paddon scoring a hat-trick.

In the *Coventry Telegraph Pink* that evening Nemo reviewed the catastrophic events of the previous seven days. He wrote: 'The factor that has shaken City followers to the core is not so much a transfer request from a star player – this is part of the everyday soccer scene. But that the capture of the most expensive player in the club's history should backfire so resoundingly after the short period of 13 matches.'

He went on: 'I do not think it is too late for City to pull themselves together and fight to re-establish themselves as contenders, even though there must be serious doubts as to whether they can, in the next few crucial weeks, find the form to do it.'

He added that several other players had been inconsistent in the first third of the season, pointing fingers at Rees, Pointer, Glazier and Kearns and concluded that Gibson's departure would not solve problems but only add to them. Hill had, in his opinion, made a mistake over Gibson but Nemo felt he should be judged at the end of the season: 'If he can salvage success out of the shambles we saw against Brighton, he will be fully vindicated.'

The knockers had their say in the newspaper as well. A Mr Sidwell criticised the manager for his team selection against Brighton and said that some of the players on Tuesday were not good enough for the Third Division let alone the First.

The following week, thankfully, was somewhat quieter and saw City reject a £15,000 offer for Ray Pointer from Oldham. Pointer, signed for £20,000 the previous December, was struggling to win a place in the side but Jimmy Hill did not want to lose money on the player. The Oldham manager was Jimmy McIlroy a former playing colleague of Pointer's at Burnley where the pair had won league championship medals in 1960. Bobby Gould realised Ray's days were numbered at Highfield Road but remembers Ray fondly: 'He was such a wonderful person. I learned a lot from Ray – he taught me how to love the game. I admired him as a boy watching him on TV for Burnley and JH did well to bring him to Coventry. The previous season he was scoring and I was largely firing blanks but it switched round and I was now scoring the goals.'

There was speculation in the Sunday papers that 'several' clubs were interested in Gibson. Hill described the stories as 'a load of fiction' and reiterated that only two clubs had shown any interest.

City travelled to Ashford in Kent on the following Monday evening for a friendly with the local Southern League team, managed by John Sillett's brother Peter. City had signed Howard Moore, a young player, from Ashford the previous season and made a promise to play a friendly there. City ran out 11-0 winners against the semi-professional side with goals from Gould (3), Key (2), Tudor (2), Farmer, Curtis, Mitten and Hill.

The following Saturday, 22 October, City went to second-placed Bolton for a league game. Bolton's star striker Wyn Davies was absent on international duty and John Byrom was in the No.9 shirt. The Trotters were without five regulars with two players struck down by a bug. Before the kick-off there was a minute's silence for the victims of the Aberfan disaster that had occurred in South Wales the previous day when 144 people, including 116 children had lost their lives when a colliery spoil tip slid into the village school. Sadly, some Bolton supporters decided to ignore the silence and shouted obscenities. Jonathan Strange was a 14-year-old schoolboy living in Swanage, Dorset at the time, and rarely watched his favourite team: 'I still think of that Bolton game in the context of the Aberfan disaster.'

In a poor first half both sides, according to Nemo in the *Coventry Telegraph*, 'seemed to be in trance'. Jimmy Hill's half-time talk had an electric effect and City played some of their best football of the season and were unlucky not to get both points. Only two superb saves from veteran keeper Eddie Hopkinson denied John Tudor goals as City dominated the second period. Thirteen minutes from time they got their reward when good work by John Mitten and Rees set up Ernie Machin to score in his home town. The goal woke Wanderers up and three minutes later a shrewd Brian Bromley pass found Byrom who, for the only time, evaded George Curtis, and his mis-hit shot slipped past Glazier and rolled into the net off a post to save Bolton's unbeaten home record.

There was another change at the top of Division Two as Ipswich beat Hull 5-4 in a thrilling top of the table clash at Portman Road with Ipswich's Ray Crawford netting a hat-trick and Town now headed the table. Other top six sides Wolves and Carlisle had home wins and City were eighth but had a game in hand on the top two.

City's away following at Bolton numbered around 500, easily the lowest travelling support of the season and reflecting the gloom of the supporters generally. In the following Saturday's *Pink* Nemo reported that a City fan had written to him complaining about Bolton fans who had set upon one of his friends after the Sky Blues had scored. Then outside Bolton railway station after the game about ten home fans went for his friend and then grabbed his scarf. An older City supporter managed to get the scarf back but police had to intervene. It was probably one of the earliest instances of hooliganism encountered by City fans.

The 'A' team's poor run continued with a 2-0 defeat to Shrewsbury Reserves whilst the 'B' team drew 1-1 with West Brom with Tom Sinclair scoring. Pat Saward had lots of injuries in his teams with Geoff Brassington needing a cartilage operation, Bob Dobbing out for a month with a thigh injury and Dudley Roberts sidelined for at least three weeks with a knee injury, just as he was pressing again for a first-team place. Meanwhile it was reported that 'A' team goalkeeper John Spiers was being released so that he could progress a career in golf in the United States.

Talks of a crisis at Highfield Road had diminished a little but the Ian Gibson saga continued. In the *Pink* that evening Nemo described how money had become tight as a result of the government's credit squeeze. Banks were reluctant to extend credit even to their favourite overdraft customers and he believed that any deal for the Scot would either be a straight player-exchange or a player and cash adjustment either way. He went on to report a quote by Jimmy Hill in a Sunday newspaper saying that 'the rift between myself and Gibson is not irreparable'. This comment had given rise to speculation that the player may settle his differences with the club and remain at Highfield Road. Nemo however was not having this: '... It's my guess that the rift IS, in fact, irreparable, and that Gibson WILL leave City. When is another matter.' The board of directors would be discussing Gibson's transfer request the following week but in the meantime he was not on the transfer list.

The next rumour to emerge concerned Bill Glazier with stories circulating that he had asked for a transfer. On the Monday following the Bolton game he told Nemo in the *Coventry Telegraph*: 'There's absolutely no truth in stories that I want a transfer. I'm perfectly happy here in Coventry. Dozens of people have asked me over the past week if these rumours are true, and I'm getting a bit fed up with the whole thing. Everything has gone as well as I had hoped since I recovered from my broken leg, and I am looking forward to a long run with this club.'

On the Tuesday night Gibson was in the reserve team that beat Southampton 3-1 alongside Dietmar Bruck, returning from injury. Bruck netted the first goal and Trevor Shepherd and Ray Pointer completed the scoring. A lanky 17-year-old Mike Channon played for Southampton.

Before the game the directors met and discussed Gibson and Burckitt's transfer requests. They recognised that Burckitt had been 'squeezed out' and were prepared to listen to offers for him. Gibson's request was not granted but Hill re-iterated the club's position: 'Any offers would have to be considered.'

Charles Harrold, the club's administrative manager, revealed that the club were not planning to run the Sky Blue Special train to the next away game at Derby. The reason given was that it wasn't economically viable to run the train for short trips in the midlands and the club would need to subsidise the fares to make it profitable. Trips were planned for the games later in the year at Huddersfield and Hull, despite the train only being three-quarters full for the Bolton trip.

On the Friday, the club revealed that 20-year-old Dave Clements, who had been in excellent form at wing-half, had been awarded a four-year contract. Clements was hopeful of regaining his Northern Ireland place after several impressive defensive performances including a man-marking job on Blackburn's Bryan Douglas in the previous home game. Strangely, it was only because of Ronnie Farmer's clash of heads with Bristol City's Brian Clark in September that Dave had emerged as a destructive wing-half.

His early-season performances on the wing had not impressed many and Farmer's injury was Dave's silver lining. Since making his international debut against Holland in March 1965, Clements had won two further caps, the last in June against Mexico in Belfast. He was the third player to be given a long contract following Rees (four years) and Glazier (five years).

Charlton Athletic, managed by former Newcastle player Bob Stokoe, were the next visitors to Highfield Road on the last Saturday of October. The Addicks' home form was good but they had only won three points on the road and had lost the last four. They were, however, fresh from a 4-0 win over Bury when Ron Saunders had scored a hat-trick.

Jimmy Hill named an unchanged team with local youngster Mick Coop on the bench. City started strongly and Bobby Gould scored after 10 minutes, pouncing when Charlie Wright failed to hold a John Mitten cross. But after the promising opening the Sky Blues struggled to dominate the defence-minded Londoners. Wright in the Charlton goal saved the Londoners from a heavier defeat with one-handed saves from Tudor, Rees and Gould. Glazier had little to do in the City goal and Mick Kearns, playing his 300th league game, looked strong at right-back. The other full-back, Brian Hill, picked up a hamstring strain and left the field after an hour to be replaced by 18-year-old Coop for his first league appearance.

As the minutes ticked by, with City holding a single-goal lead, the fans started to get nervous and although Charlton made little inroads to City's area there was relief from the 19,868 crowd at the final whistle. City had now conceded just one goal in seven home games but the lack of goals scored – 19 in 14 games was worrying.

Leaders Ipswich stayed top despite dropping a point at Plymouth and Wolves were up to second after a 4-0 victory at Northampton with Ernie Hunt scoring a hat-trick. Bolton, previously second, lost 1-0 at lowly Norwich after selling their centre-forward Wyn Davies to Newcastle for £80,000. The Sky Blues were up to sixth place, three points behind Ipswich.

The reserves lost 4-1 at West Ham despite having Gibson and Pointer on show. A strong West Ham side included former England forward Johnny Byrne who netted two goals and their substitute was a 19-year-old Harry Redknapp. Pointer was substituted with a knee injury after a heavy challenge and 16-year-old Willie Carr made his first start for the 'stiffs'. The 'A' team drew 2-2 at home to Brierley Hill after leading through goals from Malcolm Knox and Bob Dobbing. The 'B' team suffered a rare defeat, losing 2-0 to Derby's youngsters.

Top of Division Two (31 October)

		PL	*W*	*D*	*L*	*F*	*A*	*Pts*
1	Ipswich	15	8	4	3	33	25	20
2	Wolves	14	8	3	3	32	14	19
3	Bolton	14	7	4	3	26	16	18
4	Hull City	15	9	0	6	34	21	18
5	Crystal Palace	14	7	4	3	24	15	18
6	SKY BLUES	14	7	3	4	19	13	17

Chapter 5

November – Gibson is back!

POSSIBLE transfer moves dominated the local news during the first week of November with discussions between Jimmy Hill and Newcastle manager Joe Harvey ultimately coming to nothing but not before a lot of rumours. First of all, City were linked with Newcastle and former Rotherham striker Albert Bennett, as it was revealed that the north-east club, struggling at the foot of Division One, were prepared to listen to offers for all of their first team, except their £80,000 new signing Wyn Davies.

However, the following day it was revealed that Jimmy Hill wanted another of the struggling Tyneside club's players, Alan Suddick. Hill was prepared to exchange Ian Gibson for the England Under-23 international with a cash adjustment but the player, who could play at inside-forward or on the wing, had no desire to leave Newcastle and the deal was dead in the water.

Another transfer that wouldn't happen was Ray Pointer to Bristol City. Their manager Fred Ford had watched the blond striker for City's reserve team but had decided not to take matters further.

The club announced record profits of £49,000 for the year ended in May 1966. The figure was made up of a surplus on transfer fees of £23,650 (mainly the proceeds of the Hudson sale), donations of £22,325 from the Supporters' Club and an operating profit of just over £3,000. One interesting point came to light – an increase in staff and players' wages of £8,600 to £93,000. Income from home games was slightly down at £72,260 but was more than offset by the proceeds of the FA Cup run which netted over £7,000 compared to £3,000 the previous season. Most of the club's profit had been earmarked to pay off credit facilities, obtained for building work at Highfield Road and Ryton.

The Sky Blue Pool, launched in the summer, was going from strength to strength with 84,000 members signed up and the biggest weekly winner bagged a cheque for £1,289, earning his agent a £64 commission.

City travelled to the Baseball Ground on the first Saturday of November with one change – fit again Dietmar Bruck in for the injured Brian Hill who, not for the first time, had pulled a hamstring. Bruck himself was doubtful until lunchtime on the day of the game and Hill took 20-year-old Benny Glover to Derby in case 12th man Mick Coop had to step into Bruck's place. Brummie Glover had been signed two years ago from under the noses of Villa and Blues and signed as a professional only four months previously.

In less than a dozen reserve appearances the young wing-half had made rapid progress, with assistant manager Alan Dicks saying: 'If ever a young player deserves to succeed it's Benny. He's absolutely dedicated.'

Years later Benny told of his shock at the call-up: 'It was on the Friday afternoon before the Derby game when George Curtis walked up to me in the corridor outside the dressing rooms at Highfield Road and said, "Chicken or steak for lunch tomorrow, Benny?", I couldn't believe it, I was in the squad for the game.' In the event Bruck was fit to play, so Benny wasn't needed but three weeks later he would be required.

After a woeful start to the season the Rams, under manager Tim Ward, had picked up and were unbeaten in seven games scoring five goals in each of their last two home games. Despite miserably wet weather, a season's best crowd of 22,949 watched a master class from the Sky Blues. John Tudor, back in his native Derbyshire, scored after three minutes and City dominated the first half. Derby's Kevin Hector who had netted five goals in seven games since his £40,000 move from Bradford, was shackled brilliantly by Dave Clements and with Farmer shutting down Alan Durban the Sky Blues had a stranglehold on the Rams.

In total, City fashioned eight good scoring chances with a back-to-form Rees the main provider but it wasn't until the 66th minute that Ernie Machin scored the second, throwing himself at a Rees cross to head past Reg Matthews in the home goal. Gordon Hodgson did score a consolation goal near the end but City fully deserved their first ever win at the Baseball Ground.

Leaders Ipswich thrashed Northampton 6-1 with Frank Brogan scoring two penalties in a hat-trick, whilst second-placed Wolves beat Millwall 2-0 and City still trailed Ipswich by three points in fifth place. City's 'A' team had a thumping 6-2 away win at Stratford Town in the West Midlands League with new boy Trevor Shepherd scoring two goals and forgotten man Peter Denton also netting. Denton had burst on to the Sky Blue scene the previous season with a run of good first-team performances on the right-wing. He had been hailed as a 'bright young prospect with a potentially fine future'.

The previous summer he had almost joined Middlesbrough as part of the Gibson deal. Middlesbrough boss Stan Anderson had been impressed with Peter's performance the previous December at Ayresome Park and was prepared to knock £10,000 off the Gibson price to get him to sign. Jimmy Hill wanted Denton to stay and left it up to the player. At the time Peter said: 'I didn't fancy starting to swap clubs at the age of 20 and drop down a division. In any case I thought my future was more assured here (at Coventry). So, I said no.'

Now, he told Nemo: 'I suppose that psychologically it's affected the way I've been performing. Perhaps I've been trying too hard to prove to JH that I was right in deciding to stop here.' Peter was now struggling to win a place in the reserves and relegated to the third team.

There was good news that week for City's international players. Ron Rees was recalled by Wales for their Home International Championship match against world champions England at Wembley a week hence, and Dave Clements was back in the Northern Ireland team to face Scotland at Hampden Park. The Welsh selectors had watched Rees at the Baseball Ground where he had put in his best performance of the season and done enough to earn a recall to the team for what would be his 17th full cap, after being dropped for the previous game against Scotland. Clements would be playing at wing-half where he had excelled for the Sky Blues and also in the team were Tottenham goalkeeper Pat Jennings, Leicester's centre-forward Derek Dougan and the Manchester United star George Best.

On Friday of that week another increased bid for Ray Pointer from Oldham was rejected despite the former England man being unable to win a place in the City team. Jimmy Hill said: 'We cannot afford to let experienced players go at this time.'

The Sky Blues were unchanged for Saturday's visit of Crystal Palace but for the second season running the Londoners stole the points and ended City's 17-game unbeaten home league run that stretched back 11 months. Ironically, after the poor entertainment in the last home game against Charlton, this was, according to Nemo in the *Coventry Telegraph*, a 'thrilling spectacle'. At the start of play Palace were fourth in the table and by the end had risen to second, behind new leaders Wolves only on goal average.

Bill Glazier was captain for the day against his old club and was at fault for both goals. After six minutes he was slow going down to Cliff Jackson's shot which crept inside the post. City charged forward after conceding and John Mitten missed a sitter when Bobby Gould forced the Palace keeper John Jackson to drop the ball. Gould did equalise after 28 minutes after Mitten's cross-shot was palmed out by Jackson and the predatory striker netted from a narrow angle.

City's attack, however, was not firing on all cylinders and whilst the defence, the bulwark of City's season to date, had an off-day, the forwards struggled. On the hour Bobby Woodruff heaved one of his famous long throws into the City penalty area, Dyson headed the ball on and with Glazier in two minds, Steve Kember bundled the ball into the net at the far post.

The final half hour saw the Sky Blues throw everything at the visitors and it looked as though they had equalised near the end when Gould hit the bar but the ball was somehow scrambled away.

Long-serving fan Brian Chaston remembers his feelings after the setback: 'The Palace defeat got to me. I went home after the game convinced we wouldn't get promotion now. The home form hadn't been great up to then but we had kept on winning.'

There were new leaders in Division Two as Ipswich slipped up by losing 1-0 at Millwall and were leapfrogged by Wolves and Palace with only goal average separating the three clubs. Wolves drew 2-2 at Rotherham with Wagstaff and McIlmoyle on target.

City's 'A' team beat Wolves' 'A' team 1-0 with a late Pat Morrissey goal whilst the 'B' team lost 2-1 to a strong Leicester 'A' team at Ryton.

In his *Coventry Telegraph* match report of the Palace defeat Nemo summed up the position: 'What can Mr Hill do about his attack? Only 22 goals in the bag from 16 matches is clearly not promotion style.' He went on: 'City really have been living on borrowed time. Most of their results this season – results which have given hope of brighter things to come – have been based on defensive effectiveness, particularly at home. On Saturday, the thing we feared would happen sooner or later occurred; the defence showed signs of the strain knowing that any errors may prove fatal.'

Coventry City had been trendsetters the previous season by relaying closed circuit broadcasts of two away games on to giant screens at Highfield Road. The experiments had earned the club much admiration but had barely broken even financially. When asked about plans for future broadcasts Jimmy Hill was not optimistic: 'There's nothing in view at the moment. There isn't enough excitement but if we feel there is a demand for a particular game we would stage it. But it would have to be a good financial proposition.'

In the *Coventry Telegraph*, Nemo speculated that the Charlton away game on 4 March might offer an opportunity as this was the day when the League Cup Final would be staged for the first time at Wembley, and one or two London clubs were considering switching home games from that day. A Charlton official told Nemo that the club hadn't gone into the matter but it might make a difference if West Ham reached the final.

On the Tuesday evening City's reserves lost 3-1 at Crystal Palace. Coventry kid Martin Clamp made his debut in goal for the second team and Ian Gibson again appeared.

At Wembley on the Wednesday evening Rees played in a gallant Wales side overrun by the world champions England. Geoff Hurst scored two goals around the half-hour mark before Rees set up Wyn Davies for a goal. Bobby Charlton put the home side 3-1 ahead just before half-time and in the final quarter with a tired Wales wilting, England scored two more goals through Jack

Charlton and a Hennessey own goal. 400 miles away at Hampden Clements was a strong influence in the Northern Ireland side defeated 2-1 by Scotland. Huddersfield's Jimmy Nicholson gave the Irish the lead but the two Bobbys, Lennox and Murdoch, gave Scotland victory.

Both internationals were back in City colours for the trip to Huddersfield the following Saturday in what was an unchanged Coventry team. The day didn't start well for the Sky Blues as their coach broke down on the M1 near Nottingham and they had to wait 45 minutes for a relief vehicle to take them on to Leeds Road. City started the game well and John Mitten had an early snap shot saved by John Oldfield in the home goal before John Tudor's header went just the wrong side of the post.

A physical home side soon asserted themselves and dominated the first half. City were penned back for long periods and it was against the run of play when the Sky Blues took the lead six minutes before half-time. Mitten's excellent cross was splendidly controlled by Gould and lofted into the perfect space for Tudor to run in and ram the ball home from close range.

The second half saw the pattern of the game remain the same with Town pushing City back and there was little respite for the Coventry defence. Rees took a knock in the first half and was replaced by substitute Mick Coop at the break. Under continuous pressure City relied on Glazier to keep them in the lead but a goal was inevitable and it came on the hour when Dobson converted Mike Hellawell's cross.

The Leeds Road crowd erupted and four minutes later the home team took the lead. Glazier could only parry Jimmy Nicholson's fierce shot and Tony Leighton was first to react to score. City kept it at 2-1 despite barely getting out of their own half and Ron Farmer almost grabbed what would have been a fortuitous point when his ground shot thumped a post. Two minutes from time Mick Meagan made it 3-1 when his speculative shot dipped into the net to complete an afternoon of dejection for the small contingent of Sky Blues fans in the crowd of 15,192. Few City fans who travelled to Leeds Road on that cold, damp day would have put money on City remaining unbeaten for the rest of the season, for they had just witnessed the last defeat of the campaign.

Those fans that didn't make the trip to Huddersfield would have been doubly depressed on Saturday evening when they picked up their *Coventry Telegraph Pink*. Nemo's headline (written before that day's defeat) read: 'City can forget promotion if they don't boost attack'. He went on to write: 'There is something unreal about the Sky Blues promotion challenge this season. It lacks conviction and it certainly seems to lack excitement. City fans view the months ahead with hope, but they need assuring. What is wanted at Highfield Road is a spark.'

He went on to say that a strong striker was what was required – someone to play alongside Gould or Tudor. Nemo didn't realise that the 'spark' was already at the club in the shape of Ian Gibson and that the day of reconciliation between the Scot and manager Hill was close.

Wolves maintained top place by virtue of a 3-2 home win over Preston and Ipswich were back to winning ways and in second place after beating Rotherham 3-2. City, in seventh place, trailed the two leaders by five points.

On the Tuesday evening the reserves entertained Chelsea and put on a dazzling display to beat the Londoners 4-1 with goals from Tudor (2), Key and Shepherd. Chelsea put out a strong team including former Spurs star Tommy Harmer and ex-City full-back Allan Harris who had re-joined Chelsea the previous summer but had yet to start a league game for the Blues. City's star was 16-year-old Willie Carr who had the crowd really buzzing. On his home debut for the 'stiffs' he showed that he would become a big hero of the regulars at reserve games and another 5,000 plus crowd wondered if manager Hill might throw the red-headed Scot into the first team.

Nemo, writing in the following Saturday's *Pink*, understood the clamour of those who would like to see Carr blooded in league football but felt the 'fiercely-hard school' of the second division would do more harm than good to the lad. A place in the forthcoming first-team friendly with Morton might present an opportunity, however.

Jimmy Hill used his notes in the Cardiff programme to praise the reserve team's performance: 'I do not think I have seen a more entertaining game at any level at Highfield Road. The team showed great spirit, skill and running power, and as a tribute not one spectator left a second before the game ended. We all wanted it to go on all night. There is surely not a better way of spending an evening than watching these young Sky Blues performing in their own inimitable way, as they give entertainment plus and value for money that augurs well for the future.'

Ian Gibson did not play against Chelsea reserves and no reason was given for his omission but on the Friday the shock news came through that the talented Scot was back in the first team to play Cardiff the following day. The defeat in Yorkshire had taken its toll on City with injuries ruling Bill Glazier, Dietmar Bruck and Ernie Machin out of the game. Reserve goalkeeper Peter Thomas, 22, came in for his debut and Mick Coop made his first league start at full-back. Machin's place went to Gibson, recalled for his first game in seven weeks. The Scot told Nemo in the *Coventry Telegraph* that: 'I'm glad to be back but I haven't changed my mind about leaving Highfield Road. A good performance from me might make things easier for me to leave.'

And what a performance. He cut the Cardiff defence to ribbons in a dominating team performance that Nemo reported as 'City tossing away a golden chance of chalking up one of the biggest victories since they were promoted to Division Two'.

Bobby Gould had a 'howler' in front of goal and should have scored a hat-trick. The opposition was poor but City failed to turn their domination into a scoreline that reflected their superiority. As it was they had to be content with a 3-2 win.

Cardiff arrived as the bottom side in the division but buoyed by a 3-0 win over Bury a week earlier that had ended a horrendous run of five defeats in which they had conceded 25 goals including seven at Molineux. They had one bright spark, the form of 17-year-old centre-forward John Toshack who had scored twice in the victory over Bury.

John Tudor scored the first goal after 25 minutes, his fifth in nine games, when Wilson in the Cardiff goal dropped a corner under pressure from George Curtis and Tudor had an easy task. Wilson was at fault again a minute after half time and Gibson pounced to score the second goal. Nine minutes later the diminutive Scot crowned a memorable individual performance with a stunning individual third goal. Shortly afterwards Tudor was injured and replaced by another debutant, Benny Glover. City were coasting and 'Gibbo' was tearing the visitors to shreds in an effort to complete his hat-trick and more chances went begging. As the game entered the final minutes the tall, lean Toshack pounced on some lackadaisical play by City's defence and scored twice inside a minute.

There was still time however for City to create two more chances for Glover and Rees, which brought spectacular saves from Wilson.

A crowd of 19,680 went home in mixed moods. They had seen the exhilarating return of their star player and a host of scoring chances but they had been left biting their nails in the final minutes.

In a topsy-turvy day in Division Two all six clubs above the Sky Blues in the table at the start of play were beaten leaving City just three points behind joint leaders Wolves and Ipswich. Wolves lost their first game in six outings, 2-1 at Bury, whilst second-placed Ipswich lost 2-0 at Preston.

The reserves lost 2-1 at Filbert Street where Leicester-born Jeff Blockley made his reserve team debut. The 'A' team lost 3-1 at home to Shrewsbury Town reserves with Brian Cocking suffering a badly bruised leg and the 'B' team lost their fifth Midland Intermediate League game in a row, 2-1 to Birmingham City 'A'.

On the Monday after the Cardiff game all the press wanted to talk about was Ian Gibson but Jimmy Hill had his mind on other things: 'My mind is not on Gibson, but on what sort of team I can pick to beat the Wolves'. 'Gibson,' added Hill, 'is definitely in the side at Molineux – of that there is no doubt.' He did let his guard slip by saying: 'It's significant that he [Gibson] scored two goals against Cardiff – before he was dropped he scored one in 13.' Gibson's comments to the press weren't exactly indicative of a reconciliation either: 'I'm still determined to leave.'

On the Tuesday evening the Sky Blues had to fulfil a friendly with Morton at Highfield Road at a time when they could really have done with a breather bearing in mind the growing injury list. John Tudor had dislocated a bone in his knee and would be out for several weeks and Hill, Pointer and Roberts were given 'no chance' of being ready for Saturday. Glazier and Machin were rated as doubtful and Kearns had a knock but Bruck was confident of being available.

Morton, the Scottish Division Two leaders, had four Danish internationals in their squad for the friendly game including Borge Thorup, signed from Brondby the previous day. Jimmy Hill gave games to John Burckitt and Trevor Shepherd (his senior debut) and promised at least 45 minutes to substitute Willie Carr. A crowd of 4,098, less than the reserve team's average , braved the cold to see another sparkling display from Gibson. He set up goals for Rees and Gould with defence-splitting passes, goals that sandwiched a good header by Shepherd to ensure a 3-2 win and only Morton's second defeat of the season. Carr came on at the break for John Key and although a little overawed, the 16-year-old caught the eye with some delightful inter-passing with 'Gibbo'.

Carr had another reason for celebration – he had been selected to play in the Scotland international youth trial the following week at Easter Road, Edinburgh, the first step of what promised to be a colourful international career.

The busiest place in the club that week was physiotherapist Norman Pilgrim's treatment room as the 'man with magic hands' worked on City's injured list in an effort to get them fit for arguably the most important game of the season the following Saturday at leaders Wolves.

Top of Division Two (30 November 1966)

		Pl	*W*	*D*	*L*	*F*	*A*	*Pts*
1	Wolves	18	10	4	4	40	20	24
2	Ipswich	19	10	4	5	42	31	24
3	Crystal Palace	18	9	5	4	30	20	23
4	Carlisle	19	11	1	7	27	25	23
5	Bolton	18	9	4	5	32	22	22
6	SKY BLUES	18	9	3	6	26	21	21
7	Preston	19	10	1	8	32	28	21
8	Blackburn	19	8	5	6	29	29	21
9	Millwall	18	9	3	6	20	22	21

Chapter 6

December – League leaders toppled as City start surge

ON Saturday 3 December, City travelled to Molineux to face the league leaders Wolverhampton Wanderers. Despite the return of Ian Gibson the previous week and the Sky Blues' recent record against Wolves (they had done the double in two memorable clashes in 1965/66) most fans were fearing the worst.

City's following in the 27,232 crowd was nowhere near as large as the previous season when an estimated 15,000 watched in a 44,000 attendance. City's injury crisis had eased and Glazier, Bruck and Machin all returned from injury. Overnight snowfalls had left a slippery carpet of white on the pitch but the Sky Blues gave one of the best performances of the Jimmy Hill era. Beaten back on defence by the rampant Wolves for most of the game, and with less than a dozen shots, they cracked in three great goals for victory.

They owed it all to a magnificent display by their defence and particularly Bill Glazier, who stopped everything fired at him except the equaliser. Dave Clements did a fine job in curbing Wolves's danger man Ernie Hunt on his return to the ground he left to join City two years earlier and George Curtis recaptured his tremendous early season form.

Gibson scored after seven minutes, nipping in when Fred Davies failed to hold a fierce Rees shot. From that point until half-time Wolves penned City back and with Hunt pulling the strings in midfield a Wolves equaliser looked on the cards. Somehow City survived until the break but five minutes into the second half Wolves drew level when Dave Burnside headed in from a long free kick.

Many thought this would be the end of the Sky Blues but heroic defensive work and numerous brilliant saves by Glazier, together with a touch of luck, enabled City to come through 25 minutes of extreme pressure and then snatch another goal out of the blue. Kearns's long cross-field clearance found John Key who advanced before unleashing a strong shot that Davies might have stopped. Eight minutes from time City counter-attacked again and Rees, dangerous every time he got the ball, made it 3-1 with a low cross-shot. Minutes later the Welsh winger almost scored a fourth when he hit the crossbar but that would have been a bit too much.

Keith White was 16 years old at the time and has happy memories of the classic victory: 'Watching City away from home that season was a great adventure as I was going to grounds I had only read about. Wolves at Molineux with its quirky stands and huge North and South Banks was awe-inspiring. I so very nearly didn't get in to that game. When I got to the turnstiles I found out my dad had left my brother and I with very little cash. Luckily a kindly attendant let us in together so we were able to see the brilliant 3-1 win.'

Nemo summed up the result in his match report: 'Here then was a victory which will be remembered as one of the Sky Blues' finest and it came at a time when there were many doubts as to whether City could sustain yet another assault on the Division One fortress.'

Elsewhere there were more shock results with Palace, Bolton and Carlisle all in the top six at the start of play, suffering home defeats and leaving Ipswich, 2-0 victors over Bury, top of the pile and City in fourth place three points behind. Two victories and upsets for their opponents had enabled the Sky Blues to get back into the promotion race. The following Friday evening the Suffolk team were coming to Highfield Road!

City's 'A' team drew their game at Lye Town 2-2 with Don Peachey netting both goals. In midweek, the Sky Blues returned to Molineux for an FA Youth Cup second round tie and came away with an excellent 2-0 victory. In a highly professional performance Peachey scored the first goal after 76 minutes following a fine long ball from new recruit Robin Hayward, signed from Ashford Town following the friendly in October.

Peachey was on hand to score the second goal when Bloodworth's header from Paddon's cross came off the underside of the bar. It was a great victory for Pat Saward's boys whose opponents were physically stronger with four Central League regulars including Alun Evans, who two years later would become Britain's first £100,000 teenager but who, on this occasion was tightly marked by Trevor Gould.

Willie Carr impressed again, just 48 hours after playing in the Scottish youth trial in Edinburgh, and after the game Jimmy Hill was approached by an England selector enquiring about Willie's nationality. When told by JH that he was a Scot and had already been spotted north of the border the selector uttered a profanity. Hill had travelled to watch Carr in Scotland and had been spotted chatting to Celtic boss Jock Stein and a couple of other Scottish managers after the game. The next day speculation was rife in Coventry that Gibson was on his way to Celtic, rumours that were swiftly quashed by Hill.

On the same night as the youth team were winning at Molineux, the reserve team beat Ipswich 2-1 with Trevor Shepherd and Dennis Oakes on target. John Tudor had made a miraculous recovery from his knee injury but limped off after some tough challenges from Ipswich defender Derek Jefferson.

On Friday, 9 December, the new leaders Ipswich came to Highfield Road, and despite it being a miserably wet evening there were 25,715, the biggest home crowd for three months, to watch the top of the table clash. In his programme notes, Jimmy Hill explained that the game had been switched to a Friday night because the club had noticed a dip in Saturday gates in December – he imagined mums persuading dads to 'toddle off to do their Christmas shopping'. Their solution – experiment with a home game on a Friday night to keep both mums and dads happy.

Ipswich, managed by Bill McGarry, had reached the top by virtue of their strong home form but away from Portman Road they were vulnerable and had lost three out of the last four on the road. Jimmy Hill named an unchanged starting eleven – an eleven that would become his strongest line up for the rest of the season. City had the Ipswich defence in a panic from the first minute and almost scored. From then on there was no doubt whose night this was. The attack, showing more menace and ideas than for some months, continuously tore into the opposition to carve out a victory described by Nemo in the *Coventry Telegraph* as 'on a par for excitement and skill with the great one over Sunderland in the FA Cup nearly four years ago'.

After a hectic first-minute melee in Ipswich's goalmouth, and a Gibbo shot blocked on the line, the East Anglians gave away a goal after four minutes. Defender Dave Harper had time to clear but instead turned and lofted the ball towards his own goalkeeper. Unfortunately, goalkeeper Ken Hancock was already advancing and the ball went way over his head, hit the crossbar and rebounded into the path of Bobby Gould who planted it into an empty net. After 15 minutes Gibson's through ball was perfectly placed for Gould to shoot home from 15 yards.

Ipswich's Frank Brogan hit a post with Glazier beaten and John Key hit the upright at the other end before Gould completed his first senior hat-trick on 33 minutes. Ernie Machin headed back a Rees cross and Gould's header crept inside the post. The Coventry kid could have scored another two but his lunges at crosses were just short. Sadly, Ernie Machin had to limp off before half-time and was replaced by Pat Morrissey, making his senior debut.

City kept the pressure up after half-time and Key netted a fourth goal before Gibson made it 'the old five' with a goal which would be remembered for many years. The Scot had taunted, bemused and eventually demoralised the Ipswich defence. A Rees corner was headed away but only to the maestro's feet. With seven Ipswich players between him and the goal, and obviously unsighted, he chipped the ball perfectly and it went over their heads and Hancock's outstretched arms to drop just under the bar. Any doubts about the Scot had been dispelled in three stunning performances with four goals that had lifted the Sky Blues into the promotion race and raised him to legendary status amongst City fans. In his match report Nemo praised Gibson: 'Gibbo has shown why Mr Hill happily paid out £57,500 for him. There were times last night when he looked worth twice that amount.'

Bobby Gould, scorer of his first senior hat-trick, was ecstatic after the game: 'No one could have stopped us tonight. This is my greatest moment since I joined City.' Now 50 years later he tells a story from that night: 'We were all in the dressing room before the game when JH walked in. He came over to me and pointed at me. 'You young man are going to score a hat-trick tonight – I've got a feeling in my water.' He then left the dressing room and the rest of the lads are taking the mickey out of me. After just over half-an-hour I've scored three and the electronic scoreboard shows 9-9-9 (my shirt number). I've looked up at JH in the stand and thought 'you must be God'. To top it all it was my late Grandad's birthday that day – he'd first taken me to Highfield Road as a nipper and watched me making my debut at Shrewsbury in 1963.'

The following day there was a full Division Two programme and Wolves took advantage of Ipswich's loss to go top of the table, winning 2-1 at Norwich. Both sides had 26 points but Wolves had the better goal average than Ipswich and City were third ahead of Carlisle, winners at Preston, on goal average. City's 'A' team beat Lye Town 4-1 with two goals apiece from Carr and Peachey, taking Peachey's tally to six goals in eight days.

City travelled to another top-six side, Hull City, the following weekend but slight injuries to Mick Kearns and Gibson meant games for youngsters Mick Coop and John Tudor. Tudor's recovery from injury surprised everyone as he had dislocated a bone in his knee just three weeks earlier. Two eminent orthopaedic surgeons had put their heads together to diagnose the problem and could recall only one similar case in their respective experiences. The bone had been pushed back under anaesthetic and a good rest had aided his recovery. Hill made a last-minute switch of his full-backs with Dietmar Bruck coming over to the right position with the intention of marking the speedy and dangerous Ian Butler.

Hull, with a deadly strike-force of Ken Wagstaff and Chris Chilton, were the second highest scorers in the Football League with 48 goals in 20 games, 17 of them from Wagstaff, the division's leading marksman. The previous week they had put six past Crystal Palace. After 19 minutes City looked to be up against it when Ian Butler headed in following a clever corner routine. A minute after the break City were level in a rare attack when Key's low shot took a deflection past keeper Maurice Swan. The home side penned City back but Curtis and Clements had the shackles on the Hull danger-men. On 76 minutes Tudor put City in front after Bill Glazier's long kick was nudged on by Gould for the blond striker to slide the ball home. Hull's point-saver came two minutes from time when Butler's hard strike was saved well by Glazier but the winger's mis-hit second shot sailed into the net. On balance the Tigers deserved their point but City were well satisfied with theirs.

The club didn't run their Sky Blue Special train – taking the view that they would struggle to sell enough seats to make it economically viable, but a lot of fans made the trip by coach and car. For those who stayed at home there was the consolation that the game was filmed by ITV and shown in Yorkshire and the midlands the following afternoon. Hull 's crowds were their best for many years and the attendance of 25,577 was excellent for the Saturday before Christmas.

Elsewhere Wolves were beaten 3-2 at St Andrew's in the midlands derby and the Sky Blues pulled level with them on 26 points. Ipswich went back on top after a 0-0 draw with lowly Cardiff and up to second place were surprise team Carlisle United, 3-0 victors over Crystal Palace. Carlisle, like Coventry, had never played in the top division and were enjoying only the second season in their history above Division Three. Two other top-six clubs, Millwall and Hull City, had also never played in Division One.

At Ryton the 'A' team came a cropper, losing 5-2 to a strong Halesowen side but at least Brian Hill came through his first game in almost two months and scored one of the goals. At Walsall Pat Saward selected the successful Youth Cup side as the 'B' team against the Saddlers and Peachey scored another brace in the 2-0 win.

With no first-team game for nine days until Boxing Day, Jimmy Hill took some time out to give an interview with Nemo.

He discussed how many points would be required for promotion – in 1965/66 Manchester City had been champions with 59 points with Southampton in second place with 54. Hill said: 'At any time this season, I would have settled for us getting 56 points. It is a good figure for promotion. But it may be that fewer are needed this time, so tight is the race.'

Jimmy then talked about his own favourites for promotion: 'Ourselves, Wolves, Huddersfield and Ipswich – but that is only a view. Millwall and Carlisle have done well mainly because of their strength at home. But whether they have the strength to last it out is something that only time will tell.'

On Tuesday night of that pre-Christmas week the reserves drew 3-3 with Plymouth at home and the club treated their young supporters to their annual 'pop and crisps' before the game. The first-team group were all in attendance signing autographs for the children for a good 90 minutes prior to kick-off. Over 5,200 watched Brian Hill and Ray Pointer return to action after injury and the latter scored two goals to put the Sky Blues into a 3-1 lead before Plymouth took advantage of some sloppy defending to grab a point.

On the same evening Ipswich missed the opportunity to extend their lead at the top – losing 2-1 at Charlton. On Christmas Eve there were only four games played in the Football League, two of them in Division Two, and Wolves hammered Derby 5-3 to go back to the top of the table. City's 'A' team drew 2-2 at Darlaston with Pointer and Tudor on target.

Christmas 1966 arrived with the Sky Blues unbeaten in four games and spirits in the city higher than for some time. The Christmas fixtures were home and away games on successive days against Rotherham United – something of a bogey team for the Sky Blues back then.

A large Boxing Day crowd of 31,789 watched the first game at Highfield Road and certainly got their money's worth with City emerging 4-2 victors in a see-saw encounter. Mick Kearns and Ian Gibson returned after injury with Brian Hill, who had been out injured since October, on the substitutes' bench.

City took the lead after seven minutes when Ernie Machin headed on a Ron Rees corner for Bobby Gould to prod home from short range. Machin was also the creator of the second goal after 24 minutes with a beautiful through ball that Gibson clipped just inside the post. The diminutive Scot picked up a knock and had to limp off nine minutes later. As he was about to leave the pitch Rotherham winger Roy Massey, playing his first game of the season, hit a dipping volley over Glazier to reduce the lead. Six minutes later it was all-square when Rees failed to stop Wilcockson's overlapping run and Bobby Williams drove home.

Just after the hour the ball was burst when Kearns tried a shot on the run that cleared the Covered End. With the first shot with the new ball Gould restored City's lead with a spectacular effort on the turn. Visiting keeper Alan Hill left the field with a broken finger and centre-forward John Galley took the green jersey. The emergency goalkeeper was in action almost immediately as Gould, racing into the box looking for his hat-trick, was upended from behind and Ronnie Farmer slid home the spot-kick to make it 4-2.

The holiday crowd witnessed an unsavoury incident near the end when a Coventry fan climbed over the terrace wall at the Covered End and attacked stand-in goalkeeper Galley and the Rotherham trainer. Police quickly dealt with the situation but the club's reputation for well-behaved supporters was tarnished.

At Derby's Baseball Ground Wolves comfortably completed the double over Derby, winning 3-0 to retain their two-point advantage over the Sky Blues who were now up to second following Ipswich's 0-0 draw at home to Charlton. City's excellent attendance was topped at Boothferry Park where over 35,000 watched the Tigers beat Huddersfield 2-0 with Chilton and Wagstaff on the score-sheet.

The Sky Blues and the Millers moved to Millmoor for part two 24 hours later and 13,301 watched a hard-fought 1-1 draw on a gloomy, miserable afternoon. With Gibson having a knock, Brian Hill started in his place in a defensive set-up. City held the home side comfortably but were restricted to occasional breakaways to relieve the pressure. The home side seemed to bear a grudge after the previous day's game and their tackling severely provoked City players with Machin especially the target of some cynical fouls that went unpunished. Rotherham broke through in the 71st minute with a controversial goal. Clish crossed and the ball ended up in the City net but the Coventry players were adamant that Massey had palmed it in. They surrounded the referee and pleaded with the ref to consult the linesman to no avail.

City suddenly had to change their tactics to chase the game and Hill pushed Dave Clements up front to try and bring his explosive shooting into action and finally they succeeded in wresting the initiative from the home team. But as 90 minutes came and went they looked set to suffer a defeat when, two minutes into injury-time, Clements shot through a crowd of players from the edge of the box and the ball nestled in the net as the City players danced a jig of delight.

Afterwards Jimmy Hill spoke proudly of his players: 'For me that was the finest away point we have won. Everything that could break a team's spirit happened to us – but it made no difference, Rotherham will never play harder than that against any side in the next ten years.' Nemo in the *Coventry Telegraph* was effusive too: 'There are some days when muscle and heart stands a side in better stead than skills and this was one of them. City may not have looked like a leading side yesterday but their position tonight speaks for itself.'

The Christmas double-headers had significantly changed the top of Division Two. Leaders Ipswich picked up just one point whilst second-placed Carlisle suffered two defeats. Wolves, with their double over Derby, were the new leaders with the Sky Blues now in second place one point behind.

One black spot for the club came at Nottingham Forest's City Ground where the reserves lost 10-0 to Forest. Records of the club's Football Combination history are scant, but this was probably the heaviest defeat ever in that league. Former England international Alan Hinton (forced out of the Forest first team by the up and coming Ian Storey-Moore) scored four goals, Sammy Chapman and Kear both scored two with Hall and Taylor also on the score-sheet. According to the *Nottingham Post* it was a post-war Forest record reserve victory.

On New Year's Eve City entertained Portsmouth, who boasted the best away form in the division, without Ian Gibson and Ronnie Rees who had picked up knocks at Christmas. Pompey had lost just three out of 12 away games and conceded a miserly 16 goals with only Wolves letting in less. That record would go out of the window at Highfield Road.

Brian Hill's comeback from injury at Rotherham had lasted one game and he would play no further part in the campaign. Ronnie Farmer moved to wing-half, fit-again John Tudor came into the attack and John Mitten deputised for Rees. It was Tudor who put the Sky Blues on the road to a comprehensive spanking of Pompey after 19 minutes with a superb header from John Key's teasing cross. The visitors had set up to defend and despite conceding the early goal they continued to defend in depth. A patient Coventry got their reward three minutes from half-time when keeper John Milkins's miscued goal-kick went straight to Mitten who quickly fed Bobby Gould to make it 2-0.

Even so, there was little hint of the avalanche to come. Within ten minutes of the restart City had three more goals in the back of Pompey's net. Man of the match Ernie Machin had the crowd off their seats with a finely-steered header 45 seconds into the second half before Mitten took the stage. First, he coolly flicked home Farmer's free kick from close range as Pompey wilted, then he got over a splendid cross from the left on to Key's head, with another magnificent header which soared past Milkins's groping fingers.

Only Gould knows how he missed getting a sixth from Dietmar Bruck's cross and although Ray Hiron took advantage of a Curtis slip in the mud to peg one goal back after 64 minutes, it was a near-miracle that in the last 25 minutes there were no further goals as 24,981 fans went home very happy with a 5-1 home win and Pompey's promotion credentials in tatters. The Sky Blues had remained unbeaten in six games with four victories and 20 goals, 14 of them in three home games.

League leaders Wolves were held 0-0 at home by third-placed Ipswich and the two West Midlands rivals were now level on 31 points with Wolves retaining top place on goal average. Crystal Palace were up to fourth on 29 points after a 2-1 victory over Blackburn. City's 'A' team beat Boston United 3-2 at Ryton with Howard Moore (2) and Dudley Roberts on target whilst two Willie Carr goals gave the 'B' team victory at West Brom.

In the *Pink* that evening Nemo named Bill Glazier as his player of the year for 'his courageous return to the top flight of England's goalkeepers after breaking a leg badly at Easter last year'. Nemo admitted that Glazier had his off days but 'Glazier's grit to overcome a serious injury, culminating in his performance at Molineux – one of the finest from a goalkeeper I have seen – wins him the award'.

He gave Dave Clements the 'Most Improved Player of the Year' award, just ahead of Bobby Gould, and Ian Gibson picked up 'Personality of the Year'. Nemo also gave his New Year resolutions that included: 'to hail Coventry City as a First Division side for the first time' and 'that the knockers will give Ernie Machin a fair crack of the whip and have the honesty to praise the good things he does instead of always spotlighting the bad'.

It would be the last column written under the pseudonym of Nemo – from the New Year he discarded the pen name and was simply Derek Henderson. Nemo, the Latin word for nobody, had been the pseudonym of the *Coventry Telegraph* football correspondent since the early part of the 20th century. By 1967 it had become an anachronism and Henderson took the opportunity to drop it. Devon-born Henderson had been working as the *Coventry Telegraph's* main football writer, and covering Coventry City, since early 1958. By 1967 he had seen City in action on most grounds in the Football League and before his departure from the newspaper in 1973 he would take his tally to 90 of the 92 grounds. He missed Doncaster and Scunthorpe. At the same time the newspaper's rugby union writer Nimrod was revealed as David Irvine and the boxing correspondent, previously known as Leftguard, was Alex Goodman.

Top of Division Two (31 December 1966)

		Pl	*W*	*D*	*L*	*F*	*A*	*Pts*
1	Wolves	24	13	5	6	53	30	31
2	SKY BLUES	24	13	5	6	46	28	31
3	Ipswich	25	11	7	7	45	39	29
4	Crystal Palace	24	12	5	7	38	34	29
5	Millwall	24	12	5	7	27	25	29
6	Preston	25	13	2	10	47	39	28
7	Blackburn	25	11	6	8	36	34	28
8	Carlisle	25	13	2	10	37	35	28

Chapter 7

January – City hit the top but exit Cup

THE New Year started well at Highfield Road as the reserve team got over their 10-0 hammering at Forest by beating Reading 3-1 on 3 January with goals from Coop, Burckitt and Shepherd. The following evening the youth team made the long journey to Swansea for a third round FA Youth Cup tie. The club had only ever reached the fourth round once, two seasons previously, and hopes were high that Pat Saward's team could repeat that. City were below their best but took the lead in the 63rd minute when Graham Paddon slid a pass through for Trevor Gould to score. A misplaced pass in the centre circle led to the Swans' equaliser and despite Paddon clipping the bar with a header the game finished 1-1 and there would be a replay at Highfield Road.

On the first Saturday of the New Year a massive following of Sky Blue supporters, estimated at over 10,000, made the short trip to St Andrew's for the big west midlands derby game. An unchanged City team, playing in their all-red change strip, were expecting a tough game from a very sharp but inconsistent

Birmingham side who hadn't lost at home since September and had beaten Wolves three weeks earlier. Manager Stan Cullis had made the surprise signing of former Scottish international winger Graham Leggat from Fulham and gave him his debut. There were pools of water on the pitch but underneath the ground was rock-hard and the dull day meant the floodlights were on from the start.

On 23 minutes, with snow now falling, City fell behind for the third away game in a row. New man Leggat hit a high cross into the City goalmouth and Curtis went up with Blues' Geoff Vowden but Dave Clements went up as well and his slight nudge on George caused the ball to slice off the top of the skipper's head into the net. Leggat should have made it 2-0 just after half-time but Clements saved the day with a goal-line clearance. Glazier kept City in the game with a series of excellent saves but the Blues strikers squandered chances too.

The close shave seemed to spur City in a bid for an equaliser and on 52 minutes it was all-square. The ice-cool Farmer sprayed a delicious pass into the path of Clements on the left and the Ulsterman surged into the Blues' penalty area. When he drew back that explosive left foot, everyone – including keeper Jim Herriot – expected a blasting shot. But Clem surprised everyone with a neat pass inside and, as Blues' defenders hesitated, Machin drove home the leveller with telling deliberation.

From then until the final whistle it was like the Alamo as Birmingham threw everything at the Sky Blues but the brave Glazier kept them out. The only time he was beaten was when Bullock chipped the ball over his head but Dietmar Bruck popped up to head off the line.

A crowd of over 36,000 had witnessed a first-class clash full of excitement and as the relieved Sky Blue Army headed back to Coventry the news came through that Wolves had lost 1-0 at Bristol City which meant City were top of the league for the first time in the season. With Ipswich and Palace's games being postponed due to bad weather, Millwall, 2-1 winners at Northampton, were up to third and Carlisle, 3-0 victors over Cardiff, were fourth. The bookmakers now made the Sky Blues 2/1 for the championship with Wolves priced at 5/2. The 'A' team lost 1-0 at home to Port Vale's reserves whilst the 'B' team took a 7-0 beating away to Nottingham Forest.

It was FA Cup second round day and local team Nuneaton Borough pulled off probably their biggest ever giant-killing act by knocking out Third Division Swansea 2-0 at home. Swansea, who boasted former Sky Blue winger Willie Humphries and legendary Welsh international Ivor Allchurch, were outfought by the Southern League outfit. The following Monday the third-round draw gave Nuneaton a home tie with Rotherham whilst the Sky Blues were also drawn at home – to First Division Newcastle United. Assistant manager Alan Dicks, said: 'A great draw. It gives the public of Coventry and the team a chance to size up First Division standards.' The ties would be played on the last Saturday of January. In the meantime, the Sky Blues had two league fixtures to complete.

There was no January transfer window in those days – clubs could sign players at any time during the season up to the 'transfer deadline', usually around the middle of March. Jimmy Hill had been pondering a move into the market for a few weeks and that week things began to happen. The first development was John Mitten's transfer to Plymouth Argyle for £3,500, a tidy profit for a player signed on a free in 1963. Argyle, managed by Derek Ufton, an old friend of Hill's, had sold their left-winger Nicky Jennings to Portsmouth and Mitten would be the replacement.

Hill had his eyes on Portsmouth's midfield player Brian Lewis and there was the possibility of an exchange deal with City's Ray Pointer moving to Fratton Park, but on 12 January Hill told Derek Henderson in the *Coventry Telegraph*: 'It now looks as though the deal will not go through.' He would not elaborate on the matter.

Seven days after Coventry City had gone top of Division Two they played host to Norwich City. The Canaries were having a tough time, without a win in eight games and 20th in the league table. Manager Lol Morgan recalled keeper Kevin Keelan who had been dropped several weeks earlier whilst Jimmy Hill was able to recall his two star players, Ian Gibson and Ronnie Rees replacing John Tudor and Mitten.

The Sky Blues weren't on top of their game with Ian Gibson looking ring-rusty after having the best part of a month on the sidelines. They also found Keelan in top form. Time and again the keeper foiled City with saves from Machin and Rees the stand outs. Rees did beat him with a blockbuster in the second half only for the ball to bounce off defender Laurie Brown and go for a corner.

Ironically it was a freakish 30-yard free kick from Ron Farmer that secured the breakthrough on 58 minutes after all the other more likely efforts had failed. His low shot seemed to get a deflection but afterwards it was ascertained that the ball had slithered off the goalmouth sand en route, deceiving Keelan into moving too soon.

A minute later Norwich's Hugh Curran had a 'goal' disallowed for offside but five minutes from time the visitors equalised when Anderson crossed for Laurie Sheffield to head past Glazier. A draw looked likely but with one minute left on the clock Farmer produced a peach of a cross from the right for Bobby Gould to nudge the ball into the path of Machin who, for the second week running, scored an all-important goal, his third in three games. A crowd of 27,724 had watched City extend their unbeaten run to nine games with a little help from Lady Luck.

Over at Molineux, Wolves were held 1-1 by Carlisle and City had extended their lead at the top to two points. Preston, by virtue of a 1-0 win over Portsmouth, were up to third place. City's reserve team travelled to Tottenham and lost to a strong Spurs side that included Welsh international Cliff Jones, returning from injury. Jones scored one of the goals in a 2-0 victory. Dudley Roberts made his return from injury after a three-month absence. The 'A' team lost 3-1 at Cinderford Town but the 'B' team recovered from their thrashing at Forest to beat Port Vale's 'A' team 5-0 with Wilks (2), Harrison, Scott and Allen on target.

During the following week City earned a place in the fourth round of the FA Youth Cup with a 2-1 replay win over Swansea Town. Don Peachey scored both goals in front of a 3,132 crowd and Willie Carr, who had rushed back from his Scottish youth trial on the Monday, was the star man again. Talks between Pompey and City over the Lewis/Pointer transfer had stalled again as neither player was keen on the move but by the end of the week a deal looked close after Portsmouth manager George Smith watched Pointer play well in a 3-2 reserve victory over Peterborough.

The reserves were still unbeaten at home and goals from Coop, Tudor and Shepherd sealed a third successive home win. Bristol City's manager Fred Ford also watched the reserve game and after signing former England forward Chris Crowe from Nottingham Forest he may have also had his eye on Pointer. In addition, Derek Henderson reported that two Irish clubs Limerick and Sligo Rovers coveted Ray but the reporter doubted that either club could afford the asking fee. On the Friday Hill travelled to Portsmouth to have talks with Lewis and the upshot was that the player would be coming to look around Coventry the following week.

The following Saturday the club's Sky Blue Special train was on the rails again and demand was so great that an extra carriage was added and over 500 fans paid 23 shillings (£1.15) each, with juveniles paying 15 shillings (75p). In all around 3,000 City fans made the trip to follow their team at Ashton Gate, Bristol. City were unchanged against the Robins who were struggling in the lower half of the table. For the fourth away game in succession the Sky Blues conceded the first goal and, as in the other three, they stubbornly refused to acknowledge defeat and emerged with a hard-earned point.

City's attack did not function well with Rees out of form and Gould in the grip of Jack Connor throughout meaning the forwards had to rely on their defenders to score the goals. Similarly, Farmer and Dave Clements had rare off days and City were fortunate to get a draw.

In front of 21,600, Bristol took the lead when the unmarked Crowe volleyed past Glazier from a corner-kick after 11 minutes. Three minutes later George Curtis, making his 400th league start for the club, equalised with a thunderous header from a free kick but Bristol were soon back in front when Clements dithered over a clearance and Terry Bush shot home. The best goal of the match pulled City level again after 36 minutes as Dietmar Bruck hit a corking right-foot shot past Mike Gibson, the home keeper.

After half-time City had a great chance when Machin headed Gibson's sublime pass straight at the keeper who fumbled it. Machin appealed that the ball had crossed the line but got no support from the officials. In the final minutes, as Bristol piled the pressure on the off-colour Sky Blues, a Quigley shot was deflected inches wide off Bruck with Glazier relieved.

Wolves also failed to win and the point from a 0-0 draw at Blackburn ensured City's two-point lead was maintained. Carlisle pulled level with Wolves on 33 points after beating a fading Ipswich 2-1 and there were another eight teams within three points of second place in a very congested league table. The 'A' team beat Cinderford 6-2 at Ryton with Peachey and Dennis Oakes scoring two apiece whilst the 'B' team drew 2-2 with Villa. Assistant manager Alan Dicks was at St. James's Park to 'spy' on

City's cup opponents Newcastle who drew 0-0 with Nottingham Forest. The Magpies had only won five league games all season and Coventry fans were confident of taking a First Division scalp seven days hence.

The Geordies had spent serious money to try and avoid relegation including paying Bolton £80,000 for centre-forward Wyn Davies. Over Christmas manager Joe Harvey had paid £40,000 to Chelsea for winger Tommy Robson and a similar fee to Sunderland for the tough wing-half Dave Elliott. Alan Suddick, previously linked with a move to the Sky Blues, had been sold to Blackpool for £65,000 to fund the incoming transfers. Newcastle, however, still languished in 21st place with only Blackpool below them.

In the week before the big cup tie the protracted transfer of Ray Pointer and Brian Lewis was finally concluded. Pointer went to Fratton Park for a medical but there was no deal until Lewis had agreed to the move and passed his medical. Lewis and his wife, at first reluctant to come to Coventry, were won over after meeting Hill and chairman Derrick Robins as well as viewing club houses. City paid Pompey £20,000 to balance the exchange deal which effectively valued Pointer at £15,000 and 23-year-old Lewis at £35,000. Lewis couldn't play against Newcastle under the new 14-day rule but told Derek Henderson that he would be back in the city to watch the cup game. Jimmy Hill took the opportunity to praise the Sky Blue Pool whose £12,500 profit to date had made the transfer possible.

There was bad news from the reserve game against Swindon on the Tuesday evening when Brian Hill limped off after ten minutes with yet another pulled muscle. Mick Cartwright came on as City won 2-1 but it wasn't an impressive performance and Derek Henderson described it as 'an old-fashioned shocker'. City came from behind with a penalty from Dennis Oakes and the winning goal from Morrissey. Impressive in goal was young

Martin Clamp who had done so well that Jimmy Hill agreed that reserve keeper Peter Thomas could return to Irish club Waterford on a permanent basis.

As the big cup game approached 30-year-old Ron Farmer prepared for his 300th senior game for the club. The Guernsey-born player had joined City in 1958 for £4,000 from Nottingham Forest and had been a key man in the club's rise under Jimmy Hill. Hill often told the story that at the end of his first season as manager he had been on the verge of letting him go. Ron had been injured when Jimmy arrived and JH hadn't seen him play until the last few games of the season. JH decided to give Ron a chance and later told people 'he was our most accurate player'. Ron himself says that in 1962 Jimmy wanted him to go to Ards in Northern Ireland as part of the deal for Willie Humphries.

Newcastle had a famous FA Cup tradition – they had won the trophy three times in five years in the early 1950s – and although they hadn't been to Wembley since the last of those triumphs in 1955 the fans always turned out in numbers for cup games. Over 7,000 made the trip south for the cup game with hundreds arriving in Coventry on Friday night. The Precinct echoed to the sound of the Geordies' cup anthem 'The Blaydon Races' and black and white colours dominated the city centre.

In his programme notes Jimmy Hill was managing expectations: 'To lose would be disappointing for all of us, but it would be an ill-wind that might well blow favourably for us with regard to our other ambitions.' Whilst the supporters wanted a First Division scalp and an exciting cup run, Hill was realistic enough to know that promotion was the priority.

Highfield Road was a cauldron of noise from a crowd of 35,748 which generated club record receipts of £9,724. Those present saw a thrilling cup tie with the Magpies emerging 4-3 winners in a match which could have gone either way. The destiny of the game hinged more than anything else on the displays of the respective centre-forwards. Newcastle's Wyn Davies always had the upper hand in his duel with George Curtis and celebrated with a hat-trick. Bobby Gould at the other end could do nothing right. Two glaring misses in the second half cost City dearly.

Davies scored his first after just 90 seconds as he shrugged of Curtis's tackle and hit a cracking drive past Glazier. A minute later Bryan 'Pop' Robson made it 2-0 from Jim Iley's free kick but City hit back immediately when Ronnie Rees's shot cannoned into the goal off John McNamee. Rees created City's equaliser after 21 minutes with a cross that Ian Gibson met full-tilt with his head to steer it past Marshall in the visitors' goal. Gibbo was unfortunately injured in the process and left the field at half-time by which time Davies had restored Newcastle's lead from Dave Hilley's cross.

City piled the pressure on in the second half but on 75 minutes Davies completed his hat-trick with a header from Robson's cross. Within seconds City replied with Rees firing home from Machin's corner and as the minutes ticked by Gould was set up by Machin but with only Marshall to beat to force a replay he shot over from eight yards. After the game Jimmy Hill was sanguine: 'On reflection, I wasn't sorry that Bobby Gould missed that late chance. That would have meant a replay and a hard game at Bury three days later.'

The game was refereed by top official Leo Callaghan who called it 'the most exciting cup-tie I have ever handled'. Danny Lewin, the Newcastle trainer said: 'We are on the way back. Our new players are just beginning to click and the side played with terrific confidence. It was a great fight by Coventry.'

Many City fans were also unperturbed by the loss, arguing that it left the team with no distractions in its quest for promotion but Bobby Gould came in for a large amount of criticism after the game. In his autobiography *24 Carat Gould* he wrote about the miss against Newcastle: 'During the following week, I had a letter saying I was the worst player Coventry had ever signed. It continued in even more complimentary tones and ended with the remark: "You should think of committing suicide". I was very emotional about the letter and went to see JH. I was helped hugely by the arrival of many messages of support from other fans and was eventually able to laugh the hate-mail episode off, even if it cut deeply.'

Today Gould laughs off the criticism: 'I remember the miss, at the City end, I missed from three inches and just wanted the ground to open up. I still have all the poison-pen letters at home including one which said "you might as well kill yourself or we'll do it for you". JH was fantastic and said to me: "We're not having this" and told the local press. His secretary helped me reply to all the letters supporting me and the majority of fans were phenomenal to me.'

In the following Saturday's *Pink*, Derek Henderson criticised the knockers, describing Gould as one of the most whole-hearted players to wear a City shirt, he wrote: 'The knockers, ever eager to pounce on someone, are going to ludicrous extremes. "He'll never be any good" and "Jimmy Hill should sell him" are two of the more polite things they are saying.' He reminded readers that Gould had scored 15 goals that season.

Henderson went on to relate the story of what happened after the game 'in which Bobby, admittedly, had an old-fashioned shocker'. 'Walking through one of the Sky Blue bars about half-an-hour after the match to meet his girlfriend, he was roundly booed by so-called City fans. This sort of thing sickens and disgusts me. These are the sort of people football can do without. If only for one moment they would stop and put themselves in the unfortunate player's place.'

Jimmy Hill came out in support of his young striker the following day. 'People forget that Gould is in his first full season leading an attack which is expected to win the division. I think many fans will be surprised to know that Bobby is ten times as severe on himself as the nastiest anti-Gould fan. Wyn Davies was brilliant on Saturday but Bobby has scored more goals than Davies this season.'

Henderson concluded: 'There are no excuses for the sort of bad game Gould had against Newcastle. But this is no reason to pillory a promising young player who I think will eventually make his critics eat their words.'

On the last night of the month over 7,500 watched as the reserve team put on their best performance of the season. The larger than normal crowd came to see Brian Lewis pull on a sky blue shirt for the first time and left buzzing with excitement after a 6-1 victory over Fulham. Playing at inside-left, Lewis showed real class, teaming up well with the goal-hungry Tudor and scoring the second goal with a great piece of skill. Two goals each from Tudor and Denton plus one from Docker gave City an impressive victory.

Top of Division Two (31 January 1967)

		Pl	*W*	*D*	*L*	*F*	*A*	*Pts*
1	SKY BLUES	27	14	7	6	51	32	35
2	Wolves	27	13	7	7	54	32	33
3	Carlisle	28	15	3	10	43	37	33
4	Huddersfield	26	12	7	7	36	29	31
5	Preston	28	14	3	11	51	44	31
6	Crystal Palace	26	13	5	8	39	36	31
7	Millwall	27	13	5	9	30	30	31

Chapter 8

February – 'Physical' City unrelenting

ON 1 February City's youngsters bowed bravely out of the FA Youth Cup at Port Vale to a physically stronger side on a sea of mud. Both managers thought the pitch was unplayable but the referee passed it fit despite players sinking into ankle-deep mud near the touchline. Pat Saward was fuming before the kick-off and his fears were confirmed in a game where there was little football played. City's chances weren't helped when Jeff Blockley went off injured when it was 1-0 to the home side. The referee wouldn't allow his substitute Robin Hayward on to the pitch for eight minutes and by that time it was 2-0. In the end Port Vale won 3-1 to progress to the last eight of the competition in front of a good crowd of 5,397.

The first Saturday of February found the Sky Blues away to Bury. Gibson's thigh strain, picked up scoring the second goal against Newcastle, ruled him out but was not expected to sideline him for long and Brian Lewis made his debut in his place. One shock, however, was the ever-present Bobby Gould being left out in favour of John Tudor following the Newcastle game and the poison-pen letters. Gould at the time wasn't happy: 'JH was shrewd though, he knew I needed taking out of the firing line and I came on for the second half. The whole incident had made me more determined to be a successful professional footballer. The goals came thick and fast after that and I never looked back from that day forward.'

Around 2,500 City fans made the trip to Gigg Lane and turned the game into what seemed like a home match with the Sky Blue Song reverberating around the small ground. Despite Bury being a poor side in the relegation zone, City did have to rely on Glazier who fortunately was again at the top of his game. Two of his saves, one from George Jones early on, and a second – an instinctive hand to push a point-blank effort by Barry Lowes over the bar – ranked as world-class. The second save had Bury players shaking their heads in disbelief.

In a drab game City created little and at half-time substitute Gould came on for the injured John Key. His introduction livened up City's performance and on the hour he had a headed 'goal' disallowed for offside. When Ronnie Rees popped up with the winner 11 minutes from time – a crisp volley following a Machin corner – Bury drooped. And at the other end man of the match Glazier clapped his muddy hands together in satisfaction.

Derek Henderson raved about Glazier's display in his match report but he also mentioned Mick Kearns, 'one of the few unflurried ones on a day of undignified scrambling'. He wasn't impressed by City's performance and concluded that 'City must write this one down as a bad day when they emerged with the right result'.

New man Brian Lewis was unable to get into the game but summed things up: 'The thing I noticed most about playing in the side for the first time was the way everyone fought. When things aren't going well for you, this makes a big difference.'

The win extended City's unbeaten league run to 11 games as elsewhere second-placed Wolves beat Bolton 5-2 at home with two goals apiece for Ernie Hunt and Bob Hatton and dark horses Huddersfield jumped to third place with a 1-0 home win over Derby. The 'A' team lost 1-0 at Bromsgrove in a West Midlands League Cup game but the 'B' team recovered from their nightmare at Port Vale and beat Notts County 4-1 away.

The following day Jimmy Hill took his squad to Leamington for a charity game against Lockheed in aid of the Ken Shelton-Rayner Fund that had originally been scheduled for 8 January but postponed. Mr Shelton-Rayner needed a kidney machine and there was a £7,000 appeal to raise the money. The Leamington Invitation Cup was presented to Lockheed after they had beaten the Sky Blues 5-3 in front of over 2,000 spectators. City included their former player John Mitten in the starting line-up as well as reserves Mick Coop and Peter Denton, and assistant manager Alan Dicks at centre-half in place of George Curtis. City's goals came from Mitten, John Tudor and substitute Dudley Roberts.

On the Monday evening Highfield Road hosted an FA Cup second replay from the third round. Hull City and Portsmouth had fought out two drawn games and before the FA changed the rules to have a penalty shoot-out after the first replay, the clubs played on at neutral venues to find a winner. Over 18,000 fans, many of them neutrals from the Coventry area, watched a thrilling game. Former City player Albie McCann scored a first-half penalty for Pompey only for Chris Chilton, later to become a City player, to equalise. Pompey then took control and further goals from McCann and Edwards sealed a 3-1 victory and a trip Tottenham in round four. Derek Henderson reported that although Hull brought more support than Portsmouth, the local neutrals largely seemed to support Pompey and 'the Pompey Chimes song rang out in the later stages'.

The following evening the reserves dropped a rare home point in a 1-1 draw with Nottingham Forest. One of the youngest reserve sides ever fielded – Peter Denton was the eldest at 20 –

delighted the home fans and Don Peachey scored City's goal on his reserve debut.

There was a story of a different kind two days later when it was revealed that the football club were working with the police to try to thwart 'the cheats', groups of teenagers who were sneaking into Highfield Road without paying. The *Coventry Telegraph* reported that some even brought wire-cutters to chop through barbed wire and the club were trying to seal off vulnerable points. The worst affected area was behind the Covered End (west end) where gardens of houses in Nicholls Street backed on to the ground. Mrs Mary Duggan, a resident of Nicholls Street, told the newspaper: 'It's a nightmare on match days – even Tuesday night for reserve games they come down the alley, alongside the house, tramp all over our garden and climb over the iron fencing. My husband spent £5 on barbed wire a couple of years ago but most of it is down now. Unless I stand here on Saturdays after one o'clock until kick-off time they come through in droves. They're mostly teenagers.'

Jimmy Hill said of the cheats: 'We've got to stop them. They are not only cheating the club but, in a sense, they are cheating the others who pay to come in – and whose money is helping us to become a great club.' He went on to give a warning: 'Anyone caught doing it is in for trouble.' The city police agreed to keep a watch on known weak spots around the ground.

One week after dropping leading scorer Bobby Gould for the game at Bury, Hill restored him to the starting line-up to face Preston at Highfield Road on 11 February. Ian Gibson returned from injury with Brian Lewis wearing the No.7 shirt in place of the injured John Key. At the start of play North End lay fourth in the table, four points behind the Sky Blues, having lost just one league game in eight. Their strength lay in their home form at Deepdale and they had struggled away with just two wins. The good news for the Sky Blues was that Preston centre-forward

Alex Dawson, who always gave George Curtis a tough game, was missing through injury.

Preston's star player was Howard Kendall who three years earlier had been the youngest player to appear in an FA Cup final when North End had lost to West Ham. Kendall, a tireless midfielder with bags of skill, had been linked with a move to a First Division club for a long time and this would be one of his final games for Preston before an £80,000 move to Everton where he would become part of the famous midfield trio of Kendall, Ball and Harvey that took the Toffees to the League Championship in 1970.

Former club physiotherapist Norman Pilgrim recalls Preston's previous visit to Highfield Road on 1 January 1966: 'It was an evening kick-off, the pitch was frozen hard and the players and staff from both sides strolled around the pitch an hour before the kick-off trying to kick a heel or toe into the white iron. There was no enthusiasm from either side to play the game but after an inspection the referee said it was on. Back in the dressing room the players are sitting around when JH bursts in full of enthusiasm. "We're going to win this because they don't want to play but we do. The game is on we can't change that." He went on to talk about tactics, getting the ball into their penalty area as quickly as possible. "Let the mistakes happen in their half not ours." We won the game 5-1. This was long before sports psychologists. Another of the many areas where Jimmy was a man before his time.'

City's unbeaten run once again looked vulnerable especially as Preston's strong-arm tactics in the first half unsettled the Sky Blues. When a Ross free kick wasn't cleared former Busby Babe Nobby Lawton cracked home a low drive to give the visitors a half-time lead. Preston then made the mistake of defending in depth and rarely came out of their own half. The Sky Blues were well below their best but continued to press for an equaliser. Gibson was being shadowed by two or sometimes three Preston players and after one strong challenge on him by Lawton the referee had to break up a crowd of jostling players.

City had a good shout for a penalty when Godfrey tackled Gibson, then Ron Farmer had a vicious shot blocked before Mick Kearns hit the rebound over the bar. Rees saw a header beat the keeper but a defender cleared off the line before City got the breakthrough in the 80th minute when from the right by-line Gibson's chip found Machin's head and the scores were level. Two minutes later Dietmar Bruck was clean through but sliced his shot wide from 12 yards. The noise from the 29,031 home crowd was now deafening and four minutes from time Highfield Road erupted as Gould netted the winner. Kendall, a tower of strength for Preston, was caught napping when he pushed the ball too far ahead of himself, Machin whipped it off his toes, fed Farmer who teed up Bobby to finish from 15 yards.

City's refusal to be beaten had been illustrated yet again and it was an inspirational selection, albeit a gamble by Hill to recall Gould. Thrust back in front of his critics who, for once, were subdued, the young centre-forward justified his selection with an improved performance, crowned by the winning goal.

In his match report Derek Henderson in the *Coventry Telegraph* had reservations about new boy Brian Lewis: 'He looked out of place for an hour on the (right) wing, (and) did not begin to give a forceful contribution until he was moved back allowing Clements to go forward. Now the problem facing Mr Hill is finding the most suitable role for Lewis, for on this evidence he is not a winger.'

Wolves kept up the pressure by winning 3-1 at Charlton but City's lead was still two points. Carlisle were back up to third place after a 2-0 victory over Bury. The reserves drew 0-0 at Fulham after dominating the game, the 'A' team lost 3-5 to Bilston despite Trevor Gould scoring a hat-trick and the 'B' team drew 2-2 at Derby.

The following Monday Derek Henderson listed City's remaining 13 games (or hurdles as he referred to them) and posed the question: 'Is this Coventry City's year?'. He pointed out that seven of the 13 games were at home with three of their closest rivals (Wolves, Carlisle and Huddersfield) having to come to Highfield Road and that 'unlike last season, they are displaying the resilience needed in the grim tension of a tightly-fought race'. He reminded readers that the team were two points up on the same stage as the previous season in which they finished with 53 points and were pipped by Southampton for second place.

Jimmy Hill was less assured, warning: 'Saturday's game proved there is a lot of sweating to be done yet. But what has pleased me most about the last few weeks is the way the team have held on despite attempts by opponents to knock us off our perch. Even when we have been giving away the first goal, we have come back and this is a good sign that we are weathering the storm. Remember, Wolves are not losing points now. And the other clubs have been picking up points steadily, so our position is really gratifying.' Henderson concluded his piece by writing: 'I stand by my pre-season forecast that City will go up – and I have a sneaking regard for Huddersfield as the other promoted side.'

City were in discussions with other clubs about re-arranging fixtures. Their away game at Charlton, originally scheduled for 4 March, had been brought forward to the following Saturday (18 February) because of a clash with the League Cup final being played at Wembley for the first time. However, that meant the Sky Blues now had two successive free Saturdays on 4 and 11 March, the latter being FA Cup fifth round day, and Jimmy Hill wanted to bring forward one of the two Easter games with Northampton to one of those dates.

The debate was not just whether the Cobblers would agree to the switch or not, but which club would forego an Easter home game and the likelihood of a bigger gate. Discussions were ongoing but Hill was forthright in his views about Easter football: 'The whole thing is archaic. When a club fights all season to achieve something, and has to turn out three times in four days, one or two injuries could ruin their chances.' Hill was obviously thinking about the previous season when Easter defeats at Portsmouth and Derby scuppered their promotion hopes.

In midweek, City's reserves travelled to Northampton for what Derek Henderson described as 'a violent clash'. The villain was Cobblers' wing-half Graham Carr, later to be the club's manager and renowned scout for Newcastle. Two reckless challenges by Carr went unpunished and City players retaliated. Henderson hoped that 'it is not a foretaste of things to come in the two Second Division meetings later in the season ... the miracle last night was that no-one was badly hurt'. A late Billy Best goal ended City's six-game unbeaten run.

On the Saturday City travelled to the Valley to face Charlton, an encounter Jimmy Hill described as 'one of those nasty games'. The Addicks had virtually ended City's promotion hopes the previous April with a 2-0 victory and the Sky Blues had never won in seven previous visits to the Valley. Charlton had struggled all season but had been recently strengthened by the double signing of Grimsby forwards Matt Tees and Rodney Green but had not won in six games and had lost their last three home matches.

City arrived with an unchanged team and supported by around 4,000 fans. With Charlton close to the relegation zone it was always going to be tough but no-one expected a game of 41 fouls and three bookings (in an era when bookings were as uncommon as red cards today). City had the better of the first half but failed to find a goal before they took the lead in the 50th minute.

Gibson, once more displaying his wizardry, and being watched by a Scotland selector, dribbled past several Charlton players. His pass was helped on by Clements and with the home defence in tatters Gould scored from three yards. Brian Lewis, playing in a defensive role despite wearing the No.7 shirt, was the first name in the book for a knee in the back of Tees which prompted loud booing from the home fans. Minutes later Curtis won an aerial challenge against Tees which saw the Charlton man's impetus take him off the field and he seemed to collide with the touchline wall. It didn't seem that the referee was going to take action until Charlton's manager Bob Stokoe angrily protested and suddenly Curtis's name was in the book.

Three minutes from time Gould wrapped up the points with a second goal. Curtis, booed constantly after the Tees incident, broke up an attack in his own half and fed Machin who spotted Bobby racing through the middle. Ernie's great high pass split the home defence and the centre-forward ran on to plant it past Wright in the Charlton goal.

Myers scored a consolation goal with virtually the last kick of the match as City recorded their first ever win at the Valley and extended the unbeaten league run to 13 games. In the post-match press conference the atmosphere was electric as Derek Henderson described in his book *The Sky Blues*. 'It was fraught with atmosphere. It had been a fierce match that City had won 2-1, and Bob Stokoe was plainly displeased at the manner in which they had achieved it. Though friends, he and Hill were 'poles apart' in the tense moments after the game in the Charlton boardroom. Both talked to journalists only a few feet apart. It was only after a while that the electric air cleared.' The London Sunday papers were hyper-critical of City with many football reporters describing them as a 'rough' team.

Ronnie Farmer recalls the game: 'We'd lost the last two seasons at Charlton and thought we had been muscled out of both games. They were always physical when they came to Highfield Road as well. We were no angels that day – JH told us to get stuck in and we did kick them a bit.'

July 1966 *The players are back in training and they are pictured in their fine club blazers and slacks getting a pep talk from Jimmy Hill. New arrival Ian Gibson has a different coloured suit on.*

July 1966 *Pre-season photo call. Back row (L to R): Kearns, Roberts, Wesson, Glazier, Curtis, Hill. Middle row (L to R): Burckitt, Rees, Farmer, JH, Gould, Key, Pointer. Seated (L to R): Denton, Clements, Gibson, Machin, Bruck, Mitten.*

August 1966 *A new programme cover for the new season. A novel design showing the heads of the 22 captains of the Second Division teams.*

August 1966 *Hull City (home). Opening game and a shirt-sleeved crowd swelter in the heat. Bobby Gould holds the ball up as Hull goalkeeper McKechnie looks out of position.*

September 1966 *Birmingham (home). Bobby Gould lunges for a through ball as Blues' goalkeeper Jim Herriott comes out. Over 36,000 watch the Midlands derby.*

October 1966 *Carlisle (away). Sky Blues defence under pressure. Glazier looks relieved as Carlisle's Willie Carlin just fails to connect with a cross.*

J.H's PAGE . .

Conversation between Father and Daughter

Joanna : 'Why are they booing the team as they come out, Daddy ?'
J.H. : 'Because they want them to do well.'
Joanna : 'Is that the way to help them do better ?'
J.H. : 'No, not really, but it is a bad match for Coventry isn't it ?'
Joanna : 'Yes it is, do they always play as badly ?'
J.H. : 'Lately they have not found their best form, but most of them have given great service to the Sky Blues.'
Joanna : 'What does Uncle George Curtis think about it ?'
J.H. : 'Fortunately he's so busy trying to stop Brighton he hasn't the opportunity to tell them.'
Joanna : 'Why are they singing dirty songs about you Daddy ?'
J.H. : 'They like singing and dirt and they don't like me.'
Joanna : 'Why don't they like you then ?'
J.H. : 'What they really don't like is that the Sky Blues are not scoring goals and beating everybody. The results are not good enough.'
Joanna : 'They've been pretty good up to now haven't they ?'
J.H. : 'It's now that counts !'
Joanna : 'What's that Gibson/Gibson business ?'
J.H. : 'They want him in the team !'
Joanna : 'Do you want him in the team ?'
J.H. : 'I want everyone whom I think will help get the Sky Blues into Division 1.'
Joanna : 'Don't people trust you to do that ?'
J.H. : 'Obviously not at the moment.'
Joanna : 'Have they ever trusted you before ?'
J.H. : 'Yes, the week after we won the 3rd Division.'
Joanna : 'Will they trust you again ?'
J.H. : 'Yes, the week after we win the 2nd Division.'
Joanna : 'Why won't they leave it to you ?'
J.H. : 'Supporters always imagine they know better than managers—even Matt Busby, but that's what makes it so interesting.'
Joanna : 'It's a pity really because it seems such a nice club !'
J.H. : 'It's the most progressive in the country.'
Joanna : 'What are you going to do about it then ?'
J.H. : 'Win.'

3

October 1966 *Blackburn (h). Jimmy Hill's programme notes – JH's conversation with his daughter Joanna.*

October 1966 *Bolton (away). Mick Kearns (2) and George Curtis in an aerial battle with Bolton's John Byrom as Gordon Taylor (11) looks on.*

November 1966 *Crystal Palace (home). Bobby Gould scores past John Jackson in the Palace goal as John Tudor looks on. City, though, lose their unbeaten home record.*

December 1966
Ipswich (home). Bobby Gould grabs the first of his hat-trick in the 5-0 demolition of league leaders Ipswich.

Whisper quiet —
"VIVA!"
smooth, too!

The Coventry Evening Telegraph
FOOTBALL

IT'S A BEAUTY
AUSTIN 1800
SAM ROBBINS LTD.
Austin Main Dealers
COX STREET, COVENTRY.

No. 23,474 [76th Year] SATURDAY, DECEMBER 3, 1966 FOURPENCE

Ipswich on top . . . Palace, Carlisle & Bolton falter

WOLVES SNOWED UNDER!

Gibson, Key and Rees put cheer into City

WOLVERHAMPTON WANDS. 1, COVENTRY CITY 3.

WHAT an amazing performance Coventry City put on at snow-covered Molineux this afternoon. Beaten back on defence by the rampant Wolves for nine-tenths of the game and, with less than a dozen shots on target, they cracked in three great goals for victory.

The Sky Blues owed it all to a magnificent display by their defence and particularly Bill Glazier, who stopped everything fired at him except a Burnside header. The City forwards were rarely seen in attack but all credit to them for snapping up chances which brought goals for Gibson, Key and Rees

NEMO reports from Molineux

JOHN KEY . . . scored the vital second goal.

Wallabies beat Wales

Blackpool v. Fulham

McGarry's joy

December 1966
Wolves (away). The Coventry Telegraph Pink celebrates a famous away win at Molineux.

December 1966
City's first team sign autographs at the traditional 'Pop and Crisps' session for young supporters before the Plymouth reserve game on 20 December.

December 1966
Rotherham (home). Gould (partially hidden) scores the first goal in the 4-2 Boxing Day victory.

January 1967
Birmingham (away). Ernie Machin (left) scores the equaliser, watched by Gould and the creator, Clements. Over 36,000 watched the Sky Blues go top of the table for the first time.

January 1967 *Norwich (home). Gould, Key and Machin (on ground) are frustrated by the Canaries' defence.*

January 1967 Bristol City (away). George Curtis (partially hidden) bullets a header past Gibson in the Bristol goal from Rees's free-kick to make it 1-1 at Ashton Gate.

January 1967
Newcastle (home) FA Cup. A balletic Ian Gibson spectacularly heads past Marshall in the Newcastle goal to make it 2-2. Gibson pulled a muscle with his effort and had to go off.

February 1967
Bury (away). Gould, the villain seven days previously, comes off the bench but his headed 'goal' was ruled out for offside.

February 1967
Preston (home). Preston keeper Alan Kelly comes out with the ball despite five City players in the penalty area. A young Howard Kendall (6) marshals the defence.

M & B EXPORT | M & B MILD ALE

Football League Division II.
Saturday, February 11th, 1967 — Kick-off 3.15 p.m.

Coventry	THE COVENTRY EVENING TELEGRAPH	Preston
Shirts : Sky Blue Shorts : Sky Blue		Shirts : White Shorts : Blue
BILL GLAZIER	1	ALAN KELLY
MICK KEARNS	2	GEORGE ROSS
DIETMAR BRUCK	3	JOHN DONNELLY
RON FARMER	4	NOBBY LAWTON
GEORGE CURTIS	5	TONY SINGLETON
DAVID CLEMENTS	6	HOWARD KENDALL
JOHN KEY	7	ERNIE HANNIGAN
ERNIE MACHIN	8	BRIAN GODFREY
JOHN TUDOR	9	ALEX DAWSON
IAN GIBSON	10	ALAN SPAVIN
RONNIE REES	11	DAVID WILSON
To be announced	Substitutes	GEORGE LYALL

Referee :
B. J. HOMEWOOD (Sunbury-on-Thames)

Linesmen :
A. H. GOODFELLOW (Leicester)
K. McNALLY (Wirrall, Cheshire)

We thank the supporter, who wishes to be anonymous, for the gift of today's match ball

YOUR NUMBER FOR THE DRAW FOR A CUP FINAL TICKET.

17 № 0593

OUR NEXT HOME GAMES

Tuesday February 21st
GILLINGHAM
Football Combination Kick-off 7.30

Saturday February 25th
CARLISLE UNITED
Football League Kick-off 3.15

11

February 1967
Preston (home). A new-look programme includes a different, more modern, style of showing the teams.

February 1967 *Charlton (away). The referee has his lips to the whistle as an airbourne George Curtis challenges Charlie Wright in the Charlton goal.*

February 1967 *Carlisle (home). City's constant pressure pays off as Ernie Machin's 88th-minute effort sneaks in by the post despite the efforts of Willie Carlin to clear it. Ian Gibson lurks to make sure.*

February 1967 *Worthing. Jimmy Hill (flanked by Peter Hill and Alan Dicks) cracks a joke in the team talk over the breakfast table during their short break at the seaside.*

February 1967
Worthing. A photo opportunity on the front at Worthing during a short break at the seaside.

March 1967
Northampton (away). Northampton goalkeeper Harvey is beaten but three defenders ensure the ball stays out as Gould waits to pounce on any error.

March 1967
Bolton (home). Bobby Gould has his hands held high to celebrate scoring after Ronnie Rees's wonderful dribble and cross. The BBC Match of the Day *cameras are just visible on a gantry at the back of the Sky Blue Stand. Barry Lowes and Ernie Machin are about to join the celebrations.*

March 1967
Blackburn (away). That man Gould is about to pounce as Blackburn goalkeeper Barton struggles to hold a Rees cross. The vital winning goal was Bobby's 21st of the season.

April 1967
Derby (home). Ernie Machin (third from left) heads a late equaliser in the 2-2 draw. Gibson (second left) turns away to celebrate while Gould is ready, just in case.

April 1967
Crystal Palace (away). Ernie Machin appeals for an infringement as Gould comes up against three home defenders. City got a hard-earned draw in the club's first Saturday night game.

April 1967
Huddersfield (home). Gould's scrambled effort gets past Huddersfield full-backs, Chris Cattlin and Derek Parkin, to give City a 1-0 victory.

April 1967
Cardiff (away). John Key has a tap-in to give City the lead in a game that finished 1-1 and virtually guaranteed promotion.

April 1967
Wolves (home). Wolves' goalkeeper Phil Parkes is beaten by Ian Gibson's stunning goal that makes it 2-1 to the Sky Blues. Hundreds of youngsters around the perimeter are about to explode on to the pitch in celebration.

April 1967
Wolves (home). City's young fans in the Covered End celebrate Gibson's goal.

April 1967 *Wolves (home). Victory secured, chairman Robins and director Phil Mead open the champagne in the dressing room.*

May 1967
Ipswich (away). Ipswich keeper Ken Hancock is stranded with John Tudor and Ian Gibson at the far post and it looks like Tudor's goal but it is credited to Gibson. The game ended 1-1.

May 1967
Millwall (home). Only nine minutes are gone and John Key puts the Sky Blues ahead in the final match of the season.

May 1967
Millwall (home). John Tudor thumps home Brian Lewis's cross to make it 2-0 with four Millwall defenders helpless.

May 1967 *Millwall (home). City have won 3-1 and are champions after Wolves slip up. Gibson, Curtis, Glazier and Clements receive the plaudits from the massed crowds.*

May 1967 *Jimmy Hill and George Curtis hold the Second Division trophy aloft on the balcony of the Hotel Leofric as thousands of fans celebrate the success.*

May 1967 *Captain George Curtis and Rose McNulty (Sky Blue Rose) take the microphone as the team record the* Sky Blue Promotion Album.

May 1967 *Bobby Gould and his new wife, Margery at their wedding, brought forward so that Gould could go to the Caribbean. Jimmy Hill and Trevor, Bobby's brother, are present and Bobby still has his wrist in plaster.*

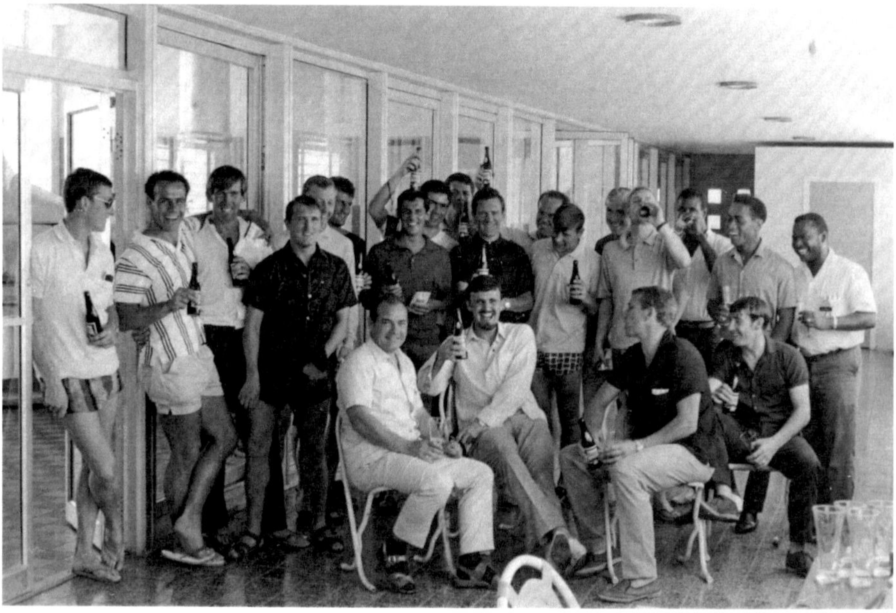

June 1967 *Barbados. City's players and staff enjoy a beer or two during their Caribbean holiday – a suitable reward for promotion.*

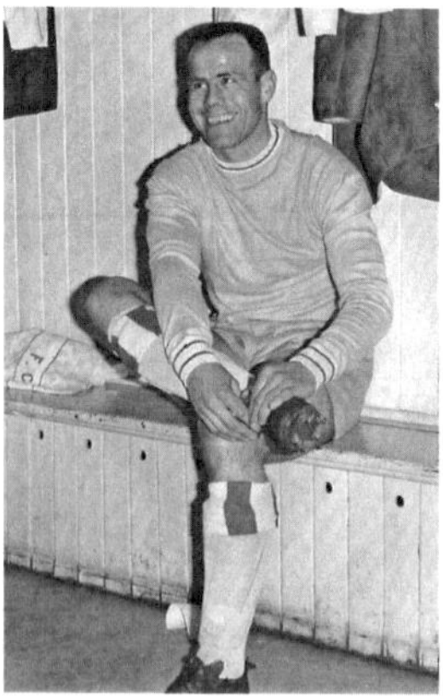

George Curtis, captain.

Bill Glazier

Dietmar Bruck

Dave Clements

Mick Coop

Ian Gibson

Bobby Gould

Ernie Machin

Alan Dicks, assistant manager

Peter Hill, trainer (pictured as a player in the early 1960s)

Pat Saward, head coach

Norman Pilgrim, physiotherapist

The men who made the Sky Blue Revolution happen. Jimmy Hill and Derrick Robins.

July 1967 *The pre-season photo shoot includes the Second Division trophy. Back row (L to R): Lewis, Curtis, Glazier, Kearns, Roberts. Middle row (L to R): Farmer, Bruck, Tudor, Coop, Machin, Hill. Seated (L to R): Key, Gibson, JH, Gould, Rees.*

With Wolves involved in FA Cup action (a 1-1 home draw with Everton), the Sky Blues extended their lead at the top of the table to four points but Wolves now had a game in hand. Third-placed Carlisle were six points behind the Sky Blues and had played the same number of games and they were City's opponents the following Saturday. City's 'A' team beat Atherstone 2-1 at Ryton with goals from Shepherd and Roberts but there was trouble between City's Dennis Oakes and Atherstone's George Awde who were ordered off for fighting. Dennis was later suspended for 14 days and fined £10. The 'B' team went down 3-1 at home to Forest.

The fixture issue was resolved that week with Northampton agreeing to switch their home game, scheduled for Easter Monday, to Saturday, 11 March and Jimmy Hill revealed that the club would play a home friendly with West Ham United on Friday, 3 March, the eve of the League Cup final. Before that Hill was taking the first-team squad to Worthing for four days to, as he put it, 'tone up for the last vital lap of Division Two games'. Worthing was looked upon as City's lucky training headquarters. They went there during the 1963 FA Cup run and the following season had spent a week there during the Third Division promotion run-in.

There was more good news from the Sky Blue Pool that week. Membership was now up to 110,000 with the weekly prize fund almost £2,000. The club were benefiting to the tune of £900 per week and Charles Harrold, City's administrative manager said: 'Although we have Coventry itself well covered, there are pockets where we could do better. We are always on the look-out for agents to help us swell the size of the pool.'

The following day it was announced that the board of directors had given the go-ahead to another major ground improvement at Highfield Road – the erection of a cantilever stand holding 3,200 seats behind the goal at the Covered End of the ground. The board were taking a big gamble, but a decision – in anticipation of First Division football – had to be made well in advance.

The new West Stand, which was estimated to cost £85,000, would be built by Banbury Grandstands, a subsidiary of Derrick Robins's company Banbury Buildings. The extra seats would take the number of seats in the ground to 10,500, one of the largest seated capacities in the Football League, and the terracing underneath would remain largely unaltered. The design of the stand would ensure an excellent view for all with each row of seats 15 inches above the one in front. The plan was for demolition of the old Covered End to commence immediately after the final league game against Millwall on 13 May and for the new stand to be ready for use for the opening home game in August. With extra season ticket revenue being generated the financial plan was that the stand would be paid for within three years.

Before flying off to the West Indies, chairman Derrick Robins spoke to the *Coventry Telegraph's* Derek Henderson: 'We have decided to go ahead with the phased programme in the knowledge that our supporters have backed us so wonderfully in the past, and that we are sure they will continue to do so.'

Jimmy Hill added: 'This situation illustrates why so few stands go up in football. No-one can foretell whether promotion will come or not. It does mean that directors of clubs under this sort of pressure mostly hesitate and then say "No". Our board is different – they hesitate and they say "Let's have a go".'

The reserves continued their impressive home form with a 3-1 victory over Gillingham with John Tudor, becoming something of a goal machine, netting two and Mick Coop the other. Tudor had now scored nine goals in 13 games for the 'stiffs'.

Third-placed Carlisle United arrived at Highfield Road on the last Saturday of February. The Cumbrians, under the management of Alan Ashman, were the surprise packet in the division and a run of six games with only one defeat since

Christmas had lifted them to the top of the pack chasing City and Wolves. There were no stars in the Carlisle team but they had an uncompromising defence and of course had got the better of the Sky Blues at Brunton Park in October and contributed to the Hill-Gibson rift.

Jimmy Hill made one change from the team that won at Charlton, recalling John Key on the right-wing and switching Brian Lewis to wing-half in place of Ronnie Farmer. Carlisle started the stronger side and almost took the lead in the fifth minute when Chris Balderstone set up Irish international winger Eric Welsh whose strong shot was tipped around a post by Glazier. Six minutes later the visitors went ahead when Welsh found George McVitie who eluded Clements and cracked a high shot over Glazier.

There was a hold-up when Key went down with a bad injury after a heavy challenge by Caldwell and the winger was replaced by substitute Farmer who came on to a tremendous reception. City reshuffled with Rees switching to the right-wing and Dave Clements moving on to the left and Lewis into defence. The Sky Blues were looking more forceful and twice missed good chances – Gibson heading over from five yards and then having his goal-bound chip shot blocked. The breakthrough came a minute before the break when Machin's header set Rees free to run at the defence and the Welshman's short cross was cracked into the top corner by Bobby Gould.

Heavy rain made the top surface slippery as the second half started and City continued where they left off, pinning the visitors back and a Farmer shot was deflected on to a post by Gibson. Then came the controversial dismissal of Carlisle goalkeeper Alan Ross. Ross jumped to hold a Curtis header and was challenged with a heavy shoulder charge from Gould. Ross produced a right hook that Henry Cooper would have been proud of to floor the City striker. Referee Maurice Fussey immediately ordered Ross from the field and it seemed that the guilty keeper was walking off as soon as the offence had been committed.

As the rain poured down, the referee turned away Carlisle's protests and defender Peter McConnell took the keeper's jersey. City were virtually camped in the visitors' half now with Glazier a mere spectator but the Carlisle defence protected McConnell and there were few shots to save. Roared on by a 29,965 crowd, the home attack had every shot and cross cleared until with two minutes remaining they scored the winner. A long cross by Clements was headed forward by Machin and in a terrific melee the ball hit a post. Carlin tried to clear it but as it rolled along the line Gibson got a touch but the ball was already over the line with credit going to Machin. The roar from the drenched crowd was more of relief that the team had, for the third home game running, pulled a victory out of the bag. Many of the soaked fans stayed on the terraces awaiting the score from Portsmouth, who had led Wolves 2-0 at half-time. The Tannoy announcement that Wolves had come back to win 3-2 was greeted with groans.

For nine-year-old Kevin Shannon it was his first visit to a City game: 'I had been pestering my dad, a lapsed City fan, to take me to the football for over a year. He finally gave in, partly persuaded no doubt, by the fact that we had already had four years of success under JH and that promotion seemed likely. From that first minute inside Highfield Road I just loved it, loved everything about the experience. The noise, the colour, the smells, the greenness of the pitch and the blueness of our kit. I was fascinated by the crowd, by the little sky blue cars that sheltered under the terrace wall on the Sky Blue Stand side, by the vendors with trays of pies at the front and tanks of tea on their backs and by the tiny slivers of rust that came down periodically onto my head from the terrace roof.

'We stood in the Covered End, behind and slightly to the right of the goal. The atmosphere was both exhilarating and slightly scary to a nine-year-old. The terrace was packed and any time the City attacked the crowd would surge forward from the back against the barriers on the terrace sometimes carrying me off of my feet. The ground tingled with excitement and anticipation. Even Carlisle taking the lead didn't dampen anyone's spirits. We all knew, even me at my first game, that City would come back. Come back they did with second-half goals from Gould and Machin. Carlisle ended with ten men as keeper Alan Ross was sent off for punching, and laying out Bobby Gould after the latter unwisely charged him. I thought things like this happened at every match!'

City's victory made it four wins out of four in the month, extended the unbeaten league run to 14 games and kept a four-point cushion with Wolves. Blackburn leap-frogged Carlisle with a 2-1 win at Bury and were two points behind Wolves. The reserves lost 2-1 at Southampton with Dennis Oakes scoring, the 'A' team lost 3-1 at Stourbridge whilst the 'B' team drew 2-2 with Walsall at Ryton with Brian Joy scoring both goals. The news on John Key's injury was bad – he was ruled out for at least a month with ankle ligament damage and there was speculation that Hill might go into the transfer market to sign a replacement.

Following Bob Stokoe's outburst after the Charlton game, Carlisle's Alan Ashman stuck the knife in during a television interview the following Monday. Ashman accused City of 'using spoiling tactics rather than skill' in their promotion campaign. 'It is not enough to have skill and courage – it seems you have got to kick as well,' he said. 'Clubs like Coventry defend this with excuses that it's a man's game. I would not wish to inflict physical stuff on our opponents.' He admitted that the referee had no alternative but to send Ross from the pitch, but added that he had 'acted under extreme provocation'.

Jimmy Hill was having none of this and retorted: 'It really is extraordinary that Mr Ashman, who has three of his players facing suspension and has had two men sent off in successive games – twice as many as we have had in my five and a half years as manager – should say things like this. We have only had four bookings all season, one each to Machin, Kearns, Lewis and Curtis. And if people describe Ernie (Machin) or Mick (Kearns) as physical they are crazy.'

The squad were now in Worthing on their break and Derek Henderson said they 'were in great spirits'. Leisure activities were restricted by the howling gale and torrential rain but on the Tuesday the weather brightened and the players played golf and squash and later had a 'brisk five-a-side work-out on the beach'. Jimmy, a fanatical horse rider had been out for morning rides at leading trainer Ryan Price's stables at nearby Findon.

On the Wednesday evening the whole squad were taken to the Dell at Southampton to watch Willie Carr make his debut for Scotland's youth team against England. Carr was one of Scotland's best players but England, boasting Peter Shilton in goal, won 1-0 with Everton's Joe Royle scoring. Other future internationals Trevor Brooking and Mick Mills also played for England.

Top of Division Two (28 February 1967)

		Pl	*W*	*D*	*L*	*F*	*A*	*Pts*
1	SKY BLUES	31	18	7	6	58	35	43
2	Wolves	30	16	7	7	65	37	39
3	Blackburn	31	14	9	8	43	37	37
4	Huddersfield	30	14	8	8	41	34	36
5	Hull City	31	15	5	11	66	46	35
6	Carlisle	31	16	3	12	46	42	35

Chapter 9

March – City move closer to the goal

WITH the transfer deadline of 16 March just two weeks away Jimmy Hill spent the Worthing mini-break thinking over his options as the final lap of the promotion season loomed. John Key's ankle x-ray had shown no break but damaged ligaments and he was likely to be out of action for about a month. JH had to decide whether to go into the transfer market for a replacement or rely on Dave Clements whom he described as 'the reluctant winger'.

Hill was fulsome in his praise for Clements's switch to the wing in recent victories over Preston and Carlisle but said 'he is loath to move away from his job as a marking defender'. Key's absence could be covered by Rees switching to the right and Clements playing on the left-wing using his 'strength and running power' to full effect. Hill also might have considered Peter Denton, who was coming back to the form that had won him a few first team games the previous season.

When pressed by Derek Henderson, Hill gave nothing away: 'Round about transfer deadline time there is always a bit of activity which blossoms forth and I am always prepared to do a deal if it is the right one.' Henderson also wondered if Hill may want some extra cover in the goalkeeping department as Glazier's deputy was local lad Martin Clamp who, although he had shown some good form for the reserves, had yet to make his first-team debut. Clamp didn't have long to wait for that taste of action – on the Friday evening he came on as a half-time substitute for Glazier in the friendly with West Ham United.

Over 18,500 turned up at Highfield Road to watch City and the Hammers play for the Winston Churchill Trophy, with many of them coming to see the Hammers' three World Cup winners. They saw few fireworks from the three heroes – Martin Peters was rested, Geoff Hurst was well marshalled by Brian Lewis and Bobby Moore eased his way through the game, occasionally showing his class with his pin-point precision passes.

City had an impressive first half and scored two early goals through Gibson and Machin but Peter Brabrook pulled a goal back from a Hurst pass. At half-time in addition to Clamp, City introduced John Tudor for Dietmar Bruck and within three minutes the Coventry-born keeper was beaten by Brabrook's 'banana' shot. Nine minutes later Hurst's shot took a deflection and squirmed past Clamp to make it 3-2 to the Londoners. Machin pulled the scores level following a goalmouth scramble and at the final whistle it was 3-3. Both managers had agreed beforehand that in the event of a draw they would have a best of 11 penalty shoot-out to decide the destination of the trophy. West Ham proved more accurate and won the competition 9-7.

The following day, with the Sky Blues not in league action, the chasing pack narrowed the gap. Wolves beat Northampton 1-0 in a scrappy game to pull within two points of City whilst Blackburn, Huddersfield and Carlisle were all successful. The likes of Ipswich, Millwall and Crystal Palace were struggling to stay in the promotion race. The 'A' team lost 2-1 at home to a strong Kidderminster Harriers side, and the 'B' team won 3-0 at Stoke with Peachey scoring two.

On the goalkeeping subject, Hill opened up more to Derek Henderson. He revealed that he was attempting to sign an amateur goalkeeper of 'international standard' to give him cover over the 'pressure period' of the last 11 matches. He went on to say: 'I don't like blocking the progress of youngsters,' but then said: 'On the other hand, this is a most vital time and one doesn't want to take undue risks.' Henderson concluded that a short-term signing was imminent. Hill was holding fire on a new winger until John Key's plaster was removed on the Wednesday: 'If he is going to be all right, our staff is good enough to do the job – I have said this all along.'

Hill didn't wait until the Wednesday – on the Tuesday he revealed that the club had paid Bury £13,000 for their 27-year-old right-winger Barry Lowes. Hill and director John Camkin had driven to Lancashire for talks with the player and Bury manager Les Shannon. Hill explained: 'The real reason I jumped in to sign him was because the report on John Key's ankle injury is that it could easily be six weeks before he is in action again. And this gives us extra cover.'

Overnight Lowes had gone from a side heading for Division Three to one looking odds-on to go into Division One. The move had come out of the blue as he described at the time: 'I was digging the back garden on Monday afternoon when I got a call to go into the club. When I got there, I was confronted by Jimmy Hill who asked me: "How about coming to Coventry and playing for me?"'

Lowes, who hailed from Barrow-in-Furness, didn't kick a soccer ball in earnest until he was 20. At that age he looked set for a future in rugby league with Barrow when he suddenly changed codes and joined the local football team as a centre-forward. Later he was converted to a winger and sold to Blackpool before four years at Workington earned him a move to Bury 12 months earlier. Before his death in 2012, Barry recalled: 'Ernie Machin said I was the only winger in the division to give Dietmar Bruck a hard time that season and Jimmy Hill signed me on the strength of that.'

A day later West Ham's 23-year-old reserve goalkeeper Alan Dickie joined the Sky Blues for £4,000 as cover for Bill Glazier during the crucial run-in. 6ft 2in Dickie had been understudy to Jim Standen and played 15 first-team games in five seasons for the Hammers. He had kept goal in the friendly the previous Friday. City agreed that he could continue to live in London and that the club would not hold him after this season. Dickie had turned down a chance to be Swansea's first-team goalkeeper and Jimmy Hill told Derek Henderson: 'That's it – we're now prepared for the last lap. There will positively be no more signings this season.'

Over at Molineux the Wolves manager Ronnie Allen was also taking no risks with promotion and that week paid Leicester £45,000 for Irish centre-forward Derek Dougan. It would prove to be an inspired signing.

A West Ham side were again at Highfield Road on the Tuesday evening as the club's reserve teams met in a Football Combination game. Goals from Howard Moore, Dudley Roberts and Tudor gave City a 3-1 win.

On Saturday, 11 March after a two-week break from league action City travelled to Northampton for a crucial local derby. The Cobblers were at the foot of the table and a second successive relegation was on the cards. The game, originally scheduled for Easter Monday had been brought forward as neither club was involved in the FA Cup – allowing a less strenuous Easter programme. New man Lowes made his debut on the right-wing in place of Key and Farmer returned in place of Brian Lewis.

An estimated 8,000 Coventry fans made the 35-mile trip to the County Ground which was packed to the gunwales with a vociferous 20,100 crowd. The covered end was completely taken over by Coventry fans expecting a comprehensive City victory. A strong buffeting wind made any slick football impossible with the more skilful players finding control difficult.

In such conditions City had to be on their mettle to ensure there was no shock result. They had the upper hand in the first period and should have gone in ahead at the break but good efforts from Farmer and Gibson were blocked by defenders on the line. Other shots hit bodies and legs as the Sky Blues tried to press home their advantage.

Early in the second half Lowes, who impressed on his debut with some direct running, sent in a shot that was belted off the line by Terry Branston and it was clearly going to be one of those afternoons. Later Cobblers' keeper Bryan Harvey stepped forward to frustrate City with several inspired stops, particularly one from Ronnie Rees.

At the other end Glazier had just one touch of fortune when he 'lost' a Theo Foley lob in the dazzling sunshine and the ball clipped back off a post. City confidently stemmed other raids to get the point that inched them closer to their greatest goal. The draw was a point dropped but extended the unbeaten run to 15 games equalling the club record set in 1937 and equalled in 1963, but it was only the second time all season that the team had failed to score.

Keith White, who was 16, recalls his first visit to the County Ground: 'Of all the grounds I had been to then [or since], the County Ground at Northampton was the strangest. At the start of the previous season when the Cobblers had just arrived in the First Division, a photo appeared in a newspaper with the caption "Where Arsenal play on Saturday!" It was the football pitch being used as a car park for the cricket team! For City's game, I had the unique experience of standing on duck boards behind a rope next to the touchline. I could smell the liniment on the players and saw at close quarters what a Curtis challenge could do.'

It was FA Cup fifth round day elsewhere and City's game was one of only three Division Two fixtures that day. Wolves weren't in action so City extended their lead over them to three points but the Wanderers now had a game in hand. City's reserves lost 3-0 at Gillingham, the 'A' team drew 1-1 in the West Midlands League with unbeaten leaders Boston United with Dudley Roberts on target and the 'B' team lost 5-3 to West Brom.

The club were also criticised by West Midland League leaders Kidderminster Harriers after the Worcestershire club had visited Ryton for a game the previous weekend. Harriers were forced to report City to the league after numerous complaints from their supporters who attended. The Kidderminster secretary told the *Coventry Telegraph* that: 'Between 200 and 300 of our supporters went to the game and were extremely disappointed with the lack of elementary facilities such as toilets and refreshments.'

City secretary Alan Leather replied to the criticism: 'Ryton is a training ground, and under the terms of the lease we are not permitted to charge on the gate. You can hardly expect facilities, although we are not saying we would not like them, but there is a limit to what we can provide. When we went into the West Midlands League everyone knew what the conditions would be at Ryton.'

On the following Tuesday night, with the transfer deadline two days away, the scouts were out in force for City's home reserve game with Crystal Palace. Watford player-manager Ken Furphy was watching Peter Denton and the managers of Bradford City and Plymouth were also present in the main stand. Assistant manager Alan Dicks who regularly played at centre-half that season, stood down to allow young Malcolm Keley to make his first reserve appearance of the season and Alan Dickie made his reserve team debut. Denton and Tudor (again) were on target in a 2-2 draw but Denton didn't convince Furphy to sign him. John Burckitt did enough to persuade Bradford boss Willie Watson to take him on loan on the understanding that if City needed him back at any time he could return – a deal that suited all parties with John getting some valuable first-team experience and City cutting their wage bill slightly.

Derek Henderson compared the ongoing 15-match unbeaten league run with the similar runs in 1937/38 and 1962/63. This term the team had collected 25 points from the 15 games compared to 23 in 1963 and 22 in 1937. Hill's team had scored 35 goals, the same as 1963 but conceded 16, two less than the 1963 side.

On the Saturday Bolton Wanderers were the visitors to Highfield Road. The Lancashire club had led the table when City had visited Burnden Park in October but inconsistent form had seen them slip to mid-table – the sale of top scorer Wyn Davies had affected them badly. They paraded new signing Bob Hatton, a £30,000 acquisition from Wolves on transfer deadline day.

City were unchanged with Ernie Machin making his 100th appearance for the club. Machin had been born just a few minutes from Burnden Park and Jimmy Hill had signed him from under the noses of Wanderers in 1962 whilst he was playing for non-league Nelson. He had emerged from a spell of heavy criticism from supporters to become one of the team's most consistent players and had been at his most effective in the weeks since Christmas.

Jimmy Hill took the opportunity to praise Machin: 'Ernie has had enough experience of crowd antagonism and nasty injuries to last him a lifetime. Let us hope it has all been crowded into the first 100 games and that things will be better for him from now on.' Since making his debut against Millwall in April 1963 he had twice suffered cartilage injuries which hampered his development but he had missed only four games the previous season and had been a virtual ever-present this campaign.

The BBC *Match of the Day* cameras were at Highfield Road for the first time with the famous Kenneth Wolstenholme doing the commentary from a temporary gantry at the top of the Sky Blue Stand. The Saturday night programme, which in those days showed highlights of only one game, had been running since August 1964 and had featured the Sky Blues at Huddersfield the previous season on BBC2. Since England's World Cup victory the programme had moved to BBC1 and millions of armchair fans got a first view of Hill's Sky Blues. The cameras were lucky to record one of the goals of the season from the Sky Blues.

After winning with late goals in their last three home games, City were this time on the receiving end of a late goal that earned the Trotters a point. The result was a travesty with Derek Henderson in the *Coventry Telegraph* describing the visitors as 'the poorest Bolton performance I have seen for years'. Henderson went on to say that 'City had enough openings to have thrashed them out of sight but tossed many of them away with careless abandon'. For once the ruthless streak that had marked so many recent performances was absent.

Henderson put the blame onto the shoulders of the attack. Gould rarely troubled their defence, Lowes looked a bundle of nerves and Gibson faded after a breezy start. Only Machin and Rees did themselves justice with the Welsh winger creating the City goal after 40 minutes with a dazzling run from his own penalty area. He beat four or five Bolton defenders before finding Gould six yards out and the centre-forward chested the ball down before shooting past the previously impregnable Eddie Hopkinson in the Bolton goal. Two minutes from time Bolton had their first effort on goal and equalised. Phillips headed goalwards from six yards, Glazier, 'his hands blue with the coldness of inactivity' and Bruck seemed to leave it to each other and the ball squirmed into the net. A frustrating afternoon but 28,580 were there to see a new club record of 16 unbeaten games set.

Wolves, parading their new signing Derek Dougan, won 1-0 at Plymouth thanks to a Peter Knowles goal and were just two points behind City with the game in hand. Blackburn and Huddersfield from the chasing pack both won away and were closing the gap. City's next match was at Ewood Park on Easter Saturday in a vital six-pointer. City's reserves notched their first away win, 3-1 at Peterborough with Tudor, Carr and Brian Hill on the scoresheet. The 'A' team drew 1-1 with Bedworth whilst the 'B' team had a week off.

The reserves were back in action in midweek and over 8,000 turned up to see City's team, a mixture of youth and experience, beat Arsenal 1-0. Barry Lowes, trying to get over his nightmare home debut, scored the winning goal, made by Willie Carr.

On Easter Saturday, 25 March, the Sky Blues travelled north to face a Blackburn side that was making a strong run for promotion after a lacklustre first half of the season following relegation from Division One the previous campaign. Manager Jack Marshall had left the club in February after the FA Cup defeat to Carlisle and his assistant Eddie Quigley had been made caretaker-manager. Quigley had steered the team to five consecutive victories that had lifted Rovers to third place in the table and they had not conceded a home goal for four and a half months. This was crunch time for Jimmy Hill's team and they came through it with a vital 1-0 victory courtesy of Bobby Gould's 21st goal of the season and his sixth in six games.

Blackburn's crowds, which had fallen to under 8,000 the previous year, were on the up but around 3,000 City fans made the trip to Lancashire and the attendance of 26,380 was easily Rovers' biggest gate of the season. A bumpy pitch and swirling wind made things difficult for both teams. Hill recalled Brian Lewis on the right wing in place of Barry Lowes against a Blackburn side who fielded several England internationals including Bryan Douglas, Ronnie Clayton and John Connelly.

The early play saw City doing most of the attacking without really threatening but there were some heavy tackles in what was a crucial game for both teams. Blackburn winger Mike Ferguson had Blackburn's best effort of the half, which Curtis had to head off the line. Four minutes before half-time City had the home defence in a tangle and keeper Barton just beat Gould to an awkward Farmer cross, then Gould got himself booked for dissent after a bit of pushing with Clayton. The niggling nature of the game spilled over just before the end of the half when Blackburn's Mike Ferguson punched Dietmar Bruck in the face and was immediately ordered off. Ferguson had a bad disciplinary record and had just completed a three-match ban for three bookings. Six minutes into the second half City scored their goal. Ronnie Rees sent over a teasing cross and Barton failed to grasp it. Gould, the ultimate predator, bundled the ball over the line to a big roar from the City following. 'It was one of the easiest goals I ever scored,' said Gould years later.

Ten-man Blackburn gave it everything in the last 40 minutes but City, with their defence packed with red shirts, kept them at bay. The travelling fans wanted them to attack Rovers but Hill's tactics were spot on and they soaked up the pressure impressively. There were a few chances, none better than when Gould was put clear by Rees only to scoop the ball over with Barton helpless. Glazier was forced into two superb saves by the tricky Douglas but City slowly drew the sting out of Rovers's brave fight.

One party of City fans who travelled to Ewood Park didn't enjoy the day. Brian Chaston who was eight years old at the time recalls: 'My mum and dad took me to virtually every game that season. My dad's company printed the Golden Goal tickets and my mum had a crimping machine to seal the tickets. He wasn't paid for the printing but got complimentary season tickets in the Sky Blue Stand, block B. We normally went to away games by car but for some reason we went to Blackburn by coach. We sat in the stand at Ewood Park and when Bobby Gould scored my dad swallowed a boiled sweet. We tried everything to get him to regurgitate the sweet without success. He was in tremendous pain all the way back to Coventry but nothing could be done. We got him to Gulson Road hospital that night and it was discovered that he had punctured a lung and had to stay in for three or four days.'

Ian Davidson, who was 13, travelled from Coventry with his father and met up with his Cheshire-based cousin, Rod Williams, to go to Ewood Park: 'We were eager to show our support and had Sky Blue balloons tied to our woollen hats. My recollection was of standing proudly behind the goal, with the balloons flapping in the wind, and at half time swapping ends to be behind the goal City were attacking. Yes, we got plenty of 'friendly' abuse from the Rovers fans as we walked around the ground but, of course, we had the last laugh with Bobby Gould scoring the only goal.'

At Molineux Wolves's new signing Derek Dougan became an instant local hero by scoring a hat-trick on his home debut in the 4-0 win over Hull City. In retrospect, it was a defining day in the season with Huddersfield's excellent run ending in a home defeat to bottom club Northampton and Palace slipping up at Selhurst Park against Millwall. City and Wolves now had a four-point cushion and it would require a massive slip-up for the two midland rivals to miss out on promotion. The 'A' team beat Stourbridge 1-0 with Pat Morrissey scoring from the penalty spot, and the 'B' team lost 3-2 at Shrewsbury to their 'A' team.

Three days later the Cobblers travelled to Highfield Road for another big game and a crowd of 38,560, City's biggest league crowd for 18 years and the fourth highest in the club's history at the time, watched the midlands derby. The relegation-threatened Cobblers, buoyed by their win at Huddersfield, boldly staved off the initial City threat. For half-an-hour they looked every bit as good as the Sky Blues and seemed quite capable of sneaking a breakaway goal that might have made it very awkward for Hill's team.

In the short space of five minutes before the break they showed signs of creaking. First Northampton keeper Bryan Harvey mishandled a cross and there followed an astonishing let-off as Ian Gibson, playing better than he had for weeks, smacked a terrific shot against the left-hand post. The ball flew along the goal line, bounced off the other upright and back into the amazed Harvey's arms.

A minute later Gould produced a stunning shot which Harvey somehow tipped over the bar. There was more drama when Brian Lewis ran in to challenge Harvey, hustled the ball away from his grasp and netted. It looked bad enough luck to have the goal disallowed but then he appeared to be butted in the face by Cobblers' defender Terry Branston who was lucky to receive only a booking.

The pattern however was set for the second half and on 62 minutes the Cobblers finally buckled. A long punt was headed down to Lewis whose cross was forced home by Machin. Seven minutes from time City broke the Northampton offside trap and Rees centred perfectly for Gould to net for the seventh time in as many games and clinch a 2-0 win.

Dietmar Bruck recalls that Jimmy Hill collared him before the game: 'He told me he'd had some phone calls saying I'd been spotted in the city the night before drinking and asked me if it was true. I told him I had been out but had only drunk lemonade. After the game, he patted me on the back and praised my performance – "I knew I could trust you".' Bruck says JH had trust in his players. 'From the early days when he took over he told us that it was our body and we should know our limitations, but woe betide if we didn't perform on a Saturday. We used to go out as a group on Tuesday nights if we didn't have a midweek game, we went to one of several pubs or working men's clubs around the city and played darts, dominoes and cribbage with the local people – it was all good for PR.'

Four points from four over Easter was good for City but Wolves had also had an excellent Easter with six points from three games and home and away 1-0 wins over Huddersfield on consecutive days meant they leapfrogged City into top place – on goal average. The two midland rivals were now six points ahead of the field and the fans were licking their lips in anticipation of the clash of the two clubs at Highfield Road on 29 April.

City secretary Alan Leather was pleased with the crowd arrangements for the Northampton game. Several people had complained they could not see but Leather said: 'Evening matches always present unique problems. People are inclined to arrive 20-30 minutes later than for a Saturday game. But we were still well below capacity.' He did reveal that the club were considering making the Wolves game all-ticket but added: 'It is very rare for a league match to be all-ticket but a firm decision has not yet been taken.'

Derek Henderson in the *Coventry Telegraph* was in no doubt about the situation: 'It is a question of who finishes top now, Wolves or the Sky Blues after an Easter programme that has established the two midland clubs as clear-cut favourites for First Division places next season. Mathematically, either side could be caught but ... anything short of a double midland triumph now would be one of the greatest shocks in modern league soccer.'

Henderson also revealed that the attendance against Northampton had pushed the club's average for the season to 26,317 and that we were now heading for a new club record. He speculated that a full house against Wolves and 30,000-plus crowds for the three other home games would take the final average to around 28,000. The record of 26,694 had been set in 1950/51 season.

The final news of what had been an exciting month at Highfield Road was the launch of a revolutionary Sky Blue Information Service. In the modern-day world of the internet and social media it sounds archaic but Jimmy Hill's idea was a telephone-answering service giving fans 15-20 seconds of the outstanding club news of the day. The club's receptionist, Rose McNulty, who became known as Sky Blue Rose, would record messages that could be heard when fans phoned in. Hill explained the sort of information that could be recorded: 'The announcement of the team, information on the Sky Blue Special (train), seat prices, news of visiting teams and suchlike. The object must be however, to keep the message concise so that people are not on the line too long.'

Top of Division Two (31 March 1967)

		Pl	*W*	*D*	*L*	*F*	*A*	*Pts*
1	Wolves	35	21	7	7	73	37	49
2	SKY BLUES	35	20	9	6	62	36	49
3	Blackburn	35	17	9	9	46	38	43
4	Ipswich	35	14	13	8	60	48	41
5	Carlisle	35	19	3	13	54	45	41
6	Millwall	35	17	7	11	41	40	41

Chapter 10

April – Promotion achieved

COVENTRY City chose April Fools' Day to give their supporters a nervous afternoon by leaving it until ten minutes from the end before grabbing a home point against Derby County. Manager Hill was able to select an unchanged side for the third game running and a good crowd of 32,041 was present on a cloudy but dry afternoon. Sky Blue fans believed it was lambs (or Rams) to the slaughter as Derby had lost seven away games in a row. Derby were without former City goalkeeping legend Reg Matthews who had a broken jaw and winger Billy Hodgson was also ruled out through injury with Nigel Cleevely deputising.

The dominant Sky Blues looked set for a comfortable win after 17 minutes when Ian Gibson jinked his way along the by-line before crossing low for Bobby Gould to slide in and convert with an outstretched leg.

Minutes later Gibson had a goal disallowed when his overhead kick was judged offside. Derby began to test a casual-looking home defence and it was no surprise when Kevin Hector equalised after shrugging off Curtis and Clements to drive a fine shot past Glazier.

Derby started the second half confidently and the home crowd were anxious, but the visitors had to survive two strong penalty claims when first Brian Lewis and then Gould went down in the box. With City looking more and more anxious there were howls of despair as Lewis blasted an easy chance over the bar. It was a costly miss as two minutes later Eddie Thomas was allowed too much room and time and hit a well-placed shot past Glazier. Hill pushed Clements forward in an effort to inject some shooting power and the Irishman connected with a Farmer cross but it went into the side netting.

Desperation was beginning to creep into City's play but the whole outcome of the game changed in the space of two minutes. First Derby's Gordon Hughes had a goal disallowed when he bundled the ball out of Glazier's arms and then flipped it over his head into the net. Then Dietmar Bruck, one of City's few stars on the day, surged forward and put over a high cross which Machin cleanly nodded in over Boulton's outstretched arms. The last ten minutes were nerve-wracking for City and at the end they were grateful for the point and the fact they had kept the unbeaten run, now 18 games, going.

Wolves' eight-game winning run came to an end at Millwall. Derek Dougan grabbed a late equaliser at the Den where it ended 1-1 and with Blackburn also drawing it was as you were at the top of the table. City's reserve team lost 4-2 at Chelsea after taking the lead and there were defeats for both the 'A' and 'B' teams at Brierley Hill and Port Vale respectively.

City's Covered End supporters got a warning about obscene chanting from director Charles Harrold. A Radio Sky Blue appeal was made over the Tannoy system after the 'choir' at the Covered End had chanted obscene words at the referee Roy Harper. An angry Harrold said: 'This is the first time for quite a while that this sort of thing has flared up, and, by and large, ours is a well-behaved crowd.' Organised chanting was now familiar at most football grounds, but Derek Henderson said: 'only occasionally does it lapse into the obscene. City obviously feel that if there is a repetition of Saturday's behaviour, they will have to pounce before it becomes a habit.'

In the *Pink* that evening Derek Henderson speculated on the likely attendance for the Wolves game four weeks hence. He felt that the ground record of 44,930 which was set against Aston Villa in 1938 could be smashed. The capacity of the ground had never been severely tested since the Sky Blue Stand had been completed in 1964. With 5,100 seats that stand added around 3,900 to the overall ground capacity which a year earlier had been pegged at 44,000 for the FA Cup game with Manchester United. 'Since little of the terrace and enclosure spacing was lost in the transformation on that side of the ground, it stands to reason that the present capacity is in the region 47-48,000.'

During that week chairman Derrick Robins and director John Camkin represented the club at an extraordinary general meeting of the Football League in London. The meeting rejected the principle of live televising of matches and supported the abolition of the players' signing-on bonus. On his return Robins was angry at the outcome. He told Derek Henderson: 'We seem to have nobody in soccer who'll take bold decisions. So little progress seems to have been made.'

Camkin supported a proposal by Manchester United that the league accept £1m for live televised games but the clubs overwhelmingly voted against it with Robins commenting: 'If they felt live TV was dangerous, why not have it for one year and see?' City opposed the abolition of the signing-on bonus feeling that the new system, which involved a ten per cent levy on transfers, would be administratively difficult and drive up transfer fees. The proposal was carried 38-10 by the clubs, a result that infuriated Robins and Hill, who said: 'The effect will be that successful Coventry City players will be subsidising players not doing so well with other clubs.'

City's reserves made a midweek trip to Swindon with a very young side including three 17-year-olds in attack. One of them, Willie Carr put City ahead but an experienced Swindon side ran out 4-1 winners.

The Sky Blues now had six league games remaining and the first of those saw the team travel to Crystal Palace for their first ever Saturday night fixture, the delayed kick-off to avoid a clash with the Grand National. The race generated so much interest that some clubs had seen a drop in attendances as people decided to stay at home and watch live TV coverage. City fans had no such plans and an estimated 8,000 planned to invade south London to watch their heroes.

The Sky Blue Special train, struggling to sell a few hundred seats in November, sold out its 730 seats in a few hours and Red House Coaches used 40 coaches to take fans to the capital. The new electrified train service from Coventry to Euston had recently been opened and a return ticket cost 29 shillings (£1.45) just four shillings (20p) more than the special train but that took you all the way to Norwood Junction, close to Selhurst Park.

Manager Hill hoped for a better performance following the lax display against Derby and made one change with Barry Lowes coming in for Ronnie Farmer. There was a surprise awaiting the Sky Blues when they arrived at Selhurst Park – the referee wouldn't let them play in their sky blue shirts, or their red change kit because of a clash with Palace's light blue shirts with thin claret stripes. Palace's kit-man dug out a set of Palace's orange change shirts and the referee allowed them to wear sky blue shorts and socks. A very bizarre outfit.

Palace, whose promotion challenge had looked so strong at one stage, had suffered two home defeats over Easter and were ten points behind the leaders. Manager Bert Head included Johnny Byrne, who had returned to his first club after five years at West Ham. The former England international, looking a little overweight, had struggled since dropping a division and had a running battle with Brian Lewis all night in a game which was competitive throughout and brutal at times. The referee let too many bad tackles go unpunished and made some inexplicable decisions. Bobby Gould was clean through with only the keeper to beat when he was yanked back by the arm by Alan Stephenson, then the referee fortunately missed Bill Glazier take a retaliatory swing at a Palace player.

Bobby Woodruff missed the best chance of an even and goalless first half but the game took off after Steve Kember gave the home side the lead in 53 minutes. The goal jolted the Sky Blues into action and for the next 25 minutes they bombarded the Palace goal with a mixture of fire and skill expected from a side on their way to Division One. The Londoners' goal led a charmed life and it looked as though the unbeaten run might be ending when Bobby Gould, who else, popped up to equalise in the 69th minute. Ernie Machin swung over a corner, Rees lobbed it back into the ruck and Gould forced it in with a header, Jackson punching the ball up into the roof of the net in an unavailing attempt to save. It took Bobby's tally for the season to 24 goals.

In his programme notes the following Saturday, Jimmy Hill wrote about the 'hysterical encouragement' given to the team by the supporters that night: 'I'm not sure how it started ... (but) it was as if the team was re-born. They had been playing what I might call our typical promotion game; rather tense, rather nervous, and thinking about not losing rather than thinking of winning. All of a sudden this was changed and we saw a brand of determined and fluent football that would do credit to any team in the land. Those of you who took part in that happening can take a bow. The point we won belonged as much to you as it belonged to the team. If ever "we will never lose" meant something on and off the field, it did last Saturday night.'

Earlier that day Wolves had beaten Rotherham 2-0 with goals from Dougan and Ernie Hunt and now led City, unbeaten in 20 games, by one point. Closest rivals Blackburn, Ipswich and Huddersfield all had good home wins and the gap was now four points, but Wolves and City had a game in hand with their pursuers. Derek Henderson was not dismayed with the dropped point: 'I would rate this away draw a successful operation, for it makes Blackburn's "salvage job" that bit more desperate.' The 'A' team drew 1-1 with Stratford at Ryton whilst the 'B' team had a weekend off.

Ronnie Rees and Dave Clements disappeared during the week to play for their respective countries in home internationals. Windsor Park was the venue for the Ireland v Wales game which ended in a 0-0 draw. There was no George Best in the Irish team so Clements won his fifth senior cap on the left-wing, a position he had vacated some months earlier for the Sky Blues, and he was alongside Wolves's Derek Dougan. Rees was winning his 18th cap on the right-wing in a game that was a 'dead rubber' in light of the two teams' earlier results against England and Scotland.

That same week the club's board of directors met to discuss the plans for the forthcoming Wolves game and announced that it would not be an all-ticket affair. The decision was made for fear if there was bad weather on the day many people, knowing their entry was assured, would leave it late to arrive and that crowd congestion would follow. Secretary Alan Leather revealed that there was going to be lots of pre-match entertainment including a display of motorcycling by the Royal Corps of Signals and urged fans to make plans to get to the ground early. The indications from Wolverhampton were that around 10,000 Wolves fans intended to make the trip.

After the meeting the directors watched the reserve team extend their unbeaten home record with a 2-1 victory over Leicester City in the penultimate home game of the season. John Key, recovered from his injury at Bury in February, scored a late winner after Dudley Roberts had scored the first goal.

Derek Henderson used his Sport Opinion column in the *Coventry Telegraph* that week to defend the Sky Blues against the criticism that they were too physical, a charge made by several opposing managers, notably Charlton's Stokoe and Carlisle's Ashman. '"Why is it," a colleague of mine asked with a distinct suggestion of disapproval, "that Coventry City always seem to be involved in physical battles these days?"

'A good question,' Henderson went on, 'And one which I feel should be answered before some of the credit for going 20 matches without defeat is lost in a welter of press notices which hint that the Sky Blues are really the villains of the piece.'

Henderson believed that part of the reason was jealousy amongst other clubs. Jealousy of the club's go-ahead ideas, high profile in the media and success. Henderson remarked: 'Many times in board rooms up and down the land must the words "I'd love to see the Sky Blue bubble burst' have been uttered. With feeling.' He believed the only way City could be taken down a peg was on the field and as teams up their game in an effort to bring the Sky Blues down 'so George Curtis and his men rise to meet the challenge. Often it means survival of the fittest. And as there are none fitter than this collection of Highfield Road professionals, you get the inevitable clash in which physical strength is invariably the dominating feature. Make no bones about it. When the tough stuff starts, City can mix it with the best of them'.

Henderson presented the statistics to prove they were not a dirty side. 'No sky blue man has been sent off during the last two seasons at senior level, and there have been only seven bookings since last August in 41 cup and league games.'

Henderson also revealed that week that Ian Gibson and Jimmy Hill had buried the hatchet. In an exclusive interview Gibson told Henderson: 'The whole episode is behind me now. As far as I am concerned, it is nothing but history.' He went on to describe how different things were at Coventry to Middlesbrough. 'I was skipper in my last season there, running everywhere for the ball, and this suited me. But it was different at Coventry with tactics and discipline being important.'

When Henderson relayed the news that Gibson was much happier and in his own words 'a more mature player' to Hill, the manager remarked: 'I am perfectly happy for Ian to stay – I have said this all along. He is doing a lot of unselfish work now, which is what I wanted.'

With five games left now the Sky Blues needed five points to be absolutely certain of promotion. On a warm sunny Saturday Huddersfield arrived to face Jimmy Hill's second-placed side. The Yorkshiremen were still on the fringe of the promotion race but knew that defeat at Highfield Road would virtually end their hopes.

John Key had come through the midweek reserve game against Leicester without a reaction and was recalled on the right-wing in place of Barry Lowes. Rees and Clements had arrived back from the international in Belfast unscathed. A good crowd of 29,709 was present as were the BBC *Match of the Day* cameras for only the second time.

The Sky Blues were tense from the start and the visitors played the better football for most of the first half with Nicholson and Dobson bossing midfield. Gibson, as ever, was at the heart of most City moves but his good work was wasted by lacklustre performances by Gould and Machin, whilst Rees on the left-wing was strangely anonymous.

Huddersfield had a good chance from a Hill free kick and Bruck and Machin had to move sharply to dispossess Mike

Hellawell, then Nicholson blasted over from a good position. City's only chance in the first half came when Rees hit a wicked shot which beat goalkeeper Oldfield but bounced off an upright.

After the break City looked a bit more composed and their best move of the game saw Gibson pick up the ball in his own half and then get on the end of a flowing move only to be dispossessed for a corner. After 63 minutes City finally broke the deadlock from a Machin corner. Curtis headed it goalwards and Oldfield failed to hold the ball and quick as a flash Gould was on hand to head home for his 25th goal of the season past Huddersfield's statuesque Chris Cattlin guarding the post. Suddenly, with the pressure off, City started to dominate play and Gould should have made it 2-0 soon afterwards. Huddersfield rarely threatened again and the game ended 1-0.

Wolves won 2-1 at Preston to maintain first place with Ernie Hunt netting both goals but third-placed Blackburn crashed 4-0 at Plymouth. This important result meant that City, seven points clear of Blackburn and Ipswich with only four games remaining, were, barring a miracle, promoted with Wolves. The 'A' team had no game but the 'B' team lost 2-1 to Shrewsbury's 'A' team.

In the *Pink* it was reported that the club were running a 720-seat Sky Blue Special train to Cardiff the following Saturday and were expecting it to sell out quickly on the Monday when tickets went on sale.

On the following Tuesday night, third-placed Ipswich's promotion hopes were ended. Over 28,000 packed into Portman Road to see the Tractor Boys beaten by their local rivals Norwich. A Bill Baxter own goal and a second from Laurie Sheffield gave the Canaries East Anglian bragging rights and virtually ensured their safety from relegation. Now only Blackburn and Carlisle could overtake City but with the Sky Blues having a vastly superior goal average a point at Cardiff would as good as secure promotion.

The reserve team made a long journey to Plymouth for a Football Combination game in midweek and faced former Sky Blue John Sillett, playing at centre forward.

Brian Hill's season went from bad to worse when he headed into his own net and was later taken off with an eye injury. Tudor equalised and Pat Morrissey scored from the penalty spot but Argyle, fighting against relegation, ran out 4-2 victors.

On the Saturday over 5,000 Coventry fans made the journey to Ninian Park to face relegation-threatened Cardiff. Dietmar Bruck remembers Jimmy Hill's pep talk in the dressing room before the game: 'He didn't talk about Cardiff. He said to us "we're still undefeated and do you realise that any result but a defeat and you'll be promoted to the First Division today? Do you realise what that means, what it means not just to the football club and the fans but to yourselves, the players? What your next step is, what your value is?" By this time we were ready to tear the door down to get on the pitch. It was unbelievably motivating and we went out and ripped Cardiff apart – we should have been three up after 20 minutes.'

As Bruck says, City, in their all-red change strip, were well on top for the opening period but could not turn their domination into goals. Cardiff goalkeeper Bobby Wilson had to palm away Bobby Gould's header, Rees had a goal ruled out for a borderline offside decision and Key looked certain to score before the ball was cleared from his toe. City finally scored on the half-hour when an impressive run and cross by Brian Lewis left Key with a tap-in.

Cardiff looked dead and buried and when Coldrick blatantly fouled Rees in the box it looked a certain penalty but to the Sky Blues' astonishment the referee waved play on. City had failed to kill the home side off and Cardiff, their status in jeopardy, and jolted by stinging half-time words from that splendid wing-half of former years, Jimmy Scoular, fought back. On the hour they equalised when Ronnie Brown's shot beat Glazier and went in off the post. This brought the home crowd to life and the team responded. With 18 minutes left Cardiff were awarded a penalty after Mick Kearns brought down Ronnie Bird. Teenager John Toshack stepped up and, with the Coventry fans booing and yelling, the youngster blasted the ball a foot wide. Toshack however was not done and in the final minute Glazier had to make a superb save to keep out a goal-bound header.

Keith White remembers his trip to Ninian Park that day: 'Somehow my dad had managed to get us half way up a large terrace on the halfway line surrounded by Welshmen with the City support far away behind the goal. My abiding memory is John Toshack sending Glazier the wrong way with a penalty only for the ball to go wide. The whole atmosphere was strange at the end of the game. I, along with many City supporters, thought we were promoted. In fact, I'm sure I heard the announcer say over the Tannoy "We congratulate Coventry City on their promotion to the First Division." We didn't have long to wait for it to be official.'

The results elsewhere meant that City were still not quite mathematically promoted. Blackburn and Carlisle, the only sides who could have overhauled them, both won but Carlisle could no longer catch them. It now meant that City had to lose their final three games and Rovers win their last three and score around 14 goals in the process. In the dressing room chairman Derrick Robins produced the champagne and the City players had a muted celebration. As George Curtis sat drinking a glass of bubbly he told Derek Henderson: 'As far as we are concerned we haven't got promotion yet,' and Hill added: 'It's not absolutely certain yet. You can work out the goal average for yourself.' Robins was not wavering however and had gone ahead and booked the plane tickets for the team's trip to the West Indies which he had promised at the start of the season if they won promotion.

Wolves beat Bury 4-1 to clinch promotion with two goals from Dougan and were now two points ahead of the Sky Blues with a superior goal average – the title seemed to be theirs. A week hence Wolves were the visitors to Highfield Road for what Jimmy Hill was describing as 'The Midlands Match of the Century'. Meanwhile, the 'A' team lost 2-1 at home to Tamworth.

One man not so happy in the dressing room in Cardiff was Bobby Gould. He had fallen on his left hand during the second half and was in a lot of pain. He recalled: 'I've got a picture taken in the dressing room at Ninian Park afterwards and JH is pictured pouring champagne with his pipe lit and I can see from the way I am holding a cup in my left hand and protecting my right that I wasn't very happy.'

He got home safely but was in so much pain the following morning that he drove himself to Coventry and North Warwickshire Hospital for an x-ray which revealed that he had broken the scaphoid (a small bone in the wrist) and would be in plaster for six weeks. Bobby remembers hearing the news: 'I was gutted because I knew I would miss the final four games of the season but more especially the Wolves game that we were all pumped up for. I had broken the same bone two years earlier and there must have been some weakness there.' The club however made light of the injury with Derek Henderson reporting that 'he will play against Wolves with the hand strapped'. In reality, the club knew he was out for the rest of the season.

On the day of the Cardiff game the club were hosts to an international game, albeit of the schoolboy variety. England Under-18 schoolboys faced Wales in front of 8,465 and won 3-0 with goals from Lappage (2) and Partridge. One England player, Alan Gowling of Stockport Grammar School, went on to enjoy a successful professional career with Manchester United and Newcastle, winning England Under-23 and Amateur caps.

On the Tuesday evening the reserves travelled to Reading and recorded their second away win of the season. John Docker scored the only goal two minutes from time but the match report in the *Coventry Telegraph* picked out Willie Carr as 'easily the outstanding player on the field.'

The Sky Blues felt sure they would have to wait at least a week for a second chance to ensure their prize. For Blackburn had a Tuesday home game against Bolton and would surely keep up the pressure by winning it. But no! With no Coventry official at Ewood Park, Rovers could only draw 0-0. And the message was soon over the wires – Coventry ARE up. At Robins's house in Kenilworth Road, Leamington the directors, manager and some of the players drank champagne. All over Coventry, in pubs and clubs, City supporters raised their glasses to toast the Sky Blues as the news came through. According to the *Coventry Telegraph*, in the Town Wall Tavern, customers were drinking champagne out of half-pint glasses and shouting 'Now we're after the championship'.

Mick Williams, who was 11 at the time, remembers waking up the next morning. 'My Dad had gone to work and left me a note next to my bed that simply said 'Blackburn 0 Bolton 0. It's First division football for Coventry next season.'

The following morning Hill arrived at a Highfield Road besieged with calls, telegrams and messages of congratulations from all quarters. He told Derek Henderson: 'It's a wonderful feeling. If anyone sees me galloping around Broadgate on a horse – the way I feel at the moment – I hope I don't get a summons.'

Derrick Robins paid tribute to Hill and the players: 'It is a wonderful and a very just reward for the hard work put in by the directors, by Jimmy, and above all else, by the players. There is no doubt there has never been a more dedicated, more disciplined team in the history of the club.'

A 20-year-old Bobby Gould suddenly had a dilemma. Fifty years on he tells the story: 'My girlfriend Margery and I were planning to get married in early June and then the club told us we had a trip to the West Indies because we had won promotion. I told Margery we'd have to bring the wedding forward, so we brought the wedding forward to 21 May and I flew off with the team ten days later.'

At Ryton, it was back to training for Saturday's game against Wolves. Derek Henderson reported that the Sky Blues expected to be at full strength. Ronnie Rees, who had left the Cardiff match ten minutes from the end with a knee injury, was back in training and expected to play, similarly Ernie Machin, who was being treated for a shoulder strain, would be fit. Gould, Henderson reported, 'will play against Wolves with the hand strapped'.

To commemorate promotion a civic reception was being planned for Tuesday, 16 May. The team would be making a tour of the city in an open coach from Highfield Road to the Hotel Leofric where the banquet, hosted by the Lord Mayor, Alderman E M Rogers, would be held. The Mayor had apparently reckoned on promotion for some time and plans were already well advanced. It was now, according to a Corporation spokesman, 'just a case of putting them into effect'.

Within days of both the Sky Blues and Wolves clinching promotion the fixture planners gave us the perfect match. In his book *The Sky Blues*, Derek Henderson wrote: 'Coventry's promotion came with the timing of an impresario ... the situation was theatrical. It cried out for a record crowd. And it got it.' Club secretary Alan Leather was anticipating a massive crowd. He drafted in crowd-packers, men inside the ground ensuring fans didn't block gangways and moved to the centre of the terraces to allow as many people as possible to get into the stadium.

He also appealed to fans to get there early: 'So we can get them all in comfortably. It would be nice if we could get about 46,000 in by three o'clock (15 minutes before kick-off) in an orderly manner.' Leather had experience with large crowds – he had been assistant secretary at Tottenham during their glory years at the start of the decade and was used to packing large crowds into White Hart Lane on their famous European nights.

The national newspapers billed it as 'a First Division match in all but name'. This was sufficient to egg on any wavering supporters and on the afternoon of 29 April all roads led to Highfield Road. Derek Henderson was making predictions as usual: 'I suppose the safest forecast of this meeting of the giants is a draw. But, because City won't take lightly to Wolves stealing a march on them on what should be their penultimate Second Division appearance at Highfield Road, I'm taking the Sky Blues for an odd-goal win. And that WILL make the last two matches intriguing.'

The Chaston family would normally drive to City home games from their home in Keats Road, near Hipswell Highway, but that day the family decided to leave the car behind and walk to the game. Brian Chaston recalls: 'I didn't understand why we couldn't drive to the game but as we got to Swan Lane I understood. The whole area was log-jammed with traffic and there were long queues at all the turnstiles.'

Another City fan there was nine-year-old Kevin Shannon, with his dad. He remembers the day well: 'On the day of the game my dad had to work a morning shift at the GEC plant at Stoke. That day the *Coventry Telegraph* was giving away, free in the paper, a Sky Blues rosette. So as my dad set off for work I went with him on the 6.30am bus, getting off at the newsagents at the Craven Arms in Binley while he carried on to work. I got the paper and the rosette, a garish sky blue and black creation made from cardboard. We were easily pleased in those days! My dad made it back from work then off on the bus again we went, a walk through Gosford Green park, up King Richard Street, round the back of the ground and onto the Covered End again through the Thackhall Street turnstiles. We only just made it before they closed the gates.'

On a bright spring day thousands of supporters were turned away as the Highfield Road turnstiles were closed 15 minutes before the kick-off on advice from the police. Hundreds of fans gained admittance illegally by climbing over walls or crawling under gates and the club felt that around 53,000 actually saw the game.

Inside, the terraces at both ends were full to overflowing and many complained of being unable to see the match. Many youngsters were plucked out of the seething mass and allowed to sit on the grass and the running track and by kick-off time the youngsters were four or five deep around most of the perimeter, many just a yard away from the touchlines. There were dozens of fans perched perilously on the base of the floodlight pylons 'like decorations on a Christmas tree' and at one stage there were more than 50 spectators sitting on the roof of the Covered End. Despite loudspeaker warnings that the roof of the tea-bars were unsafe dozens of spectators clambered on to them and when the roof collapsed on one of the bars at the Covered End four people fell through but no one was seriously injured.

Despite the importance of the game and the hullabaloo surrounding it, City kept to their match-day routine. They reported for duty at Highfield Road at 11am and had a wander on to the pitch before the coach took them to the Hotel Leofric in Broadgate where they enjoyed a light lunch before making their way to the ground before the kick-off. The coach driver Hughie Spencer edged his vehicle through the busy streets and the massive crowds around the ground before parking behind the Main Stand.

Ronnie Farmer wasn't in the team that day but was named as the substitute. He remembers his feelings well: 'I was sick not to play against Wolves. I knew I was a better player than Brian Lewis and should have been starting the game.'

Dietmar Bruck remembers feeling the nerves before the game: 'I was OK until I saw the crowds outside the ground – I'd never seen the streets so packed and everyone was in good spirits. The nerves cut in then and for the first 20 minutes or so I felt numb and nothing seemed to go right.'

With Gould ruled out with his broken thumb John Tudor was in the team for the first time since early February. He was a more than adequate replacement for Gould, having scored seven goals in 13 first team appearances and 13 goals for the reserves. Gould was in his club suit in the stand and described his feelings in his book, *24 Carat Gould*: 'My emotions were all over the place. I was gutted not to be out there and the lads knew it.'

City's unbeaten run now stretched back 22 games, a club record, whilst Wolves had gone 14 games without defeat. As far as the Second Division title was concerned, Wolves were in the driving seat, with a two-point advantage and slightly better goal average. Ronnie Allen's team was a mixture of youth and experience with several players with First Division know-how including centre-forward Derek Dougan, known as 'the Doog', speedy wingers Terry Wharton and David Wagstaffe as well as England internationals Mike Bailey and Bobby Thomson. Injuries to defenders Gerry Taylor and Leamington-born David Woodfield meant that Allen had to switch captain and driving force Bailey to right-back and bring in the precocious youngster Peter Knowles in midfield. Knowles had scored 19 goals the previous season but had found goals harder to come by this campaign.

Henry Blofeld, writing in the *Sunday Express*, was awe-struck by the scenes: 'Fans sporting light blue sat on the grass within two yards of the touchline, with City at All Stations Go. It was their finest hour. Wolves must have felt like the early Christians waiting for the lions.'

In his book *Miracle in Sky Blue,* Marshall Stewart described the atmosphere: 'When the teams came out it was to the biggest roar ever heard at Highfield Road. They saw a league clash that made the most nail-biting cup-tie seem a formality. It was tough, tense and a convincing endorsement of the ability of both sides to be in the First Division.'

The much-vaunted clash between George Curtis and Derek Dougan didn't take long to come to the boil. Curtis got the better of the first jostling duel and the next time the two clashed Curtis beat the Doog comfortably in a tight space only to be fouled by the centre-forward as he came away with the ball. The referee took Dougan's name after only nine minutes' play.

There were chances at both ends in an even first half with City's best chance falling to Tudor who shot into the side netting five minutes before half-time.

A minute later City were punished when George Curtis mis-hit a clearance to Dougan who sent Peter Knowles away and the England Under-23 international beat Bill Glazier with a cross shot at the Spion Kop end. Sky Blue hearts in the stands and terraces sagged a little.

The Sky Blues didn't become discouraged and the midfield prompting of Ian Gibson and Brian Lewis slowly began to pay dividends as did the fighting spirit that the team had served up when a goal down so often during the season.

The turning point came on the hour, when Rees sped past Bailey and centred to Gibson. He touched the ball on to Machin who drove in the equaliser despite a lunging challenge from Ernie Hunt. Henry Blofeld described the scenes: 'A triumphant yell split the heavens, and the crowd erupted on to the field.'

Marshall Stewart described the aftermath: 'The pitch became a sea of small boys and older ones who should have known better.' Five minutes later, in Blofeld's words: 'Ian Gibson, the Coventry brainbox spun "on a sixpence"', receiving a pass from Tudor, he flicked the ball over a defender's head and ran on to lob over a bemused Phil Parkes in the Wolves goal.

Stewart again: 'This time the pitch and the players were engulfed by an even greater tide of emotion. It took some time, and many policemen to clear the fans back to the side-lines, and the referee Norman Callender left the field to issue a warning that if it happened again the game would be abandoned.'

Blofeld again: 'When order was somehow restored Coventry toyed with the mighty Wolves. And wasted chances as if they were playing beach football.' There was still some life left in Wolves however and first Knowles hit a post and then Kearns had to head off the line with Glazier beaten.

Four minutes from time the drama heightened to an unforgettable level. Blofeld describes the finale: 'A peerless Gibson pass found Ronnie Rees on the left. He went like a guided missile, unleashed a great drive which sent the crowd into hysterics.' This time however none of the massed youngsters surrounding the pitch encroached – a remarkable feat of self-discipline and restraint.

Kevin Shannon disagrees with that view: 'Legend has it that as City scored their third goal that day no one ran onto the pitch in celebration. However, one young lad did run onto the pitch from the Sky Blue Stand side but quickly retreated to his place back on the touchline when he realised he was on his own. We saw him clearly from our position in front of the floodlight pylon on the terracing.'

When the final whistle blew the crowd did spill on to the pitch and into the area in front of the Main Stand. Jimmy Hill led the players and the crowd in signing the Sky Blue Song amidst scenes, which eclipsed even those which followed the famous Torquay and Sunderland games in 1936 and 1963 respectively.

Back in the dressing room the champagne flowed again and the photographs taken on the day show Bobby Gould, in club suit with his left wrist in plaster, swilling champagne and singing the Sky Blue Song.

Dietmar Bruck remembers that Hill or Robins sent a crate of champagne into the Wolves dressing room: 'We were both promoted so we had something to celebrate. We now had the upper hand in the race for the title but they sent the champagne back unopened. We thought that was petty and unsporting.' Jimmy Hill told Henry Blofeld: 'At half-time I bet all the boys sixpence – I never bet higher – we would win. They owe me 5s 6d (27p).'

The attendance was a ground record 51,455, later adjusted for league records to 51,452, over 6,000 more than the previous record of 44,930 set in 1938 for a Second Division game with Aston Villa. The receipts topped £12,000, a record, with over £10,000 taken on the day, and more than 20,000 programmes were sold. Many fans were unhappy with complaints that they couldn't see in the massive crush – and some even claimed to have left the ground before the kick-off. There were heartbreaking stories too – of two boys who got into the ground at 1pm, eventually jumped over the perimeter wall because they were worried about the congestion on the terraces before being told by police – they claimed – that they had to go back on the terrace or leave the ground. They left without seeing the game.

On a happier note the police reported that only four fans were ejected from the ground, amazing when one considers the size of the crowd. One of those fans appeared at Coventry Magistrates Court on the following Monday morning. 17-year-old coal man, Dennis Squibb, was bound over in the sum of £10 to be of good behaviour for 12 months after pleading guilty to causing a breach of the peace. According to the *Coventry Telegraph*, Squibb was ejected from the ground three times for fighting before the start of the game. Each time he was escorted from the ground he returned to cause more trouble.

In his autobiography *The Jimmy Hill Story*, JH describes the post-match fun: 'Mum and Dad helped cut the extra sandwiches needed in the Sky Blue Club for what was going to be the busiest day and night. The historic party went on, as you may imagine, moving from the ground to the Hotel Leofric. I can just remember being taxied home with Mum and Dad around five o'clock in the morning. As I was about to climb into bed, my mother appeared at the bedroom door saying that Dad had a problem – he felt the room was going round!

'He wasn't the only one. The whole world was spinning for me as a result of that extraordinary climax to my years at Coventry. It was a sensational day, and one which was personally deeply satisfying, because of the joy it brought to the friendly people who had made me so very welcome, on the face of it reserved, but under the surface extremely warm-hearted. Somebody recalled that it was a night when everything but the air turned blue – bright sky blue.' It was later revealed that Jimmy's father was taken ill with high blood pressure and had to spend four days in bed recovering.

The teams on that memorable day were:-

Coventry City: Glazier: Kearns, Bruck, Lewis, Curtis, Clements, Key, Machin, Tudor, Gibson, Rees.

Wolves: Parkes: Bailey, Thomson, Knowles, Hawkins, Holsgrove, Wharton, Hunt, Dougan, Burnside, Wagstaffe.

Over at Ryton the 'A' team were defeating Dudley 3-0 with Willie Carr netting one of the goals.

Top of Division Two (30 April 1967)

		Pl	*W*	*D*	*L*	*F*	*A*	*Pts*
1	Wolves	40	24	8	8	83	43	56
2	SKY BLUES	40	22	12	6	70	41	56
3	Blackburn	41	19	12	10	55	45	50
4	Ipswich	41	17	15	9	69	53	49
5	Carlisle	40	22	5	13	64	52	49
6	Huddersfield	40	19	8	13	54	44	46

Chapter 11

May – Champions!

THE euphoric scenes at the Wolves game could never be topped but the issues raised by the massive crowd were being addressed within days. In Monday's edition of the *Coventry Telegraph*, Charles Harrold discussing the ground's capacity said: 'Before we talk in terms of a 55,000 capacity, we must make a close study of each sector in the ground, even to the extent of using electronic equipment on the turnstiles so that when the capacity for that sector is reached, the gate will be closed. We must no longer regard this (subject) in a hit-or-miss manner. We owe it to our supporters.' Derrick Robins promised to give 'serious consideration of a special section for boys'.

On the Tuesday evening the reserve team had their own climax of the season when the Football Combination champions, Tottenham Hotspur, came to Highfield Road for the final reserve game of the season. The young Sky Blues team were unbeaten at home and keen to extend that record against the best reserve team in the south of England. Bill Nicholson put out a mixture of experience and youth. Double winners (and internationals) Bill Brown, Ron Henry and the famous Welsh winger Cliff Jones provided the experience while Keith Weller, Derek Possee and

John Pratt represented the future. City too, had a similar age mixture, with Ronnie Farmer and Brian Hill playing alongside youngsters such as Carr, Morrissey, Clamp and Keley.

City certainly ruffled the cockerel's feathers with two goals in the first six minutes, Dudley Roberts and Peter Denton on target. Mick Coop, who had a fine game against the mercurial Jones, hooked a cross-shot into his own net as the game heated up. City bombarded the Spurs' goal and Denton missed a sitter from two yards before Lowes' shot bounced along the crossbar.

It was easy to forget that City's star man, Willie Carr, was only 17, and the red-haired prodigy almost scored a third goal. But two minutes from time Possee pounced for an equaliser and the game ended 2-2. A thrilling climax for the 6,809 crowd. The reserves had averaged 5,428 for their home games, believed to be the highest in the country.

That same night BBC1 featured the Wolves match and the unprecedented crowd scenes in their *Sportsview* programme at 9.55pm. In a busy week for the team they went to Stratford racecourse on Thursday evening to take part in a Donkey Derby. A team of six Sky Blues players faced a team of National Hunt jockeys including Terry Biddlecombe and Grand National winning jockey John Buckingham. No records exist of the result of the contest.

On the Thursday, JH scotched rumours that a 'big' signing was imminent. The name mentioned in some quarters was Swindon's goalscoring winger Don Rogers. Hill diplomatically refused to discuss other teams' players and told Derek Henderson that: 'I am trying to deal with a shoal of congratulatory letters on City's promotion, and at the same time deal with players' contracts for next season, the details of the close-season tour, season tickets and the building of the West Stand. I've done enough thinking about the playing side for the moment. People can rest assured as far as a new signing is concerned, if there is a need we shall do it.'

The first team had to travel to Ipswich for the penultimate game and it seemed as though every City fan wanted to travel to Suffolk. The 'Sky Blue Special' train sold out in less than two hours and for the first time a second train was commissioned. Both trains had the traditional Radio Sky Blue piped through the carriages and bingo sessions as well as a bar and catering facilities. In the event it was estimated that over 5,000 Sky Blue fans made the trip to East Anglia and as they ran out on to the Portman Road pitch City were given a tremendous ovation for their achievements from the home fans in a crowd of 18,916.

Coventry's unchanged side started the game where they had left off against Wolves, confident and well in charge. Machin had a fierce shot blocked in the early minutes and a Brian Lewis shot was pushed on to the post by the busy Hancock in the home goal. Tudor failed to connect from six yards out after Rees had put the ball into his path and it was a surprise that it took 27 minutes for City to score. Ian Gibson, at his impudent best, tore holes through the right flank of the Ipswich defence and found Ronnie Rees on the wing. The Welshman's perfect cross was nudged home at close range at the far post by a combination of Gibson and John Tudor with the goal officially credited to 'Gibbo'.

Within a minute Joe Broadfoot thought he had equalised only to be ruled offside but City continued to dominate and were unlucky not to go two up when Gibson's overhead kick grazed the post.

The pace slackened after half-time but City continued to miss chances and with ten minutes left they were punished for their profligacy with a scrappy equaliser. A hopeful lob into the area bounced awkwardly between Curtis and the Ipswich centre-forward Crawford and the lurking Colin Viljoen had an easy task to slide it past Glazier.

At Molineux Wolves beat Norwich 4-1 with goals from Dougan (2), Ernie Hunt and Wharton. The results left Wolves a point ahead of the Sky Blues with a better goal average going into the final game and Wolves now needed a draw at Crystal Palace to clinch the title. City's 'B' team lost 3-2 to Birmingham City with Carr and Glover on target but a young Bob Latchford netted twice to give Blues the points.

Coventry hosted Liverpool for a second testimonial game for George Curtis and Mick Kearns before Millwall came to Highfield Road for the final league game. Bill Shankly's side were at virtually full strength with five of the 1966 England World Cup winning squad plus three Scottish internationals. Before the kick-off Robins and Hill thrilled the crowd by making a unique lap of honour, Robins driving the kitted Curtis and Kearns in his Rolls Royce convertible with the number plate DHR2, and Hill in full hunting gear atop a horse.

The crowd, still euphoric after the Wolves game, could not get enough of it and Liverpool fans in the crowd could not believe their eyes. City deservedly won the game 2-1 and Ronnie Rees scored the goal of the night, capping a 50-yard run with a powerful shot from just outside the penalty box that left Tommy Lawrence in the Liverpool goal grasping at thin air. A crowd of over 25,000 raised £6,000 for George and Mick's testimonial fund.

Bill Shankly, in typical acerbic style, declined to make an assessment of the Sky Blues, commenting: 'I never discuss performances in friendlies.' Never one for over-statement, he did add: 'I was impressed with the whole atmosphere here.' One player not impressed that night was Scottish international forward Ian St John, later to be City's assistant manager briefly under Noel Cantwell. He later recalled: 'Within minutes of the kick-off George Curtis performed a crunching tackle on me. I woke up being carried off on a stretcher. When I tackled George about it later he said 'It's a man's game, Saint' and that from a man we were down trying to make a few bob for.'

Geoff Moore, a Bablake schoolboy at the time remembers the game well: 'My problem was that the date clashed with Bablake School speech day. This was a three-line whip. We had no choice but to be in our places in the cathedral, in full school uniform, at 6pm. At the best of times this was an occasion the boys detested. We thought that with punishment beatings now frowned on even in traditional grammar schools, this was the best way the teachers could get their own back on the boys. We had no doubt that some really didn't like schoolchildren at all. With the mighty Liverpool in town this 'celebration' had the potential to rank as the worst couple of hours of my life so far.

'The duration of the proceedings varied, but could be close to two hours. That day we were lucky and it finished at about 7.15. We departed in the requisite orderly fashion as far as the cathedral doors, but then the race was on. It seemed that most of the school was headed for Highfield Road. Most of us were changed by the time we got to the bottom of the cathedral steps. Blazers were thrown to waiting parents and scarves collected or retrieved from under pullovers. It was a close call, but almost all the fans were inside the ground when we arrived and there were no long queues. We made it in the nick of time!'

Off the field the celebrations continued with a Sky Blue Promotion Dance on the Wednesday evening and the planning of the demolition of the old Covered End which would commence immediately after the final game with Millwall. That summer the new West Stand would be built in readiness for the first season in the top flight.

On the Saturday it was back to business and the final day of a momentous season. Wolves travelled to Crystal Palace, needing just a point for the title, whilst City entertained Millwall, who after a bright spring had lost form. On the morning of the game Jimmy Hill was quoted as saying: 'The odds must be on Wolves to get a point' whilst Derek Henderson stuck by his earlier prediction that Wolves would land the top prize. Both were left to eat their words at the end of another afternoon of roller-coaster emotions as the Sky Blues won 3-1 and Wolves crashed 4-1 at Selhurst Park.

Not for the first or last time the later kick-off at Highfield Road added to the drama and intrigue of the day. Even before the teams came out at Highfield Road for the 3.15 kick-off Sky Blue Radio told the crowd that Wolves were already trailing 1-0 and George Curtis led the team out to a deafening chant of 'Champions, champions …' By half-time the team had done their stuff, leading a decidedly inferior Millwall 2-0 with goals from John Key and John Tudor.

Harold Mayes in the *Sunday Mirror* described the goals: 'Ernie Machin laid on a magnificent 30-yard pass for Key. The winger timed his run perfectly, took the ball on three strides and cracked a beautiful rising drive wide of Lawrie Leslie. Then Key and Rees made the running for Lewis to bulldoze his way down the right and cross for Tudor to score.'

It was all so easy for the Sky Blues against the south Londoners who launched only a handful of attacks in the whole game. According to Peter Wood in the *Sunday Express*: 'But for (Lawrie) Leslie, who made several world-class saves, Coventry would have scored at least six.'

Four minutes after half-time Millwall stunned the crowd by scoring but nine minutes later, according to Peter Wood, 'Machin presented the Coventry fanatical fans with the championship from Gibson's pass'.

As the second half wore on and Wolves' embarrassment in south London became apparent the mood of the City crowd turned from a nervous nail-biting one to a euphoric, celebratory one. With 15 minutes left to play a steward raced out of the tunnel to the edge of the pitch and raised four fingers on his up-stretched arm. A stoppage in the game gave the opportunity for the Tannoy announcement confirming that Wolves had lost 4-1 and sent the crowd wild with delight as they realised that the Sky Blues, 3-1 ahead and toying with Millwall, were Second Division champions.

In the final minutes the police allowed some youngsters to come on to the running track to avoid congestion in the Covered End and then, when the final whistle was blown, the pitch was invaded and the players engulfed by young fans, among them Gibson, who had to be 'rescued' by policeman and emerged with his shirt almost torn from his back. The fans gathered behind a police cordon around the tunnel area shouting for their heroes who duly emerged in their tracksuit tops in the directors' box. In a moment to savour Hill, for the second time in two weeks, led the crowd, and the players, in the most emotional rendition of the Sky Blue Song ever.

City were champions of Division Two, unbeaten in 25 games and would play in the top division for the first time. One of the most vociferous singers was Bobby Gould, again dressed in a lounge suit and crisp white shirt. Gould was one of three key players along with Brian Hill and Ronnie Farmer who missed the run-in. Hill was still returning from injury and Farmer was the unused substitute having lost his place to Brian Lewis.

Derek Henderson summed things up: 'We thought we had seen it all a fortnight before at the Wolves game. But here were the Sky Blues with that extraordinary flair for the dramatic – landing the Second Division championship at the last hurdle amid scenes of emotional hysteria. Who else but Coventry City could eke out of an already great season, an added final triumph?' Jimmy Hill phoned Crystal Palace and gave the entire team a drink on him as a way of saying thank you, and told *Sunday Express* reporter Peter Wood: 'Marvellous, marvellous. It was impossible yet we did it.'

Over 32,000 watched the Millwall game taking the season's total to over 593,000 – an average of 28,269 and breaking the club record set in 1950-51 season. Their gates were the highest in the Second Division and the 14th highest in the country.

As soon as the last of the spectators had left the ground the demolition squad (G W Hilditch, whose sign hung from the roof of the covered end that afternoon) moved in and with the aid of floodlights the Covered End was completely demolished that weekend. By Monday morning the whole site was flattened and the building of the new stand could commence. The Covered End had become the spiritual home for City's 'choir' during the 1960s. It is difficult to pinpoint when organised singing or chanting began at the ground but it became an important part of the Highfield Road scene during the 1962/63 FA Cup run just weeks after the club launched the Sky Blue Song in December 1962. A group, normally several hundred strong would chant the songs of the day and generally cheer the side on.

The club's celebrations continued for several weeks. The following Monday the first team travelled to Nuneaton Borough's Manor Park for a testimonial game. Despite pouring rain over 7,000 turned out to see the Second Division champions play the Southern League runners-up. John Tudor was in deadly scoring form and scored four goals in seven minutes, including a hat-trick timed at four minutes (easily the fastest in the club's history) as the Sky Blues won 7-3. The same evening the 'A' team brought their season to an end at Ryton when a young team lost 5-0 to Lower Gornal Athletic. The side finished in 15th place in the table in their first season in the West Midlands League, an admirable performance considering the quality of the teams in a strong league.

The following evening the club were the guests of honour at a civic reception at the Hotel Leofric in the city centre. The championship trophy was hastily despatched from Maine Road, Manchester along with the newly struck medals and the presentations were made by Football League president Len Shipman. Hill was named the Westclox 'Manager of Tomorrow' and received a cheque for £500 to add to the £10,000 bonus paid by the club for gaining promotion to the First Division, an incentive written into his very first Coventry contract, according to his autobiography. The team were toasted by a Sky Blue cocktail, a combination of white rum, Cointreau and blue curacao invented by Ray Rastall, the Leofric's bartender who had recently won the UK cocktail championship.

A week later all City's first-team players had signed new contracts, chairman Derrick Robins kept his promise made earlier in the season and at the end of May the first-team players and the management and coaching staff flew off to the West Indies for a deserved three-week break. It wasn't all pleasure though – the team had to play six friendly games during their trip which took in Trinidad, Barbados and Bermuda.

Back at Highfield Road it was another hectic close season. In addition to the West Stand being erected at a break-neck speed, there was work going on in the Main Stand to enlarge the press box and the directors' box, the pitch, which had been pretty bare down the centre for the last two months of the season, was re-seeded.

The club announced price increases for the new season with terrace prices increasing by 6d (2.5p). Standing on the Spion Kop would now cost 5 shillings (25p) and all other terraces 6 shillings (30p). The club were expecting to sell the vast majority of the 10,500 seats as season tickets although a number would have to be retained for visiting supporters. Prices for season tickets were increased and ranged from £5 for a Kop ticket to £15 for a central seat in the Main Stand. The new West Stand seats were all priced at the competitive price of £10.

City's new price structure was very similar to Chelsea's and slightly cheaper than Tottenham who priced in guineas. Jimmy Hill told Derek Henderson that the club had tried to get a price range for the man who wanted to take his family to games: 'We are very conscious that with a family, it entails a lot of money.

But when one considers the difference, it really isn't a lot of extra money for a season of First Division football.' Within less than a fortnight the club announced they had sold their entire reserved seating accommodation of 9,800 and taken over £100,000 as result. The new West Stand had sold out completely and wasn't even built!

Before Coventry City flew off to the West Indies rumours circulated that Jimmy Hill was going to quit football for a job in television, specifically to replace David Coleman who was leaving BBC's *Grandstand* programme. When asked about the rumours by Derek Henderson, Hill said: 'As far as I am concerned there is no substance to this, simply because I have not been approached.' In the modern game responses like that can barely be trusted but back in 1967 Hill's words would have put the fans' minds at rest and quashed any rumours. However, as the summer progressed there was, as the saying goes, 'no smoke without fire'.

With wives and girlfriends left at home the trip to the West Indies was a heady mixture of pleasure and work. The team played five games in 18 days, winning them all and making lots of friends along the way with their down to earth approach to the locals and high skills on the football pitch. The only black spot on the tour was when Ronnie Rees was sent off in the fourth match, in Barbados, for what the referee later described as 'violent conduct'.

Pat Saward's youth team also had an overseas trip. On 26th May they flew out to Holland to play in two top-ranking international youth tournaments. In the first, in Rotterdam, the young Sky Blues reached the final by virtue of victories over Antwerp and Sparta Rotterdam, and draws with Go Ahead and Aalborg (Denmark). The final was a disaster however and they lost 5-0 to local team Feyenoord.

The Hague hosted the ADO tournament a week later and City got their revenge on Feyenoord, defeating them 2-0 in the group stages. Another victory over Go Ahead and a 1-1 draw with

Vasas of Hungary saw the Sky Blues through to a final against Ajax. In front of 9,000 fans Saward's boys gave Ajax a footballing lesson, winning 3-0, with goals from John Docker, Tom Sinclair and Pat Morrissey.

The ground developments continued apace during the months of June and July and on 8 July Derek Henderson reported that work on the West Stand was a week ahead of schedule. He described the new stand thus: 'It rises, with its stark white concrete, over the terraces.' He went on to describe a raft of other developments at the stadium including a new ground-level bar on the corner of the main stand closest to the west end of the stadium, an extension to the Vice-Presidents club, a new 50-seat press box to handle the demands of the much bigger coverage the club would get in the First Division and an entrance block to the West Stand from Nicholls Street. With the ticket office working at full stretch to meet the massive demand the whole ground was buzzing that summer.

In a further development, the club's administrative director Charles Harrold revealed that 20,000 programmes had been sold at the Wolves game, a club record. He also announced that a new, better programme would be produced for the coming season. City's programme – which not so long ago had been languishing in the Fourth Division in terms of ratings – had jumped into tenth place in the *Soccer Star* Programme of the Year award for 1967. The new programme would go on to win that prestigious honour in 1968.

There was to be disappointment for a few players that summer as the club made some difficult decisions about contracts. Three professionals were released: Mick Cartwright, Dennis Oakes, and Howard Moore. John Docker was not retained and the club hoped for him to go on loan to Third Division Torquay United to gain some experience. Malcolm Knox, captain of the youth team, was released but travelled to Holland to play in the tournaments whilst Paul Bloodworth and Geoff Brassington were also released. There was also some good news with four 17-year-old apprentices given professional contracts – Willie Carr, Jeff Blockley, Don Peachey and Trevor Gould. All four had outstanding seasons, making massive strides in their career with Carr very close to a first-team place.

Chapter 12

The summer of '67

AS THE cheering died away the fans started thinking about the club's first season in the First Division, with a fixture list that sparkled with names like Manchester United, Tottenham, Arsenal and Liverpool. In his book *Miracle in Sky Blue*, Marshall Stewart summed things up: 'It is worth remembering the enormity of what the Sky Blue regime has achieved already. Up from the Third Division to First. The biggest crowds in the Second Division. An unbeaten run of 25 games (the best in the club's 48-year league history). A team spirit with an unquenchable fighting flair, typified by skipper George Curtis who played in every match in the promotion season, in line with his record of having missed only three games in eight years.'

Stewart then moved on to Hill and Robins: 'Hill, the magician in the dressing room and outside, has around him a dedicated off-field team just as determined to succeed as the Sky Blue line-up itself. In the boardroom, chairman Robins adds unlimited amounts of genuine enthusiasm to his professional expertise to make Coventry City what it really is: a highly successful well-run business, with one eye on its customers and the other on the future.'

On 20 June the club party arrived back from their three-week trip to the West Indies with praise ringing in their ears about how they had conducted themselves and on the favourable impression their high standard of football left in the Caribbean. In fact, while City were still away the club received notification from the FA of a tribute from the Trinidad FA, in which the Sky Blues were praised for their impact on the islands of Trinidad and Tobago. After the final game of the trip, an 8-0 victory over a Bermuda Police XI, the local press wrote: 'Goodbye Coventry City and come back again. You showed us professional football can be played in a sporting manner.'

The players disappeared with their long-suffering families for less salubrious holidays and Bobby Gould and his new wife Margery went off on their honeymoon.

Ideally, the story should have ended there, promotion achieved, a celebration trip to the West Indies, season tickets selling like hot cakes. It was sunshine all the way. However, behind the scenes there was a storm brewing.

Throughout the so-called Summer of Love, with the hippies wearing flowers in their hair and psychedelic music everywhere, the directors and Jimmy were discussing a new contract. He had been given a five-year deal in 1964 after winning promotion to Division Two and now both parties wanted to extend that.

According to his autobiography he never considered another job and was happy at Coventry: 'I feel I belonged at Coventry City much more than I did at Fulham and saw no reason why I should not continue managing them for many years to come'. He knew however that behind the hysteria of reaching the top flight there was realism to be faced. Some members of the team would not be good enough for Division One and the club were not in a position to buy success – in those days no club could – and that the current squad of players would need to be given time to adjust to the higher level of football.

Over his five and half years at the club he had seen glimpses of the fickleness of Coventry's fans, when Bly and Hudson were sold for example, and again in the autumn of 1966 when promotion looked a pipe-dream, and the adulation for him had turned to criticism of his methods. He knew that it wouldn't be easy in Division One but he believed, given time, he could turn the Sky Blues into a team capable of challenging the best. Hill wanted time and was prepared to give it but he was a realist and foresaw a situation where the club might struggle and him being made the scapegoat and losing his job.

The board offered him an attractive £7,500 a year with a five-year contract. The money was not that important to him – he had earned less than £35,000 in his five years at Coventry – but he was after the insurance of a ten-year contract. Derrick Robins and the board were not prepared to accede to his request – they had seen the problems that Chelsea and Hull City had had after agreeing ten-year deals with managers Ted Drake and Cliff Britton respectively. Both clubs had given long term deals to their managers at the time of heady success and within 18 months or so had wanted to dispose of their managers and had to honour their long contracts. Hill listened to this argument and was disappointed, he felt his relationship with City was far deeper than Drake or Britton's.

Strangely the board did not seek a compromise. In his book Hill says he expected Robins to say 'let's split the difference and make it seven and a half years' but he didn't and Hill wouldn't budge either. The discussions dragged on with the club's directors trying to persuade him to change his mind.

The news finally broke on Thursday 17 August, two days before the first game at Burnley and no mention was made of the contract discussions. The club's official statement read: 'In the summer Mr Jimmy Hill ... told the club he wished to retire from football management. The directors have made every possible effort in recent weeks to persuade him to change his mind and regret that they have not succeeded. The board appreciated the reason for Mr Hill's decision and, recognising his tremendous work for the club in the past six years, believes it would be wrong further to prolong its persuasion. Mr Hill will retain full responsibility as the club's general manager until the board are able to obtain a new manager of suitable calibre, but he will not stay with the club after the end of the present season. Mr Hill states categorically that he would not dream of joining any club other than Coventry, where he has obtained the complete support of players, staff, directors and fans.'

At Ryton, the players were called together after training and, according to Norman Pilgrim, Jimmy told them the news. The players were in shock but Derrick Robins stood up and told them: 'We're sad that Jimmy is leaving but life goes on and we are going to appoint a top manager.' Ernie Machin's Lancastrian voice piped up from the back: 'Will he be a knight?' The players were falling off their chairs laughing. England manager Alf Ramsey had been given a knighthood in the New Years' honours list. Ernie certainly lifted the sombre mood that morning.

The shock in the city was cataclysmic. Work at the city's factories ground to a halt as the news was debated from every angle. The fans had no inkling and were planning their route and booking their train and coach trips to Burnley. Jack Patience, the secretary of the City Supporters Club said: 'I have won my bet – I said this would happen. He has done a great job of course and whoever takes over from him will have one hell of a reputation to live up to. He's ambitious and I certainly don't blame him but it will shatter a lot of City fans.' Outside his home in Canon Hill Road there were children waving rattles and chanting: 'We want Jimmy' before a police car arrived to disperse them.

The resignation was national news and the media circus descended on Highfield Road with press conferences and television cameras. The general view was that he had been offered a lucrative job in television or journalism because he already wrote a weekly column in the *News of the World* and had been impressive when called upon to do television work. A gentleman who lived just outside the ground in King Richard Street was sought out by the *Daily Express* to pronounce that it was the biggest shock of his life.

Two days later around 7,000 Coventry fans travelled to Turf Moor and watched the Sky Blues lose their 25-match unbeaten run in a 2-1 defeat. The run was just five short of the then league record of 30 games, set by Burnley in 1921. With Ian Gibson injured, Jimmy Hill resisted the temptation of throwing Willie Carr in for his debut and Ron Farmer played in Gibson's place.

City's first goal in the top flight was a late own goal by Dave Merrington, scant reward for a good performance against one of the division's best home sides. Three days later even more fans travelled to the City Ground, Nottingham to see how the Sky Blues would fare against the previous season's league runners-up. After only four minutes captain George Curtis was carried off on a stretcher with a broken leg following a challenge with Frank Wignall. City's reshuffled side, with Tudor moving back to centre-half and Bobby Gould on as substitute, took the game to Forest. Gould twice put City ahead only for Forest to equalise and it needed an Ian Storey-Moore penalty to rescue a point for Forest after Ernie Machin had scored a third City goal. Derek Henderson went into hyperbolic overdrive in his match report: 'I have seen many performances from Coventry City to make the blood tingle in the nine years I have covered their games. But never have I seen them rise to the challenge of the hour and defy all the odds as they did at Nottingham last night.' Hill described it as: 'The finest team performance in five-and-a-half years.'

It was soon clear that Curtis's leg break was a serious one and he was not expected to return quickly and Derek Henderson wrote that the injury was a bigger blow to the club than Hill's resignation: 'Luck has finally caught up with the phenomenal man who only three times since September 1958 had not turned out for Coventry City in League matches.' Hill needed a replacement and quickly, but soon found good 'stoppers' were at a premium.

After 48 hours of frantic activity he paid Southampton £25,000 for Tony Knapp who went straight into the side for City's first home game in the top flight and the inaugural game for the new West Stand, against Sheffield United. Little did the 33,000 crowd realise that over the next nine months the Sky Blues and the Blades would be bitter rivals at the foot of the table with the Blades' ultimate relegation ensuring City stayed up. Twice the Blades led and twice the Sky Blues bounced back with John Key scoring the club's first home goal in the top flight, a powerful header at the Spion Kop end. Dietmar Bruck saved a point for the Sky Blues after a Glazier howler had enabled United go in front. Three days later Forest arrived at Highfield Road and demonstrated the size of the mountain City faced in the higher league, winning 3-1 against a side already hit by injuries to key men.

The first win came in early September when old rivals Southampton were beaten 2-1, a game which marked the full debut of Willie Carr. By the time Hill left the club City had won only once more, an emphatic 4-2 home win over West Brom, a side they had the Indian sign over in the early years of life in Division One.

The search for a fresh manager took two months and both Brian Clough and Malcolm Allison came close to being appointed before, on 12 October, former Manchester United captain, Noel Cantwell, was appointed to take over. Two days later Jimmy Hill formally handed over the managerial reins, whereupon Coventry promptly lost 3-2 to Spurs.

It was a tough first season in Division One and the Sky Blues were bottom of the league at the turn of the year. But with

Maurice Setters picking up Curtis's mantle, the team hit a rich vein of home form and a goal-less draw at Southampton on the final day kept them up by one point.

What became of the cast?

The Players

Bill Glazier (Goalkeeper)

Bill was a key player in the early seasons of struggle in the top flight, saving City from heavy defeats on a regular basis. In 1970, he made a further representative appearance as a substitute for the Football League against the Scottish League at Highfield Road. He was unfortunate to have been around at a time when there were so many top English goalkeepers.

He missed only a handful of games in five seasons and was City's first choice keeper until the end of 1973/74 season, making 402 appearances for the club before losing his place to Neil Ramsbottom. The following season he was granted a testimonial match and the England World Cup winning squad honoured him by appearing at Highfield Road. In 1975, he joined Brentford but injuries forced him to give up the game soon after. He later ran a hotel in Brighton and now lives in Spain.

Mick Kearns (Right-back)

He played regularly in the first half of the 1967/68 season but following Noel Cantwell's arrival his days were numbered and his final game was against Liverpool on Boxing Day 1967. He retired from football in 1968 at the early age of 30 and he went to work in the family's bingo hall in Nuneaton. Then in 1986 George Curtis and John Sillett invited him back to the club as reserve team coach.

He later became chief scout and youth development officer but left in 1992. Now retired, he spends his days playing golf and with his grandchildren. A five-handicap player at his best, he now plays off a slightly higher mark and regularly meets up with his former colleagues Curtis, Sillett and Mick Coop.

Dietmar Bruck (Left-back)

Dietmar settled well in the top-flight and was the first choice left-back until the arrival of Chris Cattlin. He made sporadic appearances until joining Charlton Athletic in 1970 and later played for Northampton and was manager of Weymouth and several non-league sides around the midlands. In total he made 217 appearances for the Sky Blues, scoring eight goals. Dietmar is a member of the Former Players Association committee and a regular hospitality host.

Ronnie Farmer (Attacking wing-half)

Ronnie made only four appearances in the First Division and was disappointed never to play at Highfield Road in a First Division game. He joined Notts County on a free transfer in October 1967 and Jimmy Hill ensured he was well rewarded for not having a testimonial. In total he made 315 appearances for the club and scored 53 goals. After retiring with Notts County in 1969 he joined the Highfield Road staff and coached City's youth team to the FA Youth Cup Final in 1970. He later worked at Massey Ferguson and is a regular at City's home games.

George Curtis (Centre-half and captain)

Many pundits doubted whether George would be able to cope with the refinements of First Division football. Alas, we shall never know because in City's second match in the top flight, against Nottingham Forest, he broke his leg. He recovered and returned after six months but was never quite the same player and he moved to Aston Villa in December 1969 for a £25,000 fee after 543 appearances for the club.

George returned to Highfield Road in the 1970s to work in the commercial department and remained at the club for over 20 years, becoming commercial manager and later managing director. When Don Mackay left the club in April 1986 George was asked to fill the breach and in tandem with John Sillett helped stave off relegation once again. The following season, with the duo still in charge, was perhaps the most successful in the club's history with the FA Cup lifted for the first time. In 1987 Curtis stepped back upstairs when Sillett was appointed team manager.

Dave Clements (Defensive wing-half/outside-left)

After promotion Dave barely missed a game during the first four seasons, playing in a variety of roles but more often than not as an orthodox left-winger where, with his strong defensive skills, he added strength to City's frequent backs-to-the-wall away performances. He was never renowned for his speed on the wing but his strong build made him difficult to get off the ball and his cultured left foot was capable of defence-splitting passes and wicked teasing crosses.

It was a major surprise for City fans when he left City to join Second Division Sheffield Wednesday in August 1971 after 257 first team appearances for the club. In 1973 Dave moved back to the top flight by joining Everton and became one of the best midfield players of the era before finishing his career in the USA with New York Cosmos and Colorado Caribous.

He settled in the USA and makes occasional visits to the club's Legends Days.

John Key (Outside-right)

In the First Division John was one of only two City players who had top-flight experience but he made only six starts. He did have the honour of scoring City's first Division One goal at Highfield Road when he netted with a header in the 2-2 draw with Sheffield United. His last game was in the 2-1 League Cup defeat to Arsenal. He was released in March 1968 and joined Orient on a free transfer but played only 12 games before retiring to become a London cab driver. Now retired he lives in Epsom, Surrey.

Ernie Machin (Inside-forward)

When skipper George Curtis broke his leg in the club's second game in Division One there was only one candidate for the captaincy and Ernie was proud to lead the team out. He missed only three games in those first two years of struggle and was a regular, when fit, right up to the time of his departure to Plymouth in 1972. A bad car accident put him out for three months in 1970 and his knee continued to trouble him into old age.

After Plymouth, he had two years at Brighton before being persuaded by Jimmy Hill, now chairman, to return to Coventry as youth team coach. It didn't work out however and he left football and worked for Car Bodies and Massey Ferguson. Ernie sadly passed away in 2012.

Bobby Gould (Centre-forward)

In Division One Bobby made a fairy tale start, coming off the bench to replace broken leg victim George Curtis at Forest and scoring twice in a battling 3-3 draw. His eight goals in 14 games, including the club's first hat-trick in the top flight against Burnley, had the big clubs sniffing. In January 1968 City accepted Arsenal's bid of £90,000 but he never really fitted in at Arsenal and became a football nomad playing for eight different clubs after leaving Coventry including two spells with

Wolves and being substitute in the 1975 FA Cup Final for West Ham.

He was a successful manager and had two spells in charge of the Sky Blues and managed Wimbledon to FA Cup victory over Liverpool in 1988. Many of City's successful 1987 squad were signed by Gould. He also had a spell as manager of Wales and is a broadcaster with Talksport Radio.

Ian Gibson (Inside-forward)

Injuries restricted him to 15 appearances in the 1967/68 season and a similar number the following season but he never looked out of place in Division One. He was virtually injury-free in 1969/70 and had a big influence on City's qualification for Europe. That summer he was sold to Cardiff for £35,000 where he teamed up with his former Bradford boss Jimmy Scoular. In total, he made 104 appearances for the club and scored 14 goals.

His league career ended with Bournemouth and he later played non-league football with Gateshead. He died in Redcar near Middlesbrough in 2016.

Ronnie Rees (Outside-right/left)

Rees was a success in the 1967/68 season and was a virtual ever present until March 1968 when, with Noel Cantwell having to raise funds for a transfer splurge and Willie Carr champing at the bit, Rees was deemed to be expendable and he moved to West Brom for £65,000. In six seasons, he made 262 appearances for City and scored 52 goals. He won 39 full Welsh caps, 21 whilst at Highfield Road, and seven under-23 caps.

He later played for Nottingham Forest and Swansea but City fans undoubtedly saw the best of Ronnie Rees. He settled in Swansea and worked at the Ford factory in the city but had to retire at the age of 51 after a stroke. He still lives in Swansea with June and has three sons and three grandsons.

Brian Hill (Defensive wing-half)
Brian was still afflicted by injuries after promotion and played less than 20 games in 1967/68 but scored a vital goal at Fulham after coming off the bench. The following season he played as a central defender alongside either Setters or Curtis and put in some remarkable marking jobs on players such as Denis Law and Jimmy Greaves.

Perhaps his finest display was at Goodison Park in 1970 when he blotted out Alan Ball, arguably the outstanding player in the country at the time, as City held the champions-elect to a 0-0 draw. He moved on to Torquay in 1971 after 284 appearances and eight goals for City. Brian passed away in Bedworth in 2016.

John Tudor (Centre-forward)
Like a number of his team-mates, John found life hard in Division One and the goals dried up but did show his versatility by filling in as a central defender, most notably at Nottingham's City Ground in August 1967 where he went into defence to cover for George Curtis who had broken his leg.

In November 1968, after his first team opportunities became limited by the arrival of Tony Hateley, John was sold to Second Division Sheffield United for £65,000. He made 77 League and Cup appearances for the Sky Blues, scoring 15 goals. At Bramall Lane, he was a consistent scorer but really made his name as a solid goalscorer after joining Newcastle United in 1971. He developed a prolific partnership with Malcolm Macdonald and scored 58 goals in 187 games.

He later played for Stoke, Ghent in Belgium and Gateshead. He lives in Minnesota in the USA where he coached for many years. He flies to the UK often and was at Wembley in 2017 to see the Sky Blues lift the Checkatrade Trophy.

Brian Lewis (Wing-half)

In the First Division he played his part in the club's first relegation battle, making 22 league appearances and scoring twice. His last game in a sky blue shirt was in the final game that season, at the Dell, when City gained a fighting 0-0 draw to stay up. One of Brian's oddest claims to fame was being laid out by Ian St John in City's 1-1 draw with Liverpool at Highfield Road on Boxing Day. St John was sent off.

He joined Luton Town in the summer of 1968 and playing as an out-and-out striker scored 23 goals in his first season. The following year he was on the move again, to Oxford, before a transfer to Colchester later in 1970. Two months after joining the Us he was in the team that pulled off one of the greatest FA Cup shocks of all-time when they defeated the mighty Leeds United 3-2 at Layer Road. In 1972 he returned to Portsmouth and played another 40 or so games before leaving league football in 1975 to join Hastings United. He made 368 league appearances, netting 81 goals. Sadly, he died of cancer in December 1998 aged 55.

Ray Pointer (Centre-forward)

Ray scored 13 goals in 32 games for City before joining Portsmouth in February 1967. Pompey converted him into a midfield player and he went on to play 165 games, scoring 31 goals in seven seasons at Fratton Park. At the age of 37 he played for non-league Waterlooville before hanging up his boots.

He took up coaching, first at Blackpool under his old Burnley boss Harry Potts, then back at Burnley and later at Bury under former Burnley legends Martin Dobson and Frank Casper. He later ran a shop in Blackpool and died in a nursing home in 2016.

Peter Thomas (Goalkeeper)

If you mention the name Peter Thomas in the pubs of the Irish town of Waterford few middle-aged males will not know who you are talking about. The Coventry-born goalkeeper played for the local team for almost 20 years and even won two full Irish caps. In Coventry, however, Peter is largely forgotten – he played just one competitive game for the Sky Blues against Cardiff in November 1966. A week later Bill Glazier was fit again and Peter's first team career was over. In January 1967, he returned to Waterford permanently. His team dominated Irish club football for the next decade winning six league titles in eight years and represented the country in the European Cup. He played against Manchester United the year after they won the European Cup, crack Hungarian side Ujpest Dosza and Glasgow Celtic.

By 1973 Peter had become a naturalised Irishman and was in the full international squad as number two to Alan Kelly of Preston. He won two caps – against Poland in Dublin alongside City's Jimmy Holmes and against Brazil in the Maracana Stadium. He faced big names Jairzinho and Edu and a brave Irish display kept the score to 2-1. After retiring from playing he worked in insurance and now enjoys his golf and fishing near his home in Tramore.

John Burckitt (Left-back)

John was released by the Sky Blues in June 1968 after 16 first-team games and joined Walsall on a free transfer. He never appeared for the Saddlers' first team but later played for Rugby Town and Nuneaton Borough. He played 36 games for Borough scoring two goals but was released in 1971. He died at the age of 52 in 1999.

John Mitten (Outside-left)

John left Coventry in early 1967 after 41 appearances and six goals to join Plymouth where he probably had the best spell of his career. He played almost 50 games for Argyle but couldn't stop them being relegated in 1968. He dropped down to Fourth Division Exeter for three seasons before moving into non-league football with Bath City and was later manager at Sidmouth Town and Tiverton Town. He lives in Bristol and attended the 40th anniversary reunion of the 1967 team. His nephew Paul was on the books of Coventry and Manchester United in the 1990s but failed to make the grade.

Mick Coop (Right-back)

Only Steve Ogrizovic and George Curtis have made more first team appearances for the Sky Blues than Mick Coop. He played 499 first team games and but for one crazy season in 1974/75 when he fell out with the management would have overhauled Curtis's record.

In the first season in Division One Mick made 17 appearances but became a regular at right-back in 1968/69 under manager Noel Cantwell. His best season was probably 1969/70 when his form was so good that he was tipped for England Under-23 honours. Cantwell would not support his selection and sadly he was never capped. He did remain one of the most consistent full-backs in the country for several seasons.

He said: 'Being a local lad I always felt I had to do more to keep my place than other players. First Noel Cantwell tried to replace me; he paid £100,000 for Wilf Smith who took over for a while but I came back and Wilf was switched to the left to accommodate me. Then later Gordon Milne dropped me in favour of Graham Oakey and I went on loan to York for a month. But each time I worked hard and regained my position.'

In 1977/78, arguably City's most successful season of the First Division era, Mick switched to centre-back, playing alongside big Jim Holton to great effect. Mick also became the team's regular penalty taker and scored 16 penalties, missing only twice. He was sold to Derby in 1981 but had a torrid time with the Rams. The quagmire of a pitch was against good football and as Derby slumped down the Division One table, Coop's form suffered.

Mick moved into the antique trade and played briefly for AP Leamington. In 1986 George Curtis and John Sillett wooed him back to City as youth team coach and his team won the FA Youth Cup in 1987. He always kept fit and that year injuries meant he had to turn out for City's reserves at the age of 39, 21 years after his debut. Mick is still a regular golfer and lives near Warwick.

Barry Lowes (Outside-right)

Barry was one of very few bad buys by Jimmy Hill. Barry didn't think he was given the time to show his ability. JH realised he had made a mistake quite quickly and Lowes joined Swindon in the summer of 1967. Disaster struck in his first game against Brighton when he suffered a serious knee injury after a nasty challenge from a young full-back called George Dalton, later to become the Sky Blues trainer. The injury ended his career and he returned to Barrow to work as an electrician on the submarines. He died in Cumbria in 2012, aged 73.

Pat Morrissey (Attacking wing-half)

In 1967/68, with City beset by injuries to key players, Pat got another opportunity and played ten games including three as a substitute as the Sky Blues struggled with life in the First Division. His final game in a City shirt was the ignominious 2-0 defeat at Tranmere in an FA Cup replay. He signed for Torquay United in the summer of 1968 and a year later moved on to Crewe and then Chester before a £7,000 fee took him to Watford in 1971 where he was a regular for three seasons as a more attacking midfielder, notching 29 goals in 117 appearances. Three years at Aldershot followed and then a succession of non-league clubs including Dartford, Hayes, Slough, Hendon, Dunstable and Buckingham Town. At the age of 41 in 1989 he was still player-manager of Chesham United. Pat died of cancer in 2005 at the young age of 56.

Dudley Roberts (Centre-forward/centre-half)

In 1967/68 Dudley made only one appearance at Hillsborough in Jimmy Hill's last game in charge, and failed to make an impact in a 4-0 defeat. 'There was so much competition for places at Coventry at that time. I was grateful for getting an opportunity to play a few games. At the end of the day though the management obviously didn't think I had what was needed in Division One.'

In March 1968 he joined Mansfield Town for £6,000 and for the next six years he was a prolific scorer for the Stags. He scored 73 goals in 231 appearances and was the Third Division's leading scorer in the 1970/71 season. In 1974 he joined Scunthorpe where he had two successful years adding 17 more goals to his overall tally before a serious knee injury ended his career.

In 1969 he had married Rose McNulty, the original Sky Blue Rose from the Jimmy Hill era. Rose had been the first recorded voice that kept City fans up to date with news on the telephone in the days before mobile phones and text services. Rose and Dudley live in Mansfield and regularly attend the club's Legends Days.

Benny Glover (Attacking wing-half)

Benny had his 30 minutes of fame against Cardiff in November 1966 and he almost scored after being put clean through with only the goalkeeper to beat. He was substitute on two further occasions but failed to get on the pitch and had to be content with regular reserve team football for the next 12 months. The competition for midfield places was tough at Highfield Road with Willie Carr and Pat Morrissey in direct competition and in February 1968 as Noel Cantwell thinned down a big playing staff Benny was released. He joined Southern League Weymouth making over 230 appearances for the Dorset side over four years and in 1972 joined Salisbury City.

Benny now lives just outside Tewkesbury and enjoys a game of golf. One of his three children, daughter Amanda, represented

Great Britain at the 1996 Olympics in Atlanta in the beach volleyball team.

The staff

Jimmy Hill (Manager)

After handing over the managerial reins to Noel Cantwell in October 1967, Jimmy joined London Weekend Television as head of sport. He was a natural on television and virtually invented the TV pundit role working alongside Brian Moore on *The Big Match*. In 1973 he switched channels and joined the BBC and became the presenter of *Match of the Day*. His authoritative voice, insightful comments and sometimes controversial views not to mention his football knowledge made him a national treasure although 'the chin', as he was known, was often caricatured.

In 1975 he returned to Coventry City as their first paid managing director but times had changed and the club had serious financial difficulties. Although he turned things around and ran the club on sensible financial lines not all of his ideas went down well with the supporters. In 1981, in an effort to combat hooliganism, he spearheaded the club's move to make Highfield Road all-seated and then watched as crowds plummeted with fans put off by the sterile feel of the stadium, higher prices and inconvenient ticket arrangements.

An investment in North American football was unsuccessful and the club's and his personal investment was lost. In 1983 he stepped down as chairman of the club but stayed involved in football with stints as chairman of Charlton Athletic and Fulham, helping both clubs through difficult times. In 2011, in what would be his last public appearance, he unveiled his own statue at the Ricoh Arena. Sadly, Alzheimer's Disease had taken hold and Jimmy spent his last days in a care home in Sussex where he passed away in 2015.

Alan Dicks (Assistant manager)
In October 1967, after it had become clear that the Coventry directors were after a big-name appointment to replace Jimmy Hill, Alan Dicks answered a call from Second Division Bristol City to become their manager. Alan served 13 years at Ashton Gate, taking the club to the First Division in 1976 and keeping them there for four seasons until they were relegated in 1980. He spent most of the 1980s coaching overseas with jobs in Greece, Cyprus and Qatar before taking the Fulham manager's post in 1990. Eighteen months later, with the club struggling in Division Three, he was sacked. His last roles in football were in the USA with Carolina Dynamo and Charleston Battery. He lives in Bristol and was at Wembley for the club's Checkatrade Trophy final.

Pat Saward (Head coach)
After the arrival of Noel Cantwell and the departure of Alan Dicks, Pat was promoted to assistant manager. He was a logical choice being a friend of Cantwell who knew intimately how the club operated. He continued to have a big influence over the club's youth policy and is credited with their success in reaching two Youth Cup finals (1968 and 1970) and the seemingly never-ending conveyor belt of talent that reached the first team in the 1970s.

In 1970 he left City to join Brighton as their manager and led them to promotion from Division Three in his second season. However, they were relegated the following season and Pat lost his job soon afterwards. Later he managed Al-Nasr in Qatar for a period before moving to Majorca where he ran a holiday business. Alzheimer's Disease struck him down and Pat died at Newmarket in 2002, aged 74.

Peter Hill (Trainer)

After leaving the club in 1967 he went to work at the Morris factory at Courthouse Green alongside former City team-mate Harry Barratt but continued to be a regular at Highfield Road games with his wife Barbara. In 1988 manager John Sillett asked him to return and become the club's kit man. He became a key member of the staff, especially on match-days, responsible for ensuring that everything went like clockwork behind the scenes.

Peter finally retired around 1996 but not before he had groomed Andy Harvey as his replacement. Andy describes Peter as 'very quick witted and at times he could appear to be cantankerous but underneath he was a loving man who loved watching and talking about football. He was totally dedicated to Coventry City'.

Norman Pilgrim (Physiotherapist)

After Peter Hill's departure Norman had a spell as the 'sponge-man' and was seen running on to the pitch, tending players' injuries. He had his work cut out in the early years with George Curtis's broken leg, Neil Martin's back and numerous injuries incurred by Ian Gibson. Norman stayed at the club until 1976 when he set up his own private practice in Coventry. He moved to Northern Ireland in 2012 and lives in Ballyholme, Bangor. In 2017, he said: 'Looking back, what a great privilege it was to be part of the support staff in such an exciting and historic time for the club.'

Appendices

1. 1966/67 results, scorers and line-ups
2. 1966/67 Second Division – final table
3. 1966/67 appearances and goalscorers
4. 1966/67 Miscellany
5. 1966/67 Other first-team games
6. 1966/67 reserve results and scorers
7. 1966/67 Football Combination – final table
8. 1966/67 reserve appearances and goalscorers
9. 1966/67 'A' team results and scorers
10. 1966/67 West Midlands League – final table
11. 1966/67 FA Youth Cup

APPENDIX 1

No	Date		Att	Pos	Pt	F-A	H-T	Scorers, Times, and Referees	1	2	3	4	5	6	7	8	9	10	11	12 sub used
1	H	HULL CITY			W	1-0	0-0	Bruck 48	Glazier	Kearns	Bruck	Hill	Curtis	Farmer	Key	Gibson	Gould	Pointer	Rees	
	20/8		*27,933*		2				*McKechnie*	*Davidson!*	*Butler D*	*Jarvis*	*Milner*	*Simpkin*	*Henderson*	*Wagstaff*	*Chilton*	*Houghton*	*Butler I*	
								Ref: F Cowen	In a blistering heat Bruck's 35-yard groundshot creeps past a surprised Hull new boy McKechnie. Newly promoted Tigers' potent strike-force is tamed but City have to defend well near the end. Davidson off for hitting Gould. Machin is injured but Ian Gibson is the new fans' hero.											
2	A	PLYMOUTH			L	2-4	2-2	Gould 24, Pointer 44	Glazier	Kearns	Bruck	Hill	Curtis	Farmer	Rees	Gibson	Gould	Pointer*	Clements	Mitten
	24/8		*16,061*		2			*Piper 5, Jones 9, Bickle 78, 88*	*Leiper*	*Rounsevell*	*Baird*	*Piper*	*Nelson*	*Newman*	*Jones*	*Neale*	*Bickle*	*Reynolds*	*Jennings*	
								Ref: P Rhodes	A bad night for the defence and Glazier especially. Bill is at fault for at least two goals and the other two are 30-yard shots that he fails to stop. After Leiper carries outside the area Gibson's free kick is volleyed in by Pointer. City fail to press home their superiority and Bickle pounces.											
3	A	PORTSMOUTH		7	W	2-0	1-0	Clements 25, Gould 46	Glazier	Kearns	Bruck	Hill	Curtis	Farmer	Rees	Gibson	Gould	Pointer	Clements	
	27/8		*16,297*	*15*	4				*Milkins*	*Pack*	*Tindall*	*Gordon*	*Haydock*	*Harris*	*Barton**	*McCann*	*Hiron*	*Lewis*	*Kellard*	*McClelland*
								Ref: H Davies	Pompey are reeling from a 4-5 defeat to Birmingham and are no match for a fresher Gibson-inspired City. Classy Gibbo makes both goals, Clements' header and Gould's vicious shot and Curtis muffs two chances for a rout. Glazier shows his class but Rees and Pointer are off form.											
4	H	PLYMOUTH		5	W	1-0	1-0	Pointer 37	Glazier	Kearns	Bruck	Hill	Curtis	Farmer	Rees	Gibson	Gould	Pointer	Clements	
	30/8		20,343	*7*	6				*Leiper*	*Rounsevell*	*Baird*	*Piper*	*Nelson*	*Newman*	*Jones*	*Neale*	*Bickle*	*Reynolds*	*Jennings*	
								Ref: D Wells	City are lucky to beat a polished Argyle side. Pointer volleys home on the horizontal as he falls but the expected goal rush doesn't come. Bill Glazier redeems himself with several great saves and with Ian Gibson marked by Piper only the effervesent Gould troubles Derek Ufton's side.											
5	H	BIRMINGHAM		5	D	1-1	0-0	Gould 58	Glazier	Kearns	Bruck	Hill	Curtis	Farmer	Rees	Gibson	Gould	Machin	Clements	
	3/9		36,400	*1*	7			*Vowden 73*	*Herriot*	*Martin*	*Green*	*Wylie**	*Foster*	*Beard*	*Hockey!*	*Thomson*	*Bridges*	*Vowden*	*Murray*	*Fenton*
								Ref: F Nicholson	Missed chances cost City a point but they end defensive Blues' 100% record. The persistent Gould is on fire with numerous goal attempts and scores a stunning goal. Cullis's men net with their only second half chance. Hockey is sent off for fouling Ron Farmer after an earlier booking.											
6	A	MILLWALL		5	L	0-1	0-0		Glazier	Kearns	Bruck	Hill	Curtis	Farmer	Rees	Gibson	Gould	Machin	Pointer	
	5/9		*15,766*	*10*	7			*Broadfoot 65*	*Leslie*	*Gilchrist*	*McCullough*	*Jones*	*Snowden*	*Wilson*	*Broadfoot*	*Dunphy*	*Julians*	*Neil*	*Rowan*	
								Ref: D Smith	Promoted Millwall with the support of a vociferous crowd have not lost at home in 49 matches. Their physical play hampers City's football but Lawrie Leslie is the hero saving from Gould and Pointer. Joe Broadfoot scores from 35-yards and Ron Farmer's similar shot goes past the post.											
7	A	NORWICH		7	D	1-1	0-0	Gould 63	Glazier	Kearns	Bruck	Hill	Curtis	Farmer	Rees	Gibson	Gould	Machin	Clements	
	10/9		*13,454*	*19*	8			*Curran 49*	*Keelan*	*Stringer*	*Black**	*Lucas*	*Sharpe*	*Mullett*	*Anderson*	*Bryceland*	*Bolland*	*Curran*	*Punton*	*Sutton*
								Ref: A Weller	Rees skins debutant Alan Black to cross for Gould's header and a deserved draw. It takes Curran's strong header from a long free kick to rouse a sluggish and defensive Sky Blues. Lack of goals is Hill's problem with Rees and Gibbo out of form again. 600 fans cheer the rare goal.											
8	H	BRISTOL CITY		5	W	1-0	0-0	Kearns 65p	Glazier	Kearns	Bruck	Hill	Curtis	Farmer*	Rees	Gibson	Gould	Pointer	Clements	Mitten
	17/9		21,140	*20*	10				*Gibson*	*Ford*	*Briggs*	*Parr*	*Connor*	*Low*	*Peters*	*Clark*	*Down*	*Sharpe*	*Hartley*	
								Ref: H Richards	Only five sides have scored less than City. With Farmer off with concussion after a clash with Clark, Kearns gets away with a poor spot-kick after Low's handball. Boring Bristol come for a point and their best chance is headed out by Bruck. Hill rejects job with newly-formed NASL.											
9	H	BURY		4	W	3-0	1-0	Gould 5, Clements 61, Gibson 76	Glazier	Kearns	Bruck	Hill	Curtis	Clements	Key	Tudor	Gould	Gibson	Rees	
	24/9		22,076	*12*	12				*Ramsbottom*	*Leech*	*Eastham*	*Turner*	*Colquhoun*	*Parry*	*Lowes*	*Maltby*	*Aimson*	*Owen*	*Claxton*	
								Ref: J Osbourne	The game is decided on the hour. The division's top scorer Owen's 'goal' is ruled out for hands. Bury are incensed but City net within seconds with Clements' thunderous shot. Gould heads home with power and Gibson's wicked shot comes down off the bar but looks over the line.											
10	A	PRESTON		8	L	2-3	1-2	Tudor 40, Curtis 54	Glazier	Kearns	Bruck	Hill	Curtis	Clements	Key	Tudor	Gould	Gibson	Rees	
	1/10		*13,681*	*11*	12			*Dawson 2p, Hannigan 27, Wilson 59*	*Kelly*	*Ross*	*Smith*	*Spavin*	*Singleton*	*Cranston*	*Wilson*	*Hannigan*	*Dawson*	*Lawton*	*Lee*	
								Ref: N Callender	City come from 0-2 to level but throw away the initiative and settle for a point. The referee could have given two penalties apiece but only punishes Kearns' trip on Lee. Tudor clips in his first goal and Curtis heads in a corner but City are out of luck with two shots hitting wood.											

No	Date		Att	Pos	Pt	F-A	H-T	Scorers, Times, and Referees	1	2	3	4	5	6	7	8	9	10	11	12 sub used
11	A	CARLISLE		10	L	1-2	0-1	Clements 77	Glazier	Kearns	Bruck*	Hill	Curtis	Clements	Machin	Pointer	Gould	Gibson	Rees	Key
	8/10		*10,885*	6	12			*Wilson 30, Garbutt 64*	*Ross*	*Neill*	*Caldwell*	*McConnell*	*Passmoor*	*Garbutt*	*Welsh*	*Carlin*	*Wilson*	*Balderstone*	*Hartle*	
								Ref: G Kew	A disjointed City fall in Cumberland. Curtis is punished for a rare error by Wilson and Neil's cross is swept home by Garbutt. Clements is pushed forward at 0-2 and hits four stunning shots and one goes in off a post. Gould and Rees miss good chances and Gibson looks off colour.											
12	H	BLACKBURN		8	W	2-0	2-0	Tudor 7, Gould 19	Glazier	Kearns	Hill	Clements	Curtis	Farmer	Key	Machin	Gould	Tudor	Mitten	
	15/10		21,017	*10*	14				*Barton*	*Newton*	*Joyce*	*Clayton*	*Holt*	*Hole*	*Connelly*	*Ferguson*	*McEvoy*	*Douglas*	*Harrison*	
								Ref: W Holian	Relegated Rovers have several former England men and current cap Keith Newton but are no match for lively City. Farmer and Machin are back and help City defend their early lead. City are now four points behind leaders Hull. Hill denies rumours of Johnny Haynes' signing.											
13	A	BOLTON		8	D	1-1	0-0	Machin 77	Glazier	Kearns	Hill	Clements	Curtis	Farmer	Rees	Machin	Gould	Tudor	Mitten	
	22/10		*14,569*	*3*	15			*Byrom 80*	*Hopkinson*	*Hatton D*	*Cooper*	*Rimmer*	*Napier*	*Beech*	*Lee*	*Bromley*	*Byrom*	*Lennard*	*Taylor*	
								Ref: R Windle	An excellent second half display deserves both points. City's pressure is rewarded when local boy Machin slides in after good work by Mitten. Bromley sets up Byrom who is in for Davies, sold to Newcastle this week. Tudor has four chances but is foiled by ex-England man Hopkinson.											
14	H	CHARLTON		6	W	1-0	1-0	Gould 10	Glazier	Kearns	Hill*	Clements	Curtis	Farmer	Rees	Machin	Gould	Tudor	Mitten	Coop
	29/10		19,868	*15*	17				*Wright*	*Bonds*	*Kinsey*	*Reeves*	*King*	*Appleton*	*Kenning*	*Gregory*	*Saunders*	*Campbell*	*Glover*	
								Ref: V Batty	Another scrappy home win thanks to a good defensive display but it's not pretty. A nervous last ten minutes are wasted by the average visitors whose star man is 'keeper Wright who saves well from Rees and Gould. Kearns celebrates his 300th league game by keeping Len Glover quiet.											
15	A	DERBY		5	W	2-1	1-0	Tudor 3, Machin 66	Glazier	Kearns	Bruck	Farmer	Curtis	Clements	Rees	Tudor	Gould	Machin	Mitten	
	5/11		*22,949*	*17*	19			*Hodgson 80*	*Matthews*	*Richardson*	*Daniel*	*Webster*	*Saxton*	*Waller**	*Hughes*	*Hector*	*Buxton*	*Durban*	*Hodgson*	*Thomas*
								Ref: F Cowen	City put on one of their best displays of the season to notch a first-ever win at Derby. £40,000 Kevin Hector is bossed by Clements and Farmer is superb. Derby have few chances and lose for the first time in seven. But for sloppy shooting and Matthews it would have been a bigger win.											
16	H	CRYS PALACE		6	L	1-2	1-1	Gould 28	Glazier	Kearns	Bruck	Farmer	Curtis	Clements	Rees	Tudor	Gould	Machin	Mitten	
	12/11		23,035	*2*	19			*Jackson C 6, Kember 60*	*Jackson J*	*Howe*	*Bannister*	*Payne*	*Stephenson*	*Wood*	*Robertson*	*Kember*	*Dyson*	*Woodruff*	*Jackson C*	
								Ref: S Kayley	In a thriller captain for the day Glazier is at fault for both goals. Mitten misses a sitter and Jackson pulls off some great stops. Woodruff's long throw creates the second goal for the best Palace side for years. Gould's opportunism gets him a goal and he also hits the bar near the end.											
17	A	HUDDERSFIELD		7	L	1-3	1-0	Tudor 39	Glazier	Kearns	Bruck	Farmer	Curtis	Clements	Rees*	Tudor	Gould	Machin	Mitten	Coop
	19/11		*15,192*	*8*	19			*Dobson 60, Leighton 64, Meagan 88*	*Oldfield*	*Parkin*	*Cattlin*	*Nicholson*	*Coddington*	*Meagan*	*Hellawell*	*Rudge*	*Leighton*	*Dobson*	*Hill*	
								Ref: K Dagnall	Non-stop Town pressure earns a deserved victory. Gould guides Mitten's long cross into the path of Tudor. Mike Hellawell's pace sets up the equaliser before Glazier fails to hold a shot and Tony Leighton pounces. The third, a dipper, catches the otherwise brilliant Glazier off his line.											
18	H	CARDIFF		6	W	3-2	1-0	Tudor 25, Gibson 46, 55	Thomas	Kearns	Coop	Farmer	Curtis	Clements	Key	Gibson	Gould	Tudor*	Rees	Glover
	26/11		19,682	*22*	21			*Toshack 87, 88*	*Wilson*	*Coldrick*	*Ferguson*	*Williams*	*Murray*	*Harris*	*Farrell*	*Toshack*	*Brown*	*Johnston*	*Bird*	
								Ref: K Seddon	With the top six all losing City gain ground but should have had a scoring spree. Cardiff may be poor but the returning Gibson shows Hill what he has been missing with a one-man show and a sublime second goal. Gould misses a hat-full and Wilson gifts two. City relax at the end.											
19	A	WOLVES		4	W	3-1	1-0	Gibson 7, Key 73, Rees 82	Glazier	Kearns	Bruck	Farmer	Curtis	Clements	Key	Machin	Gould	Gibson	Rees	
	3/12		*27,232*	*2*	23			*Burnside 50*	*Davies*	*Wilson*	*Thomson*	*Bailey*	*Woodfield*	*Flowers*	*Wharton*	*Hunt*	*McIlmoyle*	*Burnside*	*Wagstaffe*	
								Ref: N Burtenshaw	On a snow-covered pitch City take a battering for an hour after Gibbo's snap goal. Burnside's header looks ominous but a heroic defensive play with Bill Glazier at his best and two cross-shots knock Wolves off top spot. A famous victory and three in a row over Ronnie Allen's team.											
20	H	IPSWICH		3	W	5-0	3-0	Gould 4, 15, 33, Key, Gibson	Glazier	Kearns	Bruck	Farmer	Curtis	Clements	Key	Machin*	Gould	Gibson	Rees	Morrissey
	9/12		25,724	*2*	25				*Hancock*	*McNeil*	*Houghton*	*Harper D*	*Baxter*	*Lea*	*Spearritt*	*Hegan*	*Crawford*	*Baker*	*Brogan*	
								Ref: I Jones	On a wet Friday night the scoreline does not flatter City who rip the leaders apart. Gibson is at the heart of everything and scores a memorable chipped goal over seven defenders. Gould and Rees are on fire and the former deserves his three goals, a tap-in, a vicious drive and a header.											
21	A	HULL		4	D	2-2	0-1	Key 46, Tudor 76	Glazier	Bruck	Coop	Farmer	Curtis	Clements	Key	Machin	Gould	Tudor	Rees	
	17/12		*26,577*	*6*	26			*Butler I 9, 88*	*Swan*	*Davidson*	*Butler D*	*Jarvis*	*Milner*	*Simpkin*	*Henderson*	*Wagstaff*	*Chilton*	*Wilkinson*	*Butler I*	
								Ref: L Hamer	City's defence has the upper hand against the best attack in the division. Cliff Britton's team have scored 48 and put six past Palace but leave their equaliser, a mis-hit late. Curtis and Clements master Chilton and Wagstaff and injured Gibbo is not missed. Key's goal is a deflection.											

No	Date	Att	Pos	Pt	F-A	H-T	Scorers, Times, and Referees	1	2	3	4	5	6	7	8	9	10	11	12 sub used
22	H	ROTHERHAM	2	W	4-2	2-2	Gould 7, 65, Gibson 24, Farmer 77p	Glazier	Kearns	Bruck	Farmer	Curt s	Clements	Key	Machin	Gould	Gibson*	Rees	Hill
	26/12	31,619	*16*	28			*Massey 33, Williams 39*	*Hill**	*Wilcockson*	*Clish*	*Rabjohn*	*Haselden*	*Tiler*	*Massey*	*Williams*	*Galley*	*Chappell*	*Harrity*	*Pring*
							Ref: L Callaghan	A big holiday crowd see an incident packed match and City deservedly win. Bobby Gould is again the hero with a tap-in, a thunderous shot which breaks Alan Hill's finger and he is fouled for the penalty. Gibson limps off and Galley goes in goal but is sadly attacked by a City fan.											
23	A	ROTHERHAM	2	D	1-1	0-0	Clements 90	Glazier	Kearns	Bruck	Hill	Curtis	Clements	Key	Machin	Gould	Farmer	Rees	
	27/12	*13,301*	*15*	29			*Massey 71*	*Jones*	*Wilcockson*	*Clish*	*Rabjohn*	*Haselden*	*Tiler*	*Massey*	*Williams*	*Galley*	*Chappell*	*Pring*	
							Ref: G Cooke	The Millers carry a grudge from the previous day and rough City up. Curtis and co defend desperately but with great heart. The City players are convinced that Massey handles for the goal. When it looks all over Clements levels in the 92nd minute with a shot through a crowd.											
24	H	PORTSMOUTH	2	W	5-1	2-0	Tudor 19, Gould 42, Machin 46, Mitten 52, Key 55	Glazier	Kearns	Bruck	Farmer	Curtis	Clements	Key	Machin	Gould	Tudor	Mitten	
	31/12	24,981	*12*	31			*Hiron 64*	*Milkins*	*Pack*	*Tindall*	*Gordon*	*Radcliffe*	*Harris*	*Lewis*	*McCann*	*Hiron*	*Edwards*	*Kellard*	
							Ref: P Bye	Pompey arrive with the best away record in the division, depart humbled and lucky to have got off with five. 17 goals in four home games have lit up City's season. Tudor, Machin and Key score headers, Gould profits from Milkins' bad kick and Mitten's cool flick tops a great display.											
25	A	BIRMINGHAM	1	D	1-1	0-1	Machin 52	Glazier	Kearns	Bruck	Farmer	Curtis	Clements	Key	Machin	Gould	Tudor	Mitten	
	7/1	*36,316*	*12*	32			*Curtis 23(og)*	*Herriot*	*Murray*	*Green*	*Thomson*	*Sharples*	*Beard*	*Hockey*	*Leggat*	*Bullock*	*Vowden*	*Bridges*	
							Ref: W Crossley	10,000 City fans boost Blues' biggest crowd for two years as City go top for the first time on a wet pitch. Overnight signing Leggat's cross skids off Curtis' head for a great goal. Clements's low cross when a shot looks on leaves Machin with a simple finish against a confused defence.											
26	H	NORWICH	1	W	2-1	0-0	Farmer 58, Machin 89	Glazier	Kearns	Bruck	Farmer	Curtis	Clements	Key	Machin	Gould	Gibson	Rees	
	14/1	27,354	*21*	34			*Sheffield 85*	*Keelan*	*Stringer*	*Mullett*	*Lucas*	*Brown*	*Allcock*	*Kenning*	*Bolland*	*Sheffield*	*Curran*	*Anderson*	
							Ref: H Davies	City struggle to beat lowly but gallant Norwich for whom Keelan is in top form. Ron Farmer's free kick skids off the goalmouth sand. Curran has an offside 'goal' ruled out. Sheffield's close-range header is trumped when Farmer's cross is set up by Gould for the outstanding Machin.											
27	A	BRISTOL CITY	1	D	2-2	2-2	Curtis 14, Bruck 36	Glazier	Kearns	Bruck	Farmer	Curtis	Clements	Key	Machin	Gould	Gibson	Rees	
	21/1	*21,600*	*18*	35			*Crowe 11, Bush 18*	*Gibson*	*Ford*	*Briggs*	*Parr*	*Connor*	*Low*	*Derrick*	*Crowe*	*Bush*	*Quigley*	*Peters*	
							Ref: G Roper	Unconvincing City extend their unbeaten run to ten after falling behind again. Bristol score from two errors with Crowe unmarked to volley in and dithering Clements robbed by Bush. Curtis' solid header from a free kick and Bruck's vicious shot restore parity. City hang on at the end.											
28	A	BURY	1	W	1-0	0-0	Rees 79	Glazier	Kearns	Bruck	Farmer	Curtis	Clements	Key*	Machin	Tudor	Lewis	Rees	Gould
	4/2	*9,871*	*19*	37				*Harker*	*Colquhoun*	*Eastham*	*Turner*	*Waldron*	*Lindsay*	*Lowes*	*Jones*	*Aimson*	*Owen*	*Parry*	
							Ref: P Partridge	It's like a home match with 2,500 travelling fans. The axed Gould is on at half-time for the injured Key and has an offside 'goal' ruled out. Brian Lewis makes a quiet debut and Rees nets after a partially cleared corner. Glazier is in top form and saves from Jones and Barry Lowes.											
29	H	PRESTON	1	W	2-1	0-1	Machin 80, Gould 86	Glazier	Kearns	Bruck	Farmer	Curtis	Clements	Lewis	Machin	Gould	Gibson	Rees	
	11/2	29,047	*7*	39			*Lawton 25*	*Kelly*	*Ross*	*Smith*	*Lawton*	*Singleton*	*Kendall*	*Hannigan*	*Godfrey*	*Greenhalgh*	*Spavin**	*Wilson*	*Lee*
							Ref: B Homewood	Late goals are stock in trade for City and Gould justifies his recall sliding home from Farmer's slide-rule pass. Jimmy Milne's team use rough-arm tactics and sit back after Lawton's goal. After constant attacking Machin heads in Gibson's cross in a fine move to send the crowd wild.											
30	A	CHARLTON	1	W	2-1	0-0	Gould 50, 89	Glazier	Kearns	Bruck	Farmer	Curtis	Clements	Lewis	Machin	Gould	Gibson	Rees	
	18/2	*17,914*	*16*	41			*Myers 89*	*Wright*	*Bonds*	*Gregory*	*Reeves*	*King*	*Saunders*	*Myers*	*Tees*	*Green**	*Campbell*	*Glover*	*Peacock*
							Ref: P Bye	4,000 travelling fans see City notch a deserved first-ever win at the Valley. Curtis upsets Addicks' manager Bob Stokoe when he clatters into Tees who collides with the trainer's hut. Stokoe calls City 'rough'. Gould finishes coolly after Gibbo's great dribble and Machin's perfect pass.											
31	H	CARLISLE	1	W	2-1	1-1	Gould 44, Machin 88	Glazier	Kearns	Bruck	Lewis	Curtis	Clements	Key*	Machin	Gould	Gibson	Rees	Farmer
	25/2	29,965	*6*	43			*McVitie 11*	*Ross!*	*McConnell*	*Caldwell*	*Balderstone*	*Passmoor*	*Garbutt*	*Welsh*	*Carlin*	*Wilson*	*McVitie*	*Hartle*	
							Ref: M Fussey	The fans' nerves are frayed again. Alan Ashman's gritty team hold out after Ross' sending off for striking Gould until Machin's scrambled goal beats stand-in keeper McConnell. Key has damaged ankle ligaments and the team gc to Worthing for a week's break to re-charge the batteries.											

No	Date	Att	Pos	Pt	F-A	H-T	Scorers, Times, and Referees	1	2	3	4	5	6	7	8	9	10	11	12 sub used
32	A	NORTHAMPTON	1	D	0-0	0-0		Glazier	Kearns	Bruck	Farmer	Curtis	Clements	Lowes	Machin	Gould	Gibson	Rees	
	11/3	*20,100*	*22*	44				*Harvey*	*Foley*	*Everitt*	*Mackin*	*Branston*	*Kurila*	*Walden*	*Brown*	*Large*	*Moore*	*Lines*	
							Ref: J Carr	Dave Bowen's Cobblers look doomed to another relegation. A wind-spoiled game evens the contest but City, cheered on by 8,000 fans, look the only winners. Mackin and Branston block goalbound shots and Harvey makes some good saves. City goal-less for only the second time.											
33	H	BOLTON	1	D	1-1	1-0	Gould 40	Glazier	Kearns	Bruck	Farmer	Curtis	Clements	Lowes	Machin	Gould	Gibson	Rees	
	18/3	28,674	*11*	45			*Phillips 87*	*Hopkinson*	*Hatton D*	*Farrimond*	*Rimmer*	*Hulme*	*Lennard*	*Phillips*	*Lee*	*Hatton R*	*Bromley*	*Hill*	
							Ref: H New	16 games without defeat is a new club record as *Match of the Day* make its first visit. Phillips' header is Bolton's first effort on target and gains a lucky point. Rees' mazy 60-yard run sets up Gould but despite Machin's excellent display he misses four chances. Lowes struggles.											
34	A	BLACKBURN	1	W	1-0	0-0	Gould 51	Glazier	Kearns	Bruck	Farmer	Curtis	Clements	Lewis	Machin	Gould	Gibson	Rees	
	25/3	*26,380*	*3*	47				*Barton*	*Newton*	*Wilson*	*Sharples*	*Clayton*	*Hole*	*Ferguson!*	*Joyce*	*Darling*	*Douglas*	*Connelly*	
							Ref: W Holian	A vital win and only a second home defeat for Jack Marshall's team. Rovers have won five in a row but promotion hopes are slim. Ferguson strikes Bruck seconds before the break and walks. Gould harries Barton into dropping Rees' cross and nets. The defence soaks up the pressure.											
35	H	NORTHAMPTON	2	W	2-0	0-0	Machin 62, Gould 83	Glazier	Kearns	Bruck	Farmer	Curtis	Clements	Lewis	Machin	Gould	Gibson	Rees	
	28/3	38,566	*21*	49				*Harvey*	*Foley*	*Walker*	*Mackin*	*Branston*	*Kurila*	*Walden*	*Brown*	*Large*	*Moore*	*Lines*	
							Ref: H Davey	The old foe stubbornly defend but collapse after the break. In ten wild minutes a Gibbo shot hits both posts and into Harvey's arms, Harvey tips over Gould's shot and Lewis is headbutted by Branston who is lucky to stay on. The biggest league crowd for 18 years roars the team on.											
36	H	DERBY	2	D	2-2	1-1	Gould 17, Machin 80	Glazier	Kearns	Bruck	Farmer	Curtis	Clements	Lewis	Machin	Gould	Gibson	Rees	
	¼	32,041	*15*	50			*Hector 38, Thomas 60*	*Boulton*	*Daniel*	*Richardson*	*Thomas*	*Saxton*	*Waller*	*Hughes*	*Hector**	*Buxton*	*Durban*	*Cleevely*	*Hopkinson*
							Ref: R Harper	Several players have a bad day and Tim Ward's relaxed Rams almost end the run. They score two good but soft goals and at 2-1 Hughes has a 'goal' ruled out. Finally Machin's header from Bruck's surging run and cross saves the day. Wolves' draw at the Den leave the rivals level.											
37	A	CRYS PALACE	2	D	1-1	0-0	Gould 69	Glazier	Kearns	Bruck	Lewis	Curtis	Clements	Lowes	Machin	Gould	Gibson	Rees	
	8/4	*23,247*	*8*	51			*Kember 53*	*Jackson J*	*Sewell*	*Presland*	*Payne*	*Stephenson*	*Bannister*	*Woodruff*	*Kember*	*Dyson**	*Byrne*	*O'Connell*	*Long*
							Ref: P Baldwin	A first-ever Saturday night match ends all-square after a titanic battle. Tempers are frayed and lots of fouls goes unpunished. City only start to play when a goal down and then pummel the home side. After close shaves galore Gould finally scrambles in a brave header from Rees' chip.											
38	H	HUDDERSFIELD	2	W	1-0	0-0	Gould 63	Glazier	Kearns	Bruck	Lewis	Curtis	Clements	Key	Machin	Gould	Gibson	Rees	
	15/4	29,683	*6*	53				*Oldfield*	*Parkin*	*Cattlin*	*Nicholson*	*Ellam*	*Meagan*	*Hellawell*	*Clark*	*Leighton*	*Dobson*	*Hill*	
							Ref: P Walters	Seven points clear of third-placed Ipswich City are virtually promoted. The nerve ends show and Town look the team set for Div 1. Hill gives Kearns a roasting and Glazier twice saves City. Gould's opportunism wins the day after Curtis' mighty header bounces off Cattlin.											
39	A	CARDIFF	2	D	1-1	1-0	Key 30	Glazier	Kearns	Bruck	Lewis	Curtis	Clements	Key	Machin	Gould	Gibson	Rees*	Farmer
	22/4	*19,592*	*20*	54			*Brown 60*	*Wilson*	*Coldrick*	*Ferguson*	*Williams*	*Murray*	*Harris*	*Jones*	*Brown*	*Toshack*	*King*	*Bird*	
							Ref: H New	The champagne stays on ice with one point needed for promotion after a botched job at Ninian Park. A failure to capitalise on early domination and then a Toshack penalty miss on 72 minutes lets City off. Key taps in after Brian Lewis' run and shot and Brown levels with a soft goal.											
40	H	WOLVES	2	W	3-1	0-1	Machin 59, Gibson 63, Rees 85	Glazier	Kearns	Bruck	Lewis	Curtis	Clements	Key	Machin	Tudor	Gibson	Rees	
	29/4	51,452	*1*	56			*Knowles 40*	*Parkes*	*Bailey*	*Thomson*	*Hunt*	*Hawkins*	*Holsgrove*	*Wharton*	*Knowles*	*Dougan*	*Burnside*	*Wagstaffe*	
							Ref: N Callender	Both sides are up before the 'Midlands Match of the Century' starts. A record crowd with thousands locked out see a classic with City coming from behind to rip Wolves to shreds. Two friendly crowd invasions threaten to end the game but the fans stay off when Ronnie Rees seals it.											
41	A	IPSWICH	2	D	1-1	1-0	Gibson 27	Glazier	Kearns	Bruck	Lewis	Curtis	Clements	Key	Machin	Tudor	Gibson	Rees	
	6/5	*18,916*	*4*	57			*Viljoen 80*	*Hancock*	*Carroll*	*Houghton*	*Spearritt*	*Baxter*	*Bolton*	*Broadfoot*	*Hegan*	*Crawford*	*Viljoen*	*Brogan*	
							Ref: K Walker	City let Bill McGarry's Ipswich off a drubbing after a Gibbo inspired performance. Hancock excels, the posts intervene and shots are cleared off the line as the Sky Blues thrill their 5,000 fans. Rees' cross is headed in by Gibson and 19-year-old Viljoen looks offside for the equaliser.											
42	H	MILLWALL	1	W	3-1	2-0	Key 9, Tudor 38, Machin 59	Glazier	Kearns	Bruck	Lewis	Curtis	Clements	Key	Machin	Tudor	Gibson	Rees	
	13/5	32,551	*8*	59			*Neil 49*	*Leslie*	*Gilchrist*	*Cripps*	*Rhodes*	*Kitchener*	*Plume*	*Jacks*	*Welsh*	*Neil*	*Hunt**	*Dunphy*	*Armstrong*
		Home Away					Ref: K Dagnall	With Wolves losing at Palace City clinch the title on another dramatic day. A relaxed City play flowing football which deserves more goals. Key fires in from Machin's sweet pass, Lewis sets up Tudor and Machin and Gibbo set up a classy third. Hill leads the singing afterwards.											
	Average	28,245 18,996																	

League Cup			Att			F-A	H-T	Scorers, Times, and Referees	1	2	3	4	5	6	7	8	9	10	11	12 sub used
2	H	DERBY		7	W	2-1	1-0	Farmer 33, Clements 58	Glazier	Kearns	Burckitt	Farmer	Curtis	Bruck	Rees	Gibson	Gould	Pointer	Clements	
	13/9		14,804	*22*				*Hodgson 85*	*Matthews*	*Richardson*	*Daniel*	*Webster*	*Saxton*	*Waller*	*Hughes*	*Thomas*	*Buxton*	*Draper*	*Hodgson*	
								Ref: A Dimond	**Derby fail to clear a Gibson cross and Farmer fires home. Kearns' long ball finds Clements whose first is parried but he scores from the rebound. Reg Matthews is booed after fouling Pointer. Glazier saves well from Draper but Hodgson scores before Draper's late shot goes wide.**											
3	A	BRIGHTON		8	D	1-1	1-0	Rees 18	Glazier	Kearns	Bruck	Hill	Curtis	Clements	Key	Tudor	Gould	Gibson	Rees	
	5/10		*13,007*	*3:22*				*Collins 80*	*Powney*	*Henderson*	*Baxter*	*Collins*	*Gall*	*Turner*	*Wilkinson*	*Livesey*	*Cassidy*	*Whittington*	*Gould*	
								Ref: R Paine	**After failing to kill off Archie Macauley's struggling team when they had the chances City are hanging on for dear life at the end. Glazier saves Collins' penalty harshly given against Brian Hill and saves Gould's late shot. Rees' shot is levelled when Collins' shot spins off Kearns' boot.**											
3R	H	BRIGHTON		10	L	1-3	1-2	Gould 9	Glazier	Coop	Kearns	Roberts	Curtis	Farmer	Rees*	Machin	Gould	Pointer	Clements	Mitten
	11/10		13,437	*3:19*				*Livesey 16, Cassidy 44, Wilkinson 58*	*Powney*	*Henderson*	*Baxter*	*Collins*	*Gall*	*Turner*	*Wilkinson*	*Livesey*	*Cassidy*	*Whittington*	*Gould*	
								Ref: J Mitchell	**A League Cup disaster the day after Gibson asks for a transfer means it's crisis time. Brighton, who also hit wood twice, are deserved winners over clueless City. Rees is off with damaged ligaments and Glazier errs for the first goal. The game ends with boos and Brighton in control.**											

FA Cup																				
3	H	NEWCASTLE		1	L	3-4	2-3	McNamee 4(og), Gibson 21, Rees 76	Glazier	Kearns	Bruck	Farmer	Curtis	Clements	Key	Machin	Gould	Gibson*	Rees	Morrissey
	28/1		35,748	*1:21*				*Davies 2, 30, 75, Robson B 3*	*Marshall*	*Burton*	*Clark*	*Elliott*	*McNamee*	*McGrath*	*Robson B*	*Bennett*	*Davies*	*Iley*	*Hilley*	
								Ref: L Callaghan	**After a slow start City fight back but out-of-touch Gould misses a sitter to grab a replay. The ruthless Davies is irrepressible and too much for Curtis. Iley runs the show especially after the break when Gibson is injured. Gibbo's full-tilt header and Davies' first are the pick of the goals.**											

Key:
p = penalty
* = substituted
! = player sent off
Italic font = opposition team

APPENDIX 2

1966/67 Division Two – Final Table

		Home					*Away*					
	P	*W*	*D*	*L*	*F*	*A*	*W*	*D*	*L*	*F*	*A*	*Pts*
1 COVENTRY (P)	42	17	3	1	46	16	6	10	5	28	27	59
2 Wolves (P)	42	15	4	2	53	20	10	4	7	35	28	58
3 Carlisle	42	15	3	3	42	16	8	3	10	29	38	52
4 Blackburn	42	13	6	2	33	11	6	7	8	23	35	51
5 Ipswich	42	11	8	2	45	25	6	8	7	25	29	50
6 Huddersfield	42	14	3	4	36	17	6	6	9	22	29	49
7 Crystal Palace	42	14	4	3	42	23	5	6	10	19	32	48
8 Millwall	42	14	5	2	33	17	4	4	13	16	41	45
9 Bolton	42	10	7	4	36	19	4	7	10	28	39	42
10 Birmingham	42	11	5	5	42	23	5	3	13	28	43	40
11 Norwich	42	10	7	4	31	21	3	7	11	18	34	40
12 Hull	42	11	5	5	46	25	5	2	14	31	47	39
13 Preston	42	14	3	4	44	23	2	4	15	21	44	39
14 Portsmouth	42	7	5	9	34	37	6	8	7	25	33	39
15 Bristol City	42	10	8	3	38	22	2	6	13	18	40	38
16 Plymouth	42	12	4	5	42	21	2	5	14	17	37	37
17 Derby	42	8	6	7	40	32	4	6	11	28	40	36
18 Rotherham	42	10	5	6	39	28	3	5	13	22	42	36
19 Charlton	42	11	4	6	34	16	2	5	14	15	37	35
20 Cardiff	42	9	7	5	43	28	3	2	16	18	59	33
21 Northampton (R)	42	8	6	7	28	33	4	0	17	19	51	30
22 Bury (R)	42	9	3	9	31	30	2	3	16	18	53	28

APPENDIX 3

Coventry City Appearances and Goalscorers 1966/67

	Appearances						*Goals*			
	Lge	*Sub*	*LC*	*Sub*	*FAC*	*Sub*	*Lge*	*LC*	*FAC*	*Tot*
Dietmar Bruck	38		2		1		2			2
John Burckitt			1							
Dave Clements	40		3		1		4	1		5
Mick Coop	2	2	1							
George Curtis	42		3		1		2			2
Ron Farmer	32	2	2		1		2	1		3
Ian Gibson	31		2		1		8		1	9
Bill Glazier	41		3		1					
Benny Glover		1								
Bobby Gould	38	1	3		1		24	1		25
Brian Hill	15	1	1							
Mick Kearns	41		3		1		1			1
John Key	21	1	1		1		6			6
Brian Lewis	13									
Barry Lowes	3									
Ernie Machin	34		1		1		11			11
John Mitten	8	2		1			1			1
Pat Morrissey		1				1				
Ray Pointer	7		2				2			2
Ronnie Rees	39		3		1		3	1	1	5
Dudley Roberts			1							
Peter Thomas	1									
John Tudor	16		1				8			8
Own goals									1	1

APPENDIX 4

Miscellany

Double wins: (5) Portsmouth, Bury, Charlton, Blackburn, Wolves.
Double losses: (0).

Won from behind: (3) Preston (h), Carlisle (h), Wolves (h).
Lost from in front: (2) Huddersfield (a), Brighton LC (h).

Biggest win: 5-0 Ipswich (h).
Biggest defeat: 2-4 Plymouth (a).

Red Cards City : (0)
Red cards opponents: (4) Davidson (Hull h), Hockey (Birmingham h), Ross (Carlisle h), Ferguson (Blackburn a).

Hat-tricks: (1) Gould (Ipswich h).
Opposition hat-tricks: (1) Wyn Davies (Newcastle FAC h).
Leading scorer: (25) Bobby Gould.
Fastest goal: John Tudor (Derby a) (3rd minute).
Latest goal: Dave Clements (Rotherham a) (90th minute).
Players used: 21 in league games plus two more in Cup games.

Average home attendance: 28,269 (club record).
Average away attendance: 18,996 (highest since 1951/52).
Biggest home crowd: 51,452 v Wolves (ground record).
Smallest home crowd (league): 19,682 v Cardiff.

Biggest away crowd: 36,316 v Birmingham.
Smallest away crowd: 9,871 v Bury.

Other records:
Lowest number of league defeats in a season (6).
Longest unbeaten league run (25).
Least home defeats in a season (1) (equals club record).

APPENDIX 5

Coventry City 1966/67
Other first-team games

Pre-season friendlies
6th August 1966
Dudley Town (a) 1-1 (Pointer)

10th August 1966
Varna Select (h) 1-1 (Machin)
Attendance: 9,739

12th August 1966
Hereford United (a) 5-1 (Farmer, Pointer 2, Machin 2)
Attendance: 4,540

Other friendlies
17th October 1966
Ashford Town (a) 11-0 (Farmer, Gould 3, Tudor 2, Key 2, Curtis, Mitten, B Hill)

29th November 1966
Morton (h) 3-2 (Rees, Shepherd, Gould)
Attendance: 4,098

5th February 1967
Lockheed Leamington (a) 3-5 (Gould, Lewis, Rees) (Ken Shelton-Rayner Appeal)

3rd March 1967
West Ham (h) 3-3 (Gibson, Machin 2) (West Ham won 9-7 on penalties) (Winston Churchill Remembrance Trophy)
Attendance: 18,524

9th May 1967
Liverpool (h) 2-1 (Machin, Rees) (George Curtis/Mick Kearns Testimonial)
Attendance: 25,040

15th May 1967
Nuneaton Borough (a) 7-3 (Tudor 4, Machin, Farmer, Gibson)
(Thompson/Allen Testimonial)
Attendance: 7,250

West Indies Tour
2nd June 1967
Trinidad and Tobago XI (a) 5-2 (Key, Tudor, Lewis 2, Curtis)
(at Port of Spain)

4th June 1967
South Trinidad XI (a) 4-3 (Machin, Lewis, Gould, B Hill)
(at Point Fortin)

6th June 1967
Barbados XI (a) 3-2 (Gould 2, Key)
(at Bridgetown)

12th June 1967
Barbados XI (a) 2-0 (Rees, Key)
(at Bridgetown)

18th June 1967
Bermuda Police (a) 8-0 (Rees 2, Tudor, Machin, Lewis 2, Clements, Bruck)
(at Hamilton)

APPENDIX 6

Coventry City Reserve Team 1966/67

Aug	23	H	Northampton	D	1-1	Dicks	5,640
Sep	3	A	Leicester (Cup)	D	0-0		858
	6	H	Leicester (Cup)	L	1-2	Dougan (og)	5,404
	10	A	Nottm Forest (Cup)	L	3-4	Morrissey 2, Key	1,453
	20	H	Nottm Forest (Cup)	W	4-0	Tudor 2, Key Mitten	6,640
Oct	15	A	Ipswich	L	1-2	Gibson	870
	25	H	Southampton	W	3-1	Bruck, Shepherd, Pointer	5,610
	29	A	West Ham	L	1-4	Burckitt	2,913
Nov	15	A	Crystal Palace	L	1-3	Morrissey	843
	22	H	Chelsea	W	4-1	Tudor 2, Key, Shepherd	5,417
	26	A	Leicester	L	1-2	Shepherd	881
Dec	6	H	Ipswich	W	2-1	Shepherd, Oakes	4,871
	20	H	Plymouth	D	3-3	Pointer 2, Shepherd	5,295
	27	A	Nottm Forest	L	0-10		893
Jan	3	H	Reading	W	3-1	Coop, Burckitt, Shepherd	3,400
	14	A	Tottenham	L	0-2		2,959
	17	H	Peterborough	W	3-2	Coop, Tudor, Shepherd	4,013
	24	H	Swindon	W	2-1	Oakes (pen), Morrissey	4,665
	31	H	Fulham	W	6-1	Docker, Lewis, Denton 2, Tudor 2	7,562
Feb	7	H	Nottm Forest	D	1-1	Peachey	4,594
	11	A	Fulham	D	0-0		290
	14	A	Northampton	L	0-1		2,658
	21	H	Gillingham	W	3-1	Coop, Tudor 2	4,760
	25	A	Southampton	L	1-2	Oakes	2,101
Mar	7	H	West Ham	W	3-1	Moore, Roberts, Tudor	4,986
	11	A	Gillingham	L	0-3		1,220
	14	H	Crystal Palace	D	2-2	Denton, Tudor	5,053
	18	A	Peterborough	W	3-1	Tudor, Carr, Hill	1,763
	21	H	Arsenal	W	1-0	Lowes	8,123
	30	A	Arsenal	L	1-2	?	887
Apr	1	A	Chelsea	L	2-4	Docker, Carr	626
	4	A	Swindon	L	1-4	Carr	2,131
	11	H	Leicester	W	2-1	Roberts, Key	4,878
	18	A	Plymouth	L	2-4	Tudor, Morrissey (pen)	1,029
	26	A	Reading	W	1-0	Docker	1,120
May	2	H	Tottenham	D	2-2	Roberts, Denton	6,800
Average home attendance							5,428

APPENDIX 7

1966/67 Football Combination – Final Table

Pos	*Team*	*P*	*W*	*D*	*L*	*F*	*A*	*Pts*
1	Tottenham Hotspur	32	23	3	6	83	31	49
2	Arsenal	32	18	4	10	60	41	40
3	Swindon Town	32	16	6	10	48	45	38
4	Peterborough United	32	15	7	10	66	61	37
5	Southampton	32	15	6	11	66	45	36
6	West Ham United	32	15	6	11	63	46	36
7	Leicester City	32	13	8	11	61	45	34
8	Nottingham Forest	32	14	5	13	52	55	33
9	Coventry City	32	13	6	13	56	64	32
10	Northampton Town	32	14	3	15	56	60	31
11	Chelsea	32	11	6	15	58	77	28
12	Plymouth Argyle	32	11	5	16	60	58	27
13	Gillingham	32	11	5	16	49	71	27
14	Ipswich Town	32	10	6	16	43	53	26
15	Crystal Palace	32	11	4	17	51	71	26
16	Fulham	32	9	6	17	48	60	24
17	Reading	32	8	4	20	41	78	20

APPENDIX 8

Coventry City Reserve Team 1966/67

	Appearances
Pat Morrissey	32
Benny Glover	30
Trevor Shepherd	27
John Burckitt	26
Mick Coop	25
Peter Denton	25
John Tudor	23
Alan Dicks	21
Dudley Roberts	20
Martin Clamp	17
John Docker	16
Willie Carr	16
Mick Cartwright	15
Dennis Oakes	11
Howard Moore	11
Peter Thomas	9
Brian Hill	9
Ray Pointer	8
John Mitten	7
John Key	7
Malcolm Keley	7
Bob Wesson	5
Alan Dickie	5
Barry Lowes	4
Ian Gibson	4
Brian Lewis	4
Robin Hayward	3
Don Peachey	2
Trevor Gould	2
Jeff Blockley	2
Ronnie Farmer	1
Dietmar Bruck	1
Ronnie Rees	1

	Goals
John Tudor	13
Trevor Shepherd	7
Pat Morrissey	4
John Key	4
John Docker	4
Peter Denton	4
Ray Pointer	3
Dennis Oakes	3
Willie Carr	3
Mick Coop	3
Dudley Roberts	3
John Burckitt	2
Alan Dicks	1
John Mitten	1
Ian Gibson	1
Dietmar Bruck	1
Brian Lewis	1
Don Peachey	1
Howard Moore	1
Brian Hill	1
Barry Lowes	1
own goal	1
unknown	1

APPENDIX 9

Coventry City 'A' Team 1966/67

West Midlands League

Aug	20	H	Redditch	1-1	Morrissey
Aug	23	A	Bromsgrove	1-2	Own goal
Aug	27	A	Hednesford	0-1	-
Aug	29	A	Halesowen	3-2	Tudor, Moore, Morrissey
Sep	3	A	Kidderminster	0-1	-
Sep	5	H	Darlaston	1-1	Shepherd
Sep	10	A	Atherstone	1-2	Docker
Sep	17	A	Port Vale Reserves	5-1	Tudor 2, Shepherd 2, Own goal
Sep	20	A	Bedworth	2-2	Docker, Own goal
Sep	24	A	Lower Gornal	0-2	-
Oct	1	A	Dudley	1-1	Roberts
Oct	15	H	Bromsgrove	0-4	-
Oct	22	A	Shrewsbury Reserves	0-2	-
Oct	29	H	Brierley Hill	2-2	Knox, Dobbing
Nov	5	A	Stratford Town	6-2	Denton, Shepherd 2, Docker, Oakes, Own goal
Nov	12	A	Wolves 'A'	1-0	Morrissey
Nov	19	A	Tamworth	2-3	Carr, Denton
Nov	26	H	Shrewsbury Reserves	1-3	Scott
Dec	3	A	Lye Town	2-2	Peachey 2
Dec	10	H	Lye Town	4-1	Carr 2, Peachey 2
Dec	17	H	Halesowen	2-5	Wilks, Hill
Dec	24	A	Darlaston	2-2	Pointer, Tudor
Dec	31	H	Boston United	3-2	Moore 2, Roberts
Jan	7	H	Port Vale Reserves	0-1	-
Jan	14	A	Cinderford	1-3	Own goal
Jan	21	H	Cinderford	6-2	Peachey 2, Oakes 2, Denton, Roberts
Jan	28	A	Redditch	0-1	-
Feb	11	A	Bilston	3-5	T Gould 3
Feb	18	H	Atherstone	2-1	Shepherd, Roberts
Feb	25	A	Stourbridge	1-3	Sinclair
Mar	4	H	Kidderminster	1-2	Roberts
Mar	11	A	Boston United	1-1	Roberts

Mar	18	H	Bedworth	1-1	Own goal
Mar	25	H	Stourbridge	1-0	Morrissey
Mar	27	H	Wolves 'A'	2-0	Docker, T Gould
Apr	1	A	Brierley Hill	1-2	Moore
Apr	8	H	Stratford Town	1-1	T Gould
Apr	22	H	Tamworth	1-2	Denton
Apr	29	H	Dudley	3-0	Hayward, Carr, Own goal
May	10	H	Hednesford	2-3	Moore 2
May	13	H	Bilston	5-1	Roberts 3, Shepherd, Carr
May	15	H	Lower Gornal	0-5	-

West Midlands League Cup

R1	Sep	13	A	Redditch	2-0	Morrissey, Tudor
R2	Dec	14	A	Bromsgrove	0-0	-
rep	Feb	4	H	Bromsgrove	0-1	-

APPENDIX 10

West Midlands League – Final table

	Pl	*W*	*D*	*L*	*GF*	*GA*	*Pts*
1. Boston United	42	32	6	4	139	42	70
2. Kidderminster H	42	31	5	6	123	61	67
3. Darlaston	42	22	14	6	80	44	58
4. Stourbridge	42	24	8	10	97	62	56
5. Tamworth	42	22	9	11	90	59	53
6. Halesowen	42	22	8	12	94	66	52
7. Dudley	42	22	7	13	70	50	51
8. Bromsgrove R	42	22	5	15	74	70	49
9. Bilston	42	20	7	15	88	94	47
10. Stratford Town	42	17	12	13	70	69	46
11. Atherstone	42	17	7	18	75	82	41
12. Lower Gornal	42	17	6	19	72	66	40
13. Brierley Hill	42	15	8	19	66	75	38
14. Hednesford	42	14	7	21	65	87	35
15. Coventry City 'A'	42	12	10	20	72	78	34
16. Port Vale Reserves	42	11	9	22	65	93	31
17. Cinderford Town	42	12	6	24	65	92	30
18. Redditch	42	9	10	23	36	81	28
19. Shrewsbury Town Reserves	42	11	5	26	66	98	27
20. Bedworth	42	10	7	25	50	95	27
21. Wolves 'A'	42	6	13	23	38	74	25
22. Lye Town	42	7	5	30	48	105	19

APPENDIX 11

FA Youth Cup

7th December 1966
2nd round – Wolves (a) 2-0 (Peachey 2)
Spiers: Hayward, Dobbing, Knox, Keley, Blockley, Bloodworth, Carr, Peachey, Gould, Paddon.

4th January 1967
3rd round – Swansea (a) 1-1 (Gould)
Spiers: Hayward, Dobbing, Knox, Keley, Blockley, Bloodworth, Carr, Peachey, Gould, Paddon.

18th January 1967
replay – Swansea (h) 2-1 (Peachey 2)
Spiers: Bloodworth, Dobbing, Knox, Keley, Blockley, Sinclair, Carr, Peachey, Gould, Paddon.

1st February 1967
4th round – Port Vale (a) 1-3 (Own goal)
Spiers: Bloodworth, Dobbing, Knox, Keley, Blockley, Sinclair, Carr, Peachey, Gould, Paddon.

Bibliography

I have used many books in my research but the following have been the most important:

Dean, Rod (with David Brassington, Jim Brown and Don Chalk), *Coventry City: A Complete Record 1883-1991* (Breedon Books, 1991)

Gould, Bobby and Instone, David, *24 Carat Gould* (Thomas Publications, 2010)

Henderson, Derek, *The Sky Blues, The Story of Coventry City* (Stanley Paul, 1968).

Hill, J.W.T., *The Jimmy Hill Story* (Hodder & Stoughton, 1998).

Stewart, Marshall, *Miracle in Sky Blue* (Instant Publications, 1968).